God, Reason and Theistic Proofs

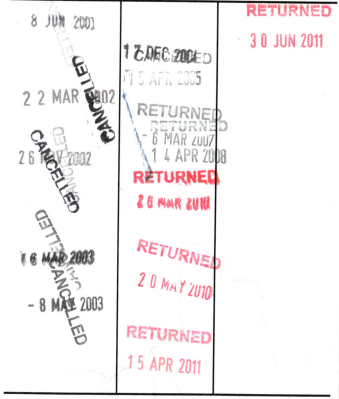

Other titles in the Reason and Religion series:

Peter Byrne: *The Moral Interpretation of Religion*
ISBN 0 7486 0784 6

C. Stephen Evans: *Faith Beyond Reason*
ISBN 0 7486 0794 3

Paul Helm: *Faith and Understanding*
ISBN 0 7486 0796 X

God, Reason and Theistic Proofs

Stephen T. Davis

Edinburgh University Press

© Stephen T. Davis, 1997

Edinburgh University Press
22 George Square, Edinburgh

Typeset in 11 on 13 pt Sabon
by Hewer Text Composition Services, Edinburgh,
Printed and bound in Great Britain by Hartnolls Ltd, Bodmin, Cornwall

A CIP record for this book is
available from the British Library

ISBN 0 7486 0799 4

The right of Stephen T. Davis to be identified as
author of this work has been asserted in accordance
with the Copyright, Designs and Patent Act (1988).

Contents

Introduction

This is a book about proofs for the existence of God. Within the discipline known as the philosophy of religion, offering arguments for the existence of God is an ancient and venerable tradition. It began, so far as we know, in ancient Greek philosophy (that is, some 2,500 years ago), and continues to this day.

Offering theistic proofs is an aspect of an enterprise that is called natural theology. Natural theology is the attempt to reach sound conclusions about (among other things) the existence and nature of God based on human reasoning alone. Natural theology uses such human cognitive faculties as experience, memory, introspection, deductive reasoning, inductive reasoning (which I will understand as including probabilistic and analogical reasoning), and inference to best explanation. It is to be contrasted with revealed theology, which is the attempt to reach sound conclusions about the existence and nature of God (among other things) based on statements that are said to be revealed by God or events that supposedly reveal something of God.

Obviously, natural theology has great importance for those who are curious about the existence and nature of God and who reject the idea of revealed theology. But for those who hold that God has revealed things to human beings – for example, most Jews, Christians, and Moslems – natural theology usually takes on only a secondary and auxiliary importance. Worrying about theistic proofs becomes somewhat *optional* for them. On the other hand, it is safe to say that most of the philosophers who have offered theistic proofs have also held to the validity, in at least some sense, of revealed theology. That is, most have believed that God could be known in other ways than through theistic proofs.

As noted, one of the most interesting facts about the enterprise of trying to prove the existence of God is its longevity. In Book X of Plato's *Laws* (written in the fourth century BC) we find a version of what we now call the cosmological argument for the existence of God.[1] Ever since then, philosophers have spent a great deal of time and effort debating various attempts to prove that God exists. The arguments that we call the ontological, cosmological, teleological and moral proofs, as well as the argument from religious experience, have been enormously fascinating to philosophers of almost every stripe, even to many who have no other particular interest in religion or the philosophy of religion. This interest continues in the twentieth century – scores of books and hundreds of articles have been written on the theistic proofs in the past hundred years or so. One could almost say that debate about the existence of God is a consuming passion of twentieth-century philosophers of religion.

It is odd that this should be the case. For several reasons, theistic proofs are widely criticized and even denigrated – by believers and unbelievers in God alike. First, most (but not quite all) of the participants in the debate concede that none of the theistic proofs succeeds in demonstrating the existence of God. Second, and perhaps for this reason, it is often pointed out that the theistic proofs are unpersuasive; few people are converted to belief in God because of one of the theistic proofs.[2] Third, theologians, religious people, and some philosophers play down or even scoff at the proofs as totally irrelevant to religious faith and practice. Believers don't need the proofs – why try to demonstrate something you already know? And the proofs, it is said, are cold, formal, and philosophical; they do not call for faith or commitment, nor do they meet our spiritual needs. Fourth, the 'God' of the theistic proofs, it is said, is a mere philosophical abstraction (a 'necessary being', the 'Greatest Conceivable Being', the 'Prime Mover', etc.) rather than the living God of the Bible. Of course many of those who defend or discuss theistic proofs assume that the God whose existence is argued for is the very same being as the God of scripture or of religious experience. But, obviously, that assumption will have to be investigated, and will be discussed later. Finally, one recent theologian, Paul Tillich, rejects the proofs because (he says) they end up denying divine transcendence. To say that 'God exists,' Tillich claims, is to place God on the same level as the creatures. God becomes a 'being' like all other existing 'beings' rather than 'the ground of being'.[3]

What good are theistic proofs, then? Why bother trying to prove that God exists? Or why bother discussing seriously the attempts of others to do so? Is this not so much wasted effort? In this book, I will try to answer these questions. I reject the idea that discussing the proofs must be a waste of time. That is, I believe the theistic proofs can be religiously and philosophically valuable. That is one of the things that I will try to show.

There are many theistic proofs, but five seem to have passed the test of time and are regarded as serious enough to be worthy of the critical efforts of philosophers of religion. These five are the arguments on which we will concentrate in this book. The first is the *ontological argument*, which is an *a priori* theistic proof. I will explain what this means in more detail in Chapter 2; for now let's simply say it means that the ontological argument is crucially based not upon empirical claims about the world – claims that we might try to verify or falsify by experience – but on certain ideas or concepts or definitions. It suggests a certain concept of God, and then offers a metaphysical argument to the effect that the concept must be instantiated.

The second category, *a posteriori* proofs, includes the other four. Briefly, *a posteriori* theistic proofs are based upon claims about reality or the world which might be investigated empirically or be verified or falsified by experience. These proofs are: the *cosmological argument*, which takes certain obvious truths (like 'Some things move' or 'Some existing things have finite lifespans') and argues metaphysically for the existence of a being – a being which is taken to be God – whose existence explains these facts; the *design* (or teleological) *argument*, which argues for the existence of a divine designer or orderer from the fact of observed order or design in the world; the *moral argument*, which argues for the existence of a divine source of the human experience of morality or as the source of the highest good; and the *argument from religious experience*, which argues that the existence of God is the best explanation of the fact of human religious experience. These proofs are all *a posteriori* in this sense – observation of certain facts about the world, or about the whole of reality, is crucially relevant to the proof.

Let me note here something that will become abundantly clear later, namely, that each theistic proof comes in a great variety of versions. This makes studying them both fascinating and frustrating – fascinating because of the almost infinitely many versions that we find under each category; frustrating because the great variety of versions makes it particularly difficult to reach definitive conclusions about the worth of a given theistic proof.

One of the obvious implications of this fact is that in any discussion of theistic proofs, including this book, there is inevitably a process of selection at work. Since all theistic proofs come in different versions, the versions that I have chosen to discuss might well be different from the versions other philosophers might choose. I have tried to select versions that at least have some possibility of being successful theistic proofs (that is, they are not obviously fallacious) and that can be explained without a great deal of presupposed technical expertise on the part of the reader.

I should also note that while I will try to be fair to the texts from Anselm, Aquinas, Paley and other famous theistic provers whose arguments we will consider, my emphasis in this book is not on exegetical considerations. I will not spend much time on the historical setting of the theistic proofs, nor in most cases will I spend much time on detailed textual analysis. My emphasis will be on the question of whether a serious theistic proof can sensibly be found in the text, and what it seems to me to be.

Let me now provide an outline of how the book will proceed. In Chapter 1 I will try to explain exactly what a theistic proof is; what theistic proofs presuppose; and what they try to accomplish. The question of what constitutes a good or successful argument for the existence of God will also be addressed. I will also discuss briefly some criticisms of the enterprise of trying to prove the existence of God. Chapter 2 is a discussion of the famous ontological argument. I will focus primarily on the version offered by Anselm in Chapter II of his book *Proslogion*.

Chapter 3 concerns the relationship between theistic proofs and religious realism. The issue is important because the contemporary theological and philosophical scenes include several versions of nonrealism, and some of them are relevant to the problem of trying to prove the existence of God. Inspired in part by Anselm, I will offer a critique of one version of nonrealism in the contemporary philosophy of religion. Chapter 4 is a discussion of the cosmological argument. Our primary, but not only, focus here will be the first three 'Ways' of proving the existence of God offered by Thomas Aquinas.

Chapter 5 is called 'Theistic proofs and foundationalism'. In it, I will define the epistemological position known as foundationalism, consider some current critiques of it, and discuss in some detail the question of its relevance to theistic proofs. In Chapter 6 we will consider the famous 'design' or 'teleological' argument for the existence of God. Although we will look at some earlier versions of the argument, our main focus will be on contemporary defences, and criticisms, of the design argument. In Chapter 7 we will complete our tour of the major theistic proofs with an analysis of the argument from religious experience. Here too our main focus will be on contemporary discussions of it.

Chapter 8 is called 'Other theistic proofs'. The idea here is that I will discuss briefly several arguments, some of them different versions of arguments that we have already considered, that seem to me to raise interesting new issues. Chapter 9 introduces the large topic of alternatives to theistic proofs, that is, other ways of trying to argue for theism besides offering theistic proofs. I will concentrate on two such arguments, Pascal's famous 'wager' argument and William James' almost (but not quite) equally famous argument in his essay 'The Will to Believe'. Finally, in Chapter 10 I will try to reach some sensible conclusions about three remaining issues. Just how important is the question of the existence of God? Is the being that is purportedly proved to exist in the theistic proofs the same being as the God that Jews, Christians and Moslems worship? And in the end, how valuable has the enterprise of offering theistic proofs turned out to be?

I would like to thank several friends and colleagues – William L. Craig, Paul Helm, Jeff Jordan and Linda Zagzebski – who read the initial draft of this book and supplied helpful criticisms and suggestions. Doug Geivett, John Hick and Richard Swinburne read and commented on parts of the manuscript. These scholars saved me from making several errors, and I deeply appreciate their suggestions.

Portions of this book appeared in different forms in a variety of publications. The author and publisher wish to thank the editors of these publications for their permission to use the listed material in the form in which it appears in this book.

'Anselm and Gaunilo on the "Lost Island"', *The Southern Journal of Philosophy*, Vol. XIII, No. 4, Winter, 1975.

'Does the Ontological Argument Beg the Question?', *International Journal for Philosophy of Religion*, Vol. VII, No. 4, Winter, 1976.

'Anselm and Question-Begging: A Reply to William Rowe', *International Journal for Philosophy of Religion*, Vol. VII, No. 4, Winter, 1976.

Faith, Skepticism, and Evidence: An Essay in Religious Epistemology (Lewisburg, Pennsylvania: Bucknell University Press, 1978).

'What Good Are Theistic Proofs?', in Louis Pojman (ed.), *Philosophy of Religion: An Anthology* (Belmont, California: Wadsworth Publishing Company, 1987).

'Why God Must Be Unlimited', in Linda J. Tessier (ed.), *Concepts of the Ultimate* (London: Macmillan, 1989).

'Pascal on Self-Caused Belief', *Religious Studies*, Vol. 27, No. 1, March, 1991.

'Hierarchical Causes in the Cosmological Argument', *International Journal for Philosophy of Religion*, Vol. 31, No. 1, February, 1992.

'Against "Anti-Realist Faith"', in Joseph Runzo (ed.), *Is God Real?* (London: Macmillan Press, 1993).

'Anselm and Phillips on Religious Realism', in Timothy Tessin and Mario van der Ruhr (eds), *Philosophy and the Grammar of Religious Belief* (New York: St Martin's Press, 1995).

NOTES

1. Edith Hamilton and Huntington Cairns (eds), *The Collected Dialogues of Plato* (New York: Pantheon, 1961), 1,455–79 (894A-899C). Antecedents to the tradition of theistic proofs are found in the search of the pre-Socratic philosophers for a universal *arche* (starting-point, principle of order, principle of explanation). See L. P. Gerson, *God and Greek Philosophy: Studies in the Early History of Natural Theology* (London: Routledge, 1990), pp. 1–32.

2. Bertrand Russell tells the following charming story about his days as a Cambridge undergraduate: 'I remember the precise moment, one day in 1894, as I was walking along Trinity Lane, when I saw in a flash (or thought I saw) that the ontological argument is valid. I had gone out to buy a tin of tobacco; on my way back, I suddenly threw it up in the air, and exclaimed as I caught it: "Great Scott, the ontological argument is sound"' (Bertrand Russell, *The Basic Writings of Bertrand Russell*, ed. Robert E. Egner and Lester E. Denonn (New York: Simon and Schuster, 1961), p. 42). Of course Russell's impression of the soundness of the ontological argument did not stick, and for the rest of his life he was a confirmed atheist or at least agnostic.

3. See Paul Tillich, *Systematic Theology*, I (Chicago: University of Chicago Press, 1951), pp. 235–8.

1

What is a Theistic Proof?

I. DEFINING THE CONCEPT

A theistic proof is an attempt to prove, by argument, that God exists. But what exactly is an argument? What is a proof? And who or what is God? Obviously, we need to begin by defining these and other terms.

Let us say that 'God' is the God of theism. That is, when I speak in this book of God, I refer (unless otherwise noted) to a unique, eternal, all-powerful, all-knowing, and personal spirit who created the heavens and the earth and who works for the salvation of human beings. The three great monotheistic traditions – Judaism, Christianity, and Islam – all worship a God with these properties. Other religions surely do as well.

Let us say that an 'argument' is a finite set of words arranged in sentences, consisting of one or more premises and a conclusion, and whose premises are designed to prove, entail, or provide intellectual support for the conclusion. (Here, we are considering only *deductive* arguments; other sorts will be noted later.) Clearly some arguments have different aims from others, and some arguments are better than others in achieving those aims. This is a point that we will have to discuss further.

We had best define two terms – 'valid' and 'sound' – that are often used to describe arguments. Let us say that a 'valid' argument is one in which no mistake in logic is made. For example, the argument:

1. Some of my students are red-headed;
2. Smith is one of my students;
3. Therefore, Smith is red-headed

is clearly invalid. (3) does not follow from (1) and (2). A more rigorous way of stating the criterion of validity is this: in a valid argument it is logically impossible for the premises to be true and the conclusion false. It is perfectly possible for (1) and (2) to be true and (3) false; thus, the (1)–(3) argument is invalid. But it is possible for a valid argument to provide no intellectual support for the conclusion. Observe this argument:

4. All Californians are male;
5. Mother Teresa is a Californian;
6. Therefore, Mother Teresa is male.

Notice that no mistake in logic has been made here; if (4) and (5) are true then (6) must be true. But of course the reason that this argument is a poor argument is that both of its premises are in fact false. Accordingly, let us say that a 'sound argument' is a valid argument in which all the premises are true.

The next question we need to ask is: What would constitute a good or successful theistic proof?[1] Validity and soundness will have to be mentioned here, as well as other points. Let us see if we can answer our question by considering various theistic proofs. Suppose we begin with the following:

7. All the people in Claremont are people;
8. Some people believe in God;
9. Therefore, God exists.

Now this is obviously a feeble attempt to prove the existence of God. Probably the most noticeable problem is that the argument is invalid – the conclusion does not follow from the premises. Let us then try to remedy this difficulty by coming up with a theistic proof that is formally valid:

10. If God exists then God exists;
11. God exists;
12. Therefore, God exists.

But this argument too is feeble – doubtless few atheists or agnostics will come to believe in the existence of God because of it. More importantly, it is obvious that no one *should* come to believe in the existence of God because of it. It is true that the argument is formally valid: if (10) and (11) are true, (12) must be true. That is, it is impossible for (10) and (11) to be true and (12) false. But the argument assumes in premise (11) exactly what it is trying to prove; accordingly, no sensible person who doubts the conclusion will grant premise (11). Classically, then, this is an argument that commits the informal fallacy of 'begging the question'. The argument, then, is informally invalid.

Consider also the following two arguments:

13. Everything the Bible says is true;
14. The Bible says that God exists;
15. Therefore, God exists;

and

16. Either God exists or $7 + 5 = 13$;
17. $7 + 5$ does not $= 13$;
18. Therefore, God exists.[2]

These arguments too beg the question. As far as the first is concerned, it does so because no one who denies or doubts (15) will grant that both (13) and (14) are true. Premise (14) is perhaps beyond reproach, but (13) will be singularly unappealing to atheists or agnostics. The second argument is a bit more complicated; it is surely formally valid, and those who believe in God, as I do, will hold that it is also sound. Nearly everyone will grant (17), and I for one am happy to grant (16). But the problem again is that no sensible person who denies or doubts the conclusion will grant (16); there is no reason to grant (16) apart from a prior commitment to the existence of God. Thus this argument too begs the question.

Another major informal fallacy is that of 'equivocation' – that is, using the same word without acknowledgement in two different senses – as for example in the following argument: 'The audience gave her a hand; therefore, the audience gave her something; therefore, the audience gave her something with five fingers.' A theistic proof that commits the fallacy of equivocation might be stated as follows:

19. I believe in God;
20. Therefore, God exists;
21. Therefore, God exists.

Here the word exists is apparently used in two different ways. If premise (19) all by itself is to entail premise (20), then the word 'exists' in (20) must mean something like 'exists in my mind' (or as Anselm would have said, exists *in intellectu*). But if the above argument is to count as a theistic proof, then the word 'exists' in (21) must mean something quite different. It must mean something like 'exists independently of my mind' (exists *in re*, as Anselm would have it). Thus this argument too is quite worthless as an attempt to prove the existence of God.

We appear then so far to have arrived at two criteria that a theistic proof must satisfy in order to count as successful; it must be formally valid (at least if it is a deductive argument, as opposed to one that is inductive or probabilistic), and it must be informally valid. That is, it must be the case that the truth of the premises logically requires the truth of the conclusion, and it must be the case that the argument avoids question begging, equivocation, arguing in a circle, and all other informal fallacies. But clearly these criteria are insufficient. Notice the following argument:

22. Anything everyone believes is true;
23. Everyone believes in the existence of God;
24. Therefore, God exists.

This argument seems to me to satisfy both of the above criteria – it is valid both formally and informally – but it is clearly a poor attempt at a theistic proof. It fails because (22) and (23) are both false – the argument is unsound. (As implied earlier, an argument is unsound if *any* of its premises is false, let alone if both or all of them are.) Thus it seems we must add some third criterion that has something to do with the truth of the premises. But here too we find complications; how exactly shall we specify this third criterion?

Which of the following shall we say that the premises of a successful theistic proof must be?

(a) possibly true;
(b) known to be possibly true;
(c) more reasonable or plausible than their denials;
(d) known to be more reasonable or plausible than their denials;
(e) reasonable or plausible;
(f) known to be reasonable or plausible;
(g) true;
(h) known to be true;
(i) necessarily true; or
(j) known to be necessarily true?

Some of these candidates can surely be ruled out – (a) and (b) are doubtless too weak; if they were acceptable the (22)–(24) argument might well count as a successful theistic proof, for both (22) and (23) are possibly true and known to be so. And (i) and (j) are doubtless too strong.

Of the remaining candidates – (c), (d), (e), (f), (g) and (h) – I will opt for either (c) or (d). Obviously, the strongest of the remaining criteria are (g) and (h); a theistic proof whose premises are either true or known to be true has a chance of being a powerful argument. But I believe a theistic proof can be a successful argument even if it is not possible to show that its premises are true. If it is possible to show that the premises are either acceptable in themselves ((e) and (f)) or more acceptable than their denials ((c) and (d)), then an otherwise impeccable theistic proof can be considered successful. Between these two pairs, I will opt for (c) and (d). This is for two reasons. First, I believe that most of the theistic provers (i.e. those who offer and defend theistic proofs) whom we will be discussing in this book would want to be interpreted as holding that the premises of their arguments were more reasonable or plausible than their denials. Second, in the vast majority of cases, if a premise can be shown to be more plausible or reasonable than its denial, this will also show that it is, in itself, plausible or reasonable.

But it will not be possible fully to answer our question – Which properties must characterise the premises of a successful theistic proof? – until we ask about the goal or purpose of a theistic proof. Let us then ask: What is or ought to be the aim, goal, or purpose of a theistic proof?

II. THE GOAL OF A THEISTIC PROOF

Here too we find difficulties. There are several ways of envisioning the goal or purpose of a theistic proof. There is perhaps a common assumption behind most discussions of theistic proofs, an assumption made by both defenders and critics of these arguments, namely, that theism is in better epistemic shape, so to speak, if a theistic proof succeeds than it is if none succeeds. But beyond that point of general (but not quite universal) agreement, there are at least three ways in which we might try to define success for a theistic proof.

One possibility is to say that a successful theistic proof is one that convinces people that God exists. But which people? (a) Perhaps a successful proof convinces everyone who hears and follows it that God exists. But of course it is extremely doubtful that any proof of *any* conclusion will ever do that. (b) Perhaps then a successful proof is one that convinces every *rational* person who hears and follows it that God exists. This notion is more promising than the first (indeed, in the end I will embrace something like it), but one difficulty is that we might never be able to tell whether a proof is successful because we have no precise criteria for determining which people are rational. (c) Perhaps we ought to say that a successful proof is one that convinces all rational people *who believe its premises* that God exists. (I am assuming both here and elsewhere that it makes sense to speak of both believers and unbelievers in a proposition *p* as 'being convinced' that *p* is true; in the second case but not the first a change of mind is involved.) But this is surely too liberal a notion of success. On the basis of this notion, the (13)–(15) and the (16)–(18) arguments above are probably successful theistic proofs, and that is something we should not grant. (d) Perhaps we ought to say that a successful theistic proof is one that convinces at least *some* of the people who hear and follow it that God exists. But this notion is also too liberal – probably lots of feeble theistic proofs (possibly including some of the ones mentioned above) will convince somebody somewhere that God exists.

A second possibility is to define a successful theistic proof as one that strengthens the faith of theists, that is, strengthens the conviction of those who already believe in God. But although some theistic proofs probably do achieve this end, and some people will consider this an end worth achieving, it is doubtful that we ought to understand success for a theistic proof in this way. For one thing, possibly something like the (13)–(15) argument above would strengthen the faith of some theists, but we will not want to call that argument a successful proof. Furthermore, in the case of the actual theistic proofs discussed by philosophers – for example, the ontological, cosmological, teleological, and moral arguments – stronger aims than this one are clearly had in mind by the people who propose them.

Suppose we consider a third possibility. A successful theistic proof, we might say, is one that demonstrates the existence of God. This entails (among other things) that it is one that substantiates or provides good grounds for belief in the existence of God. It creates a situation in which rational people who hear and follow the proof should rationally believe in the existence of God. But here too we face the question, To whom is a theistic proof addressed? Does a successful proof demonstrate to *everyone* the rationality of belief in God? Or just to some of the persons who hear and follow the proof? Or – and this as noted is the option that seems best – to all rational persons?

What then is the purpose of a theistic proof? It seems that the third of the above possibilities is by far the most promising. Without claiming that this was precisely what such defenders of theistic proofs as Plato, Anselm, Aquinas, Paley, Kant, and so on had in mind, I will hold that the purpose, aim, or goal of a theistic proof is to demonstrate the existence of God and thus the rationality of belief in the existence of God. That is, what a theistic proof aims to do is substantiate the theist's belief in God, give a good reason for it, show that it is credible, show that it is *true*. And theistic proofs, I suggest, try to demonstrate the rationality of theistic belief to all rational persons (whoever exactly they are). So far as the premises of the theistic proof are concerned, one fine way to do this is to show that they are more probable or plausible than their denials.

So it seems that the third criterion (besides formal validity and informal validity) of a good or successful theistic proof is either (c) or (d) above.

That is, the premises of a good or successful theistic proof must be either more reasonable or plausible than their denials or else known to be so. Let's say that if the premises are merely more reasonable or plausible than their denials, a person can rationally believe them; and that if they are known to be so, it is irrational for a person (or at least the knower) not to believe them. Of course a theistic proof would be even more able to demonstrate the rationality of theism if it satisfied the stronger criterion that its premises must be known to be true. But I opt for the slightly weaker criterion because there are premises that have not been proved and that may not be known to be true but that, being recognised as at least plausible or rational, can appear as premises in a successful theistic proof.

I think for example of that statement that appears in many versions of the ontological argument, namely 'The Greatest Conceivable Being is a possible being.' Many (including me) would claim to know this statement, but surely many others would dispute such a claim. And I see no way of proving the statement apart from showing that the Greatest Conceivable Being is actual (all actual beings are possible beings). Nevertheless, if this being seems to me to be a possible being, and if I have apparently answered successfully all the known arguments to the contrary, then I know to be plausible the statement 'The Greatest Conceivable Being is a possible being.' Accordingly, I can rationally believe the statement, and I can use it as a premise in a successful theistic proof.

Between candidates (c) and (d) for the third criterion of a successful theistic proof, (d) is to be preferred. It is crucial that the premises of a successful theistic proof be known to be more plausible than their denials. But known to whom? They must be knowable by any rational person; and ideally they must be known by the people to whom the rationality of belief in the existence of God is to be demonstrated (including, presumably, the person who offers the proof). If the premises of a theistic proof are more plausible than their denials but the relevant people do not know that fact, the rationality of theism will not be demonstrated to them. Neither believers nor unbelievers in the existence of God will receive the intended benefit, namely, recognition of the rationality of belief in the existence of God.

Of course there may be premises that some people know to be more plausible than their denials and others don't. Notoriously, this situation frequently occurs in discussions of theistic proofs, for example, with statements like 'Every existing thing has a reason for its existence,' or 'The universe is like a watch.' If these premises appear in an otherwise successful theistic proof, then the rationality of belief in the existence of God will have been demonstrated to those who know that the premises in question are more plausible than their denials (if there are any such people) but not to those who do not.

In summary, then, a good or successful deductive theistic proof satisfies the following criteria:

> It is formally valid;
> It is informally valid; and
> Its premises are known to be more plausible than their denials.

A theistic proof that satisfies these criteria (if any such argument ever does) demonstrates the existence of God. It shows that rational people can rationally believe in the existence of God.

III. ASSUMPTIONS OF THEISTIC PROOFS

One grand presupposition of all theistic proofs (as well as of virtually all philosophy and science) is that the world we experience is a cosmos rather than a chaos. That is, reality as such has a rational structure that can (at least in part) be discovered by human reason. Our rational faculties are (usually) reliable; we are capable of using them and arriving at truth. Without that assumption, no one could ever have any faith that human argument about the nature of reality could validly lead to the conclusion that God exists. Of course, critics of theistic proofs (which in this book we will often call TPs for short) make this assumption about the orderliness and intelligibility of the world too; indeed, so does everyone who wants to argue rationally for some conclusion or another.

In that vein, let me note three related assumptions typically made by theistic provers – assumptions that need to be made if theistic proofs are to be helpful or probative.[3] The first is that theistic proofs presuppose a realist notion of truth. Thus theistic provers oppose coherence or pragmatic theories of truth, theories that make truth equal to some kind of epistemic status of statements or beliefs (warranted, rational, etc.), or even views that de-emphasise robust notions of truth. Theistic proofs presuppose some such notion as 'A statement (proposition, belief . . .) is true if and only if what the statement says to be the case actually is the case.'[4] It is also assumed that religious statements can be true or false, and that the words 'true' and 'false' mean similar things in such contexts to what they mean when we use them about nonreligious statements.[5]

Second, theistic provers presuppose an ability to get clear on what is meant by the term 'God'. The claim is not that we can know everything that there is to know about God, or that the notion of God is transparent to human reason, but rather that we can attain enough clarity about God to ensure that both those who offer, and those who resist, theistic proofs know what they are talking about. As Anselm said in the context of the ontological argument, both the believer and the atheist can at least understand the words 'that than which no greater can be conceived'. This assumption is opposed to all views which for either theological or philosophical reasons end up affirming the radical inexpressibility of God, views which insist that any definition or verbal understanding of God can only misconstrue God.[6]

Third, theistic provers presuppose the view that philosophy is capable of arriving at truth, and even at truth about God. In other words, the existence of God is capable of rational justification or refutation. Reasoning about God can be a helpful thing to do. As noted, most theistic provers in the history of philosophy were also believers in revelation. Like Aquinas, they held that most of what we know or can know about God is to be learned by divine revelation; and that only a few things about God (God's existence and perhaps a few other items) can be learned by natural theology. Still, all theistic provers presuppose that at least some things about God can be learned via human reason alone. They also accept the idea that providing rational support for religious belief is a good thing.

Can such assumptions as these be proved? Messer argues strongly that they cannot be non-circularly supported.[7] Although I do not agree with him I will not argue against Messer's claim because it will not matter much for theistic provers even if he is right. These assumptions provide the most basic axioms against which other assertions are measured in order to evaluate them; as Aristotle showed (discussing the laws of logic),[8] once we arrive at the most basic axioms of all, the question of proof cannot arise. But there is no big danger here for theistic provers. As long as our three assumptions are agreed upon (whether proved or not), TPs can still be offered and debated, and perhaps some will be successful arguments.

IV. WHAT IF A THEISTIC PROOF WERE SUCCESSFUL?

What then would be the result if some logician or philosopher of religion were able to produce a successful, or at least apparently successful, theistic proof? Suppose it were an argument of the form we call *modus ponens* and went something like this:

25. If p is true, then God exists;
26. p is true;
27. Therefore, God exists.

Or perhaps the argument might run as follows:

28. If q is true, it is highly probable that God exists;
29. q is true;
30. Therefore, it is highly probable that God exists.

Now arguments of this form would surely be formally valid. Suppose that they were also informally valid and that the premises were known to be more plausible than their denials. What would or should our reaction be?

Our first thought might be to return to the various criticisms mentioned in the Introduction to this book that have been raised against theistic proofs. We might wonder what ought to be said about them in the light of the existence of an apparently successful theistic proof. So let us now take a second look at those criticisms. The first point was not so much a criticism as a recognition of the odd fact that debate about theistic proofs thrives despite general but not universal agreement that no actual theistic proof succeeds. But even if all this were true, it constitutes no good argument against the continued thriving of the industry. Perhaps the majority is wrong; perhaps some existing theistic proof succeeds despite the failure of the majority to recognise its success. (I myself hold that there are versions of the ontological argument that have not been refuted.) Or even if the majority is right and no theistic proof succeeds, perhaps engaging in the enterprise of discussing theistic proofs is valuable anyway, that is, for some other reason.

The second point was that theistic proofs don't often convince religious sceptics and unbelievers to believe in the existence of God. That is surely true, but perhaps it is merely because no successful theistic proof yet exists; or perhaps it is because defenders of successful theistic proofs have thus far done a poor job of defending them; or perhaps it is because atheists and agnostics are too stubborn. Few arguments possess irresistible force; few coerce people on pain of irrationality, so to speak, into accepting their conclusions. So even if a successful theistic proof existed, we should expect (as Norman Malcolm once suggested)[9] few conversions. It is always possible to find some reason to reject an argument whose conclusion one finds repugnant.

The third point was that theistic proofs are irrelevant to religious faith and practice. And it does seem odd to try to prove something that you already know – for example, that San Francisco is north of Los Angeles, or that your mother loves you. But perhaps it is not so odd to try to prove something you believe but do not know (which is how many theists would describe their cognitive state *vis-à-vis* the existence of God). And it is surely not at all odd to try to prove something you believe or even know, when the proof is aimed at someone else who neither knows nor believes it. It is also true that the theistic proofs do not do a good job of meeting human spiritual needs – the cosmological argument, for example, calls few people to religious commitment. The teleological argument does not tell us how to worship or pray. The moral argument does not teach us any lessons about forgiving each other. But why is that a problem? Naturally, there are many crucial human tasks that theistic proofs do not succeed in doing – for example, feeding hungry people. There are even crucial intellectual tasks that theistic proofs do not succeed in doing – for example, solving the problem of evil. Is the fact that they fail to do these things a reason for us all to opt out of the debate over theistic proofs? Of course not. Perhaps there are other crucial tasks the theistic proofs can perform. (What they might be I will discuss below.)

The fourth point was that the 'God' spoken of in the theistic proofs is a philosophical abstraction rather than the living God of the Bible. One can appreciate what is being said here. As is well known, Aquinas finishes each of his 'Five Ways' of demonstrating the existence of God with some such statement as 'and this everyone understands to be God'. It has been frequently pointed out that what he claims here is not necessarily true. It is logically possible for a first mover, a first cause, and a necessary being that owes its necessity to no other being to exist without possessing such characteristic properties of God as omnipotence, omniscience, compassion, and so on. The beings whose existence Aquinas tries to prove, in short, do not have to be God. (We will discuss this point in more detail in Chapter 10.) Furthermore, the beings spoken of in typical theistic proofs do sometimes seem more like metaphysical principles than living beings. But the criticism of theistic proofs that we are considering here would be immeasurably stronger, in my view, if it could be shown that such beings as 'the Greatest Conceivable Being', 'the Designer of the Universe', 'the Prime Mover', and so on, *cannot* be God, that is, if some of their properties are inconsistent with some of the properties of the living God of the Bible. But that has not been shown and (I would claim) is not true.[10]

The fifth point was Tillich's insistence that God is not a 'being' and that to try to prove 'the existence of God' is illicitly to place God on the same level as finite beings. But I confess I have never been able to grasp how it lessens or destroys God's transcendence over the creatures to say that God is a being. Why can't we state that God 'is a being' and 'exists' without denying that God's existence is of a radically different sort from ours? And whether or not we choose to regard God as sharing some of our properties – for example, the property of being a being, the property of knowing the sum of six and five, the property of desiring peace on earth – we will still want to be free to ask whether God is real, whether the atheists are right or wrong. And I see no significant danger in using the word 'exist' to ask the relevant questions or make the relevant affirmations. As long as we recognise the limitations of all human talk about God, and as long as we recognise that God 'exists' in a different sense from that in which we do, the enterprise of proposing, criticising and defending theistic proofs can continue.

V. DO THEISTIC PROOFS ACCOMPLISH ANYTHING?

What good, then, do theistic proofs do? Why spend time arguing about them? I would prefer to approach the question by asking, What good would a *successful* theistic proof do (if one existed)? Naturally, the question and its answer might be quite different if I were instead to ask, What good is done by the existing theistic proofs discussed by philosophers, that is, the ontological argument, the moral argument, and so on? I choose to proceed in the way I do because the main point behind discussions of these arguments seems to me in any case to be to see whether or not they are successful. Those who defend them think they are or might be (although their notions of 'success' sometimes appear to differ from mine); those who criticize them think they are not.

In my view, there are two closely related benefits that would derive from a successful theistic proof.[11] The first is this: Theistic proofs show that theists do or at least can make full and thoroughgoing use of their rational faculties in arriving at or continuing in belief in the existence of God. I say this because it is frequently charged (oddly, by some who look sympathetically on religious faith as well as by some who do not) that faith in God is essentially irrational or at least arational, that is, is based on an 'existential choice' that is not supported by evidence, arguments, or reasons.

The second and most important benefit that would derive from a successful theistic proof is that belief in the existence of God will have been shown to be rational or intellectually justified. (I do not claim, of course, that this is the only way such a belief can be shown to be rational.) The standard criticism of belief in the existence of God, namely, that it is naive or credulous or gullible or irrational to believe in the existence of something you can't see or measure or test or prove, will have been answered. I consider that this result will constitute a very great benefit indeed for theism.

If such a proof existed, the temptation for theists would be to use it as an evangelistic device. That is, they might try to use the proof to convince nonbelievers in the existence of God to become believers. And it is possible there might be some converts – a successful theistic proof might at least lead some folk to consider God more seriously than they had been doing, or it might for some folk remove intellectual obstacles to belief in the existence of God. But that is about all it should be expected to do. As noted above, few arguments are intellectually coercive; doubtless there never will exist a discursive, deductive theistic proof that convinces all the rational people who attend to it.

One reason this is true is that in the face of even a successful theistic proof a stubborn atheist always has the option of denying one of its premises. And in some cases this might be a rational thing for an atheist to do. Similarly, if someone were clever enough to construct, from premises that I believe, a proof of the *non*-existence of God, I am quite sure that the first thing I would do would be to consider which of those premises to deny. The strength of my commitment to theism would outweigh my commitment to at least one of those premises. And, I claim, this might well be the rational thing for me to do.

But when might it be rational for a person to deny a previously accepted premise in order rationally to reject a conclusion it entails or helps to entail? This is a complicated matter; I will suggest some criteria, but they should be taken as tentative suggestions only. Let us imagine an atheist, Jones, who is faced with the theistic proof with which we began:

7. All the people in Claremont are people;
8. Some people believe in God;
9. Therefore, God exists.

Let us further suppose something that is obviously not in fact true, namely, that this is a valid argument. And if it were valid, then it would also be sound, since surely premises (7) and (8) are true. Now since these premises seem to be not only true but known to be plausible, this argument – so we are supposing – meets our requirements of a successful theistic proof. Finally, let us suppose that Jones knows that these premises are both plausible and more plausible than their denials. What, then, can or should Jones do in the light of this imagined successful theistic proof?

It seems that Jones has three options. First, Jones might agree that our theistic proof is successful but still deny its conclusion. Second, Jones might agree that our theistic proof is successful and accept its conclusion, that is, become a theist. Third, Jones might deny that our theistic proof is successful by denying the plausibility of premises (7), (8), or both. (Let us imagine it is the contingently true premise (8) that Jones would decide to dispute.) Now the first option is obviously unacceptable and must be rejected as irrational. The second option, however, is clearly acceptable; in the light of our successful theistic proof, we would want to say, Jones rationally should accept the truth of (9).

Whether the third option is acceptable seems to depend on various considerations. First, is Jones willing to pay the price of rationally rejecting (9)? That is, is Jones willing to deny the apparently plausible premise (8)? Second, how important in Jones's world view is the denial of (9)? Is it central or important enough to outweigh the cost of denying premise (8)? Third, how probable is the denial of (9) (that is, atheism) versus the probability of (8)? I would argue, then, that if Jones is willing to deny (8), and if the denial of (9) is crucial to Jones's world view, and if Jones's best judgement is that the denial of (9) is more probable than the truth of premise (8), then Jones is rational in denying (8), despite its initial plausibility, in order rationally to deny (9).

In short, if you think a statement p is plausible or even true; and you are utterly convinced that another statement q is false; and if you discover that p entails q; then you can rationally change your mind about p and deny it if you are willing to pay the price of doing so, if the denial of q is crucial to your world view, and if the denial of q seems far more probable to you than the truth or plausibility of p.

NOTES

1. Helpful work on this question has been done by George Mavrodes in his *Belief in God* (New York: Random House, 1970), pp. 17–48, and by James F. Ross in his *Philosophical Theology* (Indianapolis: Bobbs-Merrill, 1969), pp. 3–34.
2. This argument is discussed by Alvin Plantinga in *The Nature of Necessity* (Oxford: Clarendon Press, 1974), pp. 217–18.
3. My analysis of the assumptions made by theistic provers is not quite the same as Richard Messer's; still, I need to express a debt of gratitude to Messer's illuminating discussion of this and other related matters in his *Does God's Existence Need Proof?* (Oxford: Clarendon Press, 1993); see especially pp. 1–73.
4. William P. Alston, *A Realist Conception of Truth* (Ithaca, New York: Cornell University Press, 1996), p. 5 (ellipses in original). Alston's book is an excellent defence of a realist notion of truth.
5. In Chapter 3 we will discuss some of the views of D. Z. Phillips, who is often interpreted as rejecting this assumption.
6. Phillips seems to hold views like these as well.
7. Messer, *Does God's Existence Need Proof?*, p. 131.
8. Aristotle, *Metaphysics*, trans. by Richard Hope (Ann Arbor, Michigan: University of Michigan Press, 1960), Book Gamma, 3–4.
9. See Norman Malcolm, 'Anselm's Ontological Arguments', in John Hick (ed.), *The Existence of God* (New York: Macmillan, 1964), p. 68.
10. See my *Logic and the Nature of God* (London: Macmillan, 1983), pp. 145–53.
11. Another possible benefit of theistic proofs, which I will not discuss in much detail here, is their use in a cumulative, nondeductive argument for the broad truth of the theistic world view. Some contemporary philosophers have been engaged in making such a case; see, e.g., Basil Mitchell, *The Justification of Religious Belief* (New York: Oxford University Press, 1981), and Richard Swinburne, *The Existence of God* (Oxford: Clarendon Press, 1979).

2

The Ontological Argument

I. INTRODUCTION

Let us begin with the ontological argument. It is unlike many of the other theistic proofs in several ways. One of those ways is this: with several of the proofs, we do not know their origin, that is, who first thought of them. But with the ontological argument (or OA for short) we do: the argument was first conceived by Anselm of Canterbury (AD 1033–1109), an eminent medieval philosopher, theologian and churchman. He was Abbot of a monastery at Bec and later Archbishop of Canterbury.

Another difference, already noted, is that this is an *a priori* argument. That is, it is an argument which is crucially based on a certain definition or concept. This is as opposed to *a posteriori* arguments, which are based upon claims that can be verified or falsified by experience. Doubtless most of the things that we know are items of *a posteriori* knowledge, items that we learn from experience, through the use of the senses. My knowledge that Lincoln was assassinated in 1865, my knowledge that there are eucalyptus trees on the lawn outside my office window, my knowledge of my wife's opinion of Monet – all are items of *a posteriori* knowledge. But some philosophers think that some things can be known *a priori*, that is, apart from or 'prior to' experience. Take the statement '2 + 2 = 4'. Some philosophers hold that this statement can be known *a priori* because we do not come to know it or verify it by looking around in the world and gathering evidence. If we understand the meaning of '2,' the meaning of '+,' the meaning of '=,' and the meaning of '4,' then we simply *see* or *grasp*, by an act of what might be called mental intuition, that '2 + 2 = 4.'

Similarly, the ontological argument is an attempt to prove *a priori* that God exists. It does not involve looking around at various properties of the world with the senses; it rather asks the reader to think hard about a certain concept, that is, a definition of God, together with certain other metaphysical or necessary truths. It tries to prove, on that basis, that God exists.

Anselm did not use the term 'the ontological argument'. His argument was not called that till much later. The term 'the *a priori* argument' would have been much more accurate, but it is by now far too late. The argument has come to be called 'the ontological argument' by philosophers, and that name will stick.

The ontological argument is one of the most incredibly fascinating arguments in the history of philosophy.[1] One reason for this is that there are serious disagreements among readers of Anselm about how to interpret *Proslogion* II and III. Some see one argument there; some see two. Some of those who see two hold that the first argument is the superior one; some of them hold that it is the second. Some believe that the OA is designed to prove the existence of God to atheists or to all sensible people; others believe that Anselm had no such intention in mind and was not offering a 'theistic proof' in anything like the traditional sense.[2] (It goes without saying that I do not accept this last view.) Not wishing to become involved in debates about the proper exegesis of Anselm's work, let me simply state that the argument I will discuss in this chapter is the way that I find myself (and the way many other philosophers have found themselves) interpreting *Proslogion* II–III. It is probably possible, even with careful exegesis, to extract several different arguments from the pages of Anselm's text.

The second reason the OA is fascinating is that there are many difficult and controversial philosophical issues involved in evaluating it. So it is not surprising that philosophers have rated the argument variously. Some think it so obviously fallacious as to be uninteresting. Many think that it is a serious argument but that it has been refuted, for example, by Immanuel Kant in his claim that '"exists" is not a real predicate.' (This, indeed, is probably the view of the majority of contemporary philosophers.) Some think the OA fallacious, but are prepared to admit that it is exceedingly difficult to show how or why it fails. (This seems to be a more common view than it was, say, thirty or forty years ago.) Some few think there are versions of the OA that have not yet been refuted.

It should be noted that Anselm intended the OA as a proof not only of the existence of God but of God's properties (or at least some of them) as well. In his prayer at the beginning of *Proslogion II* he said: 'And so, Lord, do thou . . . give me . . . to understand that thou art as we believe; and that thou art that which we believe'.[3] And what is it that 'we' believe about God, according to Anselm? It is that God is 'a being than which nothing greater can be conceived' (a term that surely either has no referent at all or else has as its referent God or a God-like being).

Now the OA will constitute a successful proof of the existence of God if, and only if, two conditions are satisfied: (1) the notion of 'a being than which nothing greater can be conceived' is a coherent notion whose only possible referent is God; and (2) the OA itself is a sound argument. (The second condition actually includes the first – the OA couldn't very well be sound if Anselm's term for God were incoherent – but it is useful to think of there being two separate conditions here.)

What did Anselm mean by the term 'a being than which nothing greater can be conceived'? Anselm clearly did not mean the greatest being that can be adequately imagined by you or me. Our conceiving or imagining abilities are limited; perhaps we are unable to conceive (in some sense of the term 'conceive') of the being Anselm has in mind. But this need not bother Anselm; what he meant was the greatest being that it is logically possible for *any* conceiver to conceive of. It would not trouble Anselm one bit if there are senses of the term 'conceive' where only 'a being than which nothing greater can be conceived' will be able to conceive of 'a being than which nothing greater can be conceived'.

Since philosophers who discuss the OA often refer to Anselm's 'a being than which nothing greater can be conceived' (let's call it ABTW for short) as the 'greatest conceivable being' (GCB) or the 'greatest possible being' (GPB), we might discuss briefly the appropriateness of this move. There are two (closely related) issues here – first, are the logical properties of the terms ABTW, GCB and GPB the same or at least so very nearly the same as to justify their exchangeability? And second, are the limits of conceivability equal to the limits of possibility?

On the first question, there is one point where the terms ABTW and GCB seem to differ in their implications. The term GCB entails that the being in question *can be conceived* (by some conceiver or other) while the term ABTW does not entail this. But this surely is merely a momentary irritant. Let us assume a premise that seems quite beyond reproach, despite the fact that it is not an explicit part of Anselm's argument, namely, that ability to conceive of oneself is a great-making property. (In a moment I will explain the notion of a 'great-making' property.) That is, if we have two beings, A and B, who are alike in greatness as much as possible except that A is able to conceive of itself and B is not, then A is greater than B. If so, it follows that for any being that cannot conceive of itself, no matter how great this being is, we can conceive of a greater being, namely, one just like it in every possible way except that it *is* able to conceive of itself. The ABTW, then, *must* be a being that can conceive of itself, and the two terms ABTW and GCB turn out to be equivalent.

Let us notice that some properties of beings are relevant to the greatness or likeness to God of those beings and some are not. The property of *being red-headed*, for example, is not (as we might say) a great-making or Godlike-making property because a red-headed being is not (other things being equal) necessarily greater or more Godlike than a non-red-headed being. But other properties clearly are relevant to the greatness or God-likeness of the beings that have them. The property of *being all-powerful*, for example, is a great-making or Godlike-making property because an all-powerful being *is* (other things being equal) necessarily greater or more Godlike than a being that is not all-powerful. Let us call these sorts of properties, properties that make the beings that have them greater or more Godlike, G-properties.

Let us also notice that some properties admit of degrees or increments and others do not. For example, the property of *being a prime number* admits of no degrees – a being either possesses this property or it does not. The same would be true of properties like *being six feet tall*, *being either a horse or a non-horse*, and so on. But some properties do admit of degrees, for example, *being tall*. Some tall people are taller than other tall people. Now, of the properties that admit of degrees, we notice that some of them possess, so to speak, an intrinsic or conceivable maximum and some do not. For example, the property of *being tall* possesses no intrinsic maximum – no matter how tall we imagine a tall person to be we can always imagine a taller person. But some properties do possess an intrinsic maximum – for instance, the property of *having scored well in a golf match*. A score that cannot be bested would be achieved by that golfer who scores 18 in an 18-hole match, that is, who makes a hole-in-one on each hole. Perhaps the property of *being powerful* is also such a property. A being who is omni-powerful or omnipotent at a given time is roughly a being who can bring about any state of affairs that it is not logically impossible for that being to bring about at that time. This is a degree of power that cannot be bested.

The second point is far more thorny and complex. There are many things that might be meant by the word 'conceivable' and several things that might be meant by the word 'possible'. By 'possible' let's just stipulate that we mean 'logically possible' in the sense of broad logical possibility standardly used by most philosophers these days.[4] It is possible for me to run the mile in two minutes flat but not for me to meet a married bachelor or truthfully to say, 'I am Richard Nixon.' But clearly we can, if we want, draw the limits of conceivability wider than the limits of possibility (I can *conceive*, in some sense of that term, of married bachelors) or equal to them (married bachelors, in this sense of the term, are *inconceivable*).

By the term 'conceivable', we might mean something like 'logically possible'; something like 'mentally picturable'; something like 'definable'; or something like 'nameable'. Anselm himself seemed to use the term in each of the first two ways. He claimed in *Proslogion* IV that in one sense of the word 'conceivable' (what he calls 'conceiving of the word') at least one logical impossibility can be conceived (the fool can conceive of God's non-existence). But as long as philosophers make clear their usage and stick to it consistently, I see no serious difficulty in their simply stipulating that for them conceivability equals possibility. (Perhaps this is precisely what Anselm himself did for the other use of the term 'conceive' – 'conceiving of the thing' – that he mentioned in *Proslogion* IV. This is the sense in which he supposed that the non-existence of God is inconceivable.) I propose in this chapter to make this very move; I will stipulate that conceivability equals possibility; and so I will feel no compunction in using the term GCB in my discussion of the OA.

The final difficulty that I will discuss in coming to grasp the meaning of Anselm's term 'a being than which nothing greater can be conceived' is the word 'greater'. Sadly, this is one of the gaps in Anselm's argument; Anselm nowhere said exactly what he meant by 'greater' or what it is that constitutes 'greatness' for a being. But we can, as it were, try to work backward and figure out what he must have meant or at least what his argument requires. That is, we can ask what notions of 'greatness' might make the OA succeed. There is some textual evidence that Anselm wanted us to interpret 'greatness' in terms of goodness,[5] but I prefer to follow another path. If we read greatness as, say, *red-headedness* or *running speed* or *largeness* the OA will clearly not succeed. (There logically can be no 'red-headedest conceivable being', 'fastest-running conceivable being', or 'largest conceivable being'.) But if we read greatness as *power*, *ability*, *freedom of action* (where the GCB is then omnipotent), the OA just might succeed. (Perhaps other notions of greatness will also make the OA succeed.) I make no exegetical claim that this notion of 'greatness' is Anselm's intended notion, although it is clearly in the spirit of the concept of God he worked with in the *Proslogion* and the *Monologion*. Nor do I claim that power is the *only* great-making property for beings or persons. I claim merely that my criterion is intelligible and has a chance of allowing the OA to succeed.

Now if all this gives us a reasonably helpful handle on the meaning of Anselm's term 'a being than which nothing greater can be conceived', we must proceed to the next question, namely, is the term coherent? That is, does the notion of a GCB make sense? The notion will make sense, I think, on two conditions.[6] First, it must be the case that beings are comparable or commensurable with respect to greatness; and second, it must be the case that greatness admits of a maximal case. I believe that both conditions are satisfied. Though much of the groundwork has been done above, let me explain further.

Clearly, there are notions of greatness on which beings are not readily comparable. Suppose we say that one being is greater than another if it is *more of a prime number* than the other. But how can one being (say, the number three) be *more of a prime number* than another being (say, the number seven)? An OA based on *this* notion of greatness cannot even get going. But if we define greatness as above, that is, as *power, ability,* or *freedom of action*, comparisons clearly can be made, even among beings of widely different kinds. In some cases it will be difficult to decide (is a possum more powerful than a raccoon?), and in nearly all cases it will be difficult to be mathematically precise (exactly how much more powerful is a typewriter than a nail?). Nevertheless, we do frequently compare different items as to their power, ability to act, freedom, and so forth. Geese are more powerful than stones; humans are more powerful than cocker spaniels; President Clinton is more powerful than the mayor of Washington D.C.

Furthermore, as Tom Morris[7] has pointed out, Anselm's argument can go through even if for some reason it is false that all beings are commensurable, that is, even if there are some beings that cannot sensibly be compared with each other in greatness. All Anselm strictly needs is that all beings be comparable in greatness with God. So even if there are two beings, X and Y, that are not comparable with each other in greatness (that is, it makes no sense to ask which of them is greater), the OA can still succeed just as long as it is still true that both X and Y are less great than the GCB.

Is greatness a property that admits of a maximal degree? Surely not on some notions of greatness. But on the notion of greatness I have been using, it does. There logically can be no more powerful being than a being who is omnipotent, as defined above. It looks, then, as if both conditions for the coherence of the concept of the GCB are satisfied. Beings *are* comparable with respect to greatness (as defined), and greatness (as defined) *does* admit of a maximal case. Thus if the term GCB refers to God, and if there are sound versions of the OA (naturally, the latter is a very big if), we have found in the OA a piece of natural theology that successfully argues for the existence of God.

II. ANSELM'S ARGUMENT

Let us now consider Anselm's argument. It is important to remind ourselves that the OA is what we might call an '*a priori* existential' argument. That is, it is an argument that tries to prove the existence of something (namely, the GCB), and as noted it tries to do so primarily by *a priori* means, that is, by examining concepts or ideas or definitions. (This is as opposed to a more common '*a posteriori* existential' argument, one which argues for the existence of something on the basis of probabilistic appeals to experience.) The OA I will present here is a version of the so-called 'first form' of Anselm's argument, the one that is found in *Proslogion* II.

Here is what Anselm said:

> And so, Lord, do thou, who dost give understanding to faith, give me, so far as thou knowest it to be profitable, to understand that thou art as we believe; and that thou art that which we believe. And, indeed, we believe that thou art a being than which nothing greater can be conceived. Or is there no such nature, since the fool hath said in his heart, there is no God? (Psalms xiv.1). But, at any rate, this very fool, when he hears of this being of which I speak – a being than which nothing greater can be conceived – understands what he hears, and what he understands is in his understanding; although he does not understand it to exist . . .
>
> Hence, even the fool is convinced that something exists in the understanding, at least, than which nothing greater can be conceived. For, when he hears of this, he understands it. And whatever is understood, exists in the understanding. And assuredly that, than which nothing greater can be conceived, cannot exist in the understanding alone. For, suppose it exists in the understanding alone; then it can be conceived to exist in reality; which is greater.
>
> Therefore, if that, than which nothing greater can be conceived, exists in the understanding alone, the very being, than which nothing greater can be conceived is one, than which a greater can be conceived. But obviously this is impossible. Hence, there is no doubt that there exists a being, than which nothing greater can be conceived, and it exists both in the understanding and in reality.[8]

The argument that follows is my attempt to state, in logical form and as clearly as I can, the argument that Anselm presents in *Proslogion* II. The argument begins with:

1. Things can exist in only two ways – in the mind and in reality.

A thing exists 'in the mind' if somebody imagines, defines or conceives of it. A thing exists 'in reality' if it exists or is real independently of anyone's ideas or concepts of it, and if it exists as a concrete thing that has causal properties.[9] Thus there are four (what we might call) 'modes of existence' – a thing might exist both in the mind and in reality (for example, Bill Clinton); it might exist in the mind but not in reality (for instance, Stephen Davis's ninth daughter); it might exist in reality but not in the mind (for instance, some undiscovered but existing chemical element); or it might exist in neither way (for example, nuclear weapons in the year AD 1550).

The argument continues with:

2. The GCB can possibly exist in reality, that is, is not an impossible thing.

All premise (2) means is that since we can find no contradiction or other sort of incoherence in the term 'greatest conceivable being', it looks as if this being can possibly exist. It either exists in reality or else (like unicorns and my ninth daughter) contingently fails to exist. Unlike married bachelors and square circles (whose definitions *are* contradictory), logic does not require the non-existence of the GCB.

The next premise is:

3. The GCB exists in the mind.

This simply means that someone (Anselm, you the reader, or whoever) has conceived of the GCB. Of course, Anselm was not suggesting that anyone conceives of God in the sense of understanding all about God – as a Christian theologian, he knew that no human could do that. (We will return to this point in Section III.) He simply suggested that someone has conceived of God in the sense of understanding his term for God, 'greatest conceivable being'.

The next premise might be called Anselm's hidden premise, because he nowhere stated it in the *Proslogion*. It is clear, however, that his argument needs some such step as:

4. Whatever exists only in the mind and might possibly exist in reality might possibly be greater than it is.

The intuitive idea here is that things are greater if they exist both in the mind and in reality than they would be if they existed just in the mind. Anselm was not comparing different sorts of things – he was not saying, for example, that a given clod of dirt in the flower bed in my front yard, since it exists in both ways, is greater (in the sense defined earlier) than Paul Bunyan, who exists only in the mind. He was comparing the same thing in different modes of being – he was implying, for example, that the clod of dirt is greater than it would be if it existed only in the mind, and that Paul Bunyan would have been greater than he in fact is had the legendary woodsman existed in reality as well as in the mind. In terms of our earlier definition of 'greater', Anselm should accordingly be taken as suggesting that things that exist both in the mind and in reality are more powerful, freer, more able to do things than they would be if they existed merely in the mind.

Premises (1) through (4) constitute the basic assumptions of the OA. Like any deductive argument, the soundness of the OA depends on the truth of its assumptions. If any of them is false, the argument is unsound. Next Anselm suggested a premise that he wanted to reduce to absurdity:

5. The GCB exists only in the mind.

Anselm thus asked us in effect to assume that the GCB does not exist. He did this because he thought that this assumption, together with the earlier premises of the OA, leads to a contradiction. *Reductio ad absurdum* (reduction to absurdity) is an ancient and well-recognised logical device which allows us to negate any premise that is responsible for producing a contradiction or other absurdity. Thus Anselm was trying to prove that the GCB exists by showing that premise (5), together of course with (1) through (4), entails a contradiction.

The next three premises constitute the logical outworking of the assumptions of the OA. Here Anselm showed that premise (5) is unacceptable and should be negated. First, he suggested that if premises (5), (2) and (4) are true, then the premise

6. The GCB might be greater than it is

must be true as well. Now because there might be confusion here, let me explain this point in a bit more detail. Clearly we are able to use and understand the term 'GCB'; the question is what ontological status to assign to the GCB – to that to which the term 'GCB' refers (if it refers to anything). Is the GCB a *mere concept* (like 'Stephen Davis's ninth daughter') or rather an *existing thing* (like 'Stephen Davis's second son'?)[10] Note that existing things are *greater* (in the sense of 'greater' defined above) than the mere concepts of those things. That is, existing things are more powerful, freer, more able to do things than the mere concepts of those things. Mere concepts presumably have some abilities – they can sometimes help stimulate us to think or act, for example – but not nearly so many as existing things. What premise (6) claims, then, is as follows: the ontological status that the GCB has (given premise (5)) is such that (given premise (2)) the GCB might be an existing thing rather than a mere concept; and if it were an existing thing, then (given premise (4)) it would be greater than it is. As a mere concept, the GCB is not particularly great; as an existing thing it would be greater.

But it can be pointed out that this is to open the OA to an objection. What is needed to make the OA work, it will be said, is that something like the following proposition be coherent:

6a. The mere concept of the GCB might be an existing thing.

But it will then be charged that (6a) is incoherent – a concept cannot literally *be* an existing thing. A concept, after all, is just an idea, not an existing thing. What does make sense (it will be said) is:

6b. The mere concept of the GCB might be an instantiated concept

(that is, a concept that names or refers to or corresponds to an existing thing), which does not help the OA at all. For Anselm apparently made no claims about the greatness of concepts (for instance, about instantiated concepts being greater than uninstantiated concepts); rather, he claimed that existing things are greater than the mere concepts of those things. If (6a) is incoherent (so the objection concludes), then (6) cannot be coherently stated, and the OA fails.

But in answer to this objection we need only ask what is meant or referred to by the term 'GCB'. If there exists no GCB in reality, then the 'GCB' exists, as Anselm would have it, only 'in the mind'. And if the GCB exists (as he would say) 'in reality', then of course the term 'GCB' refers to or denotes an existing thing. Accordingly, Anselm needed to push no arguments and have no opinion about whether instantiated concepts are greater than uninstantiated ones. He *did* need to argue, however, that existing things are greater than the mere concepts of them. His point, then, was that if the GCB is a mere concept it is still true that the (non-existent) thing described by that concept might exist (just as Stephen Davis's ninth daughter might possibly exist); and that if it did exist, it would be greater than it (the mere concept) in fact is. It is true that premise (6a) sounds odd – perhaps a concept cannot literally *be* an existing thing, but the point is that the thing the concept describes or refers to might be an existing thing.

But of course this is to invite the following query: what exactly is this 'thing' that the concept describes or refers to? In reply, let's look at what we've thus far said about this 'thing'. We've said it is non-existent; we've said it possesses properties (a non-existent GCB, for example, still has the property of *being a concept*); and we've said it can be referred to. But can we refer to non-existent, property-bearing things? Of course we can. The following sentences are not only coherent but true: 'Paul Bunyan is a woodsman,' 'Davis's ninth daughter is a daughter', 'Charles De Gaulle is a former President of France.' The 'thing' the concept describes or refers to, then, is simply what we might call a 'possibly existing thing' (dare we call it a PET, for short?). A possibly existing thing is simply a set of compossible properties that might or might not be real (or exist in reality, as Anselm would say). Some PETs exist in reality and are thus also concrete objects; some exist only as PETs and thus are merely abstract objects. I am a PET, and so is Bill Clinton; Paul Bunyan is a PET, and so is my ninth daughter. There certainly can be mere concepts of PETs, but a PET is not just and without remainder a mere concept, for surely there are PETS of which no conceiver has ever had any concept. Thus a non-existent GCB can best be thought of as a set of compossible properties that constitute a PET. And premise (6) is to be taken as saying that the GCB, a non-existent PET, might be an existing PET; and that if it were an existing PET, it would be greater than it in fact is.[11]

Having returned to premise (6), let us notice that it is at least implicitly contradictory; what it says is that 'the greatest conceivable being might be greater than it is.' Another way of expressing this implicit contradiction, and one that is directly entailed by premise (6), is:

7. The GCB is a being than which a greater is conceivable.

Now since (7) is an explicit contradiction, then by *reductio ad absurdum* we are allowed to search for whatever premise above it in the argument is responsible for producing the contradiction. Realistically, we must look to the assumptions of the argument, that is, (1) through (5). Now (1), (2), (3), and (4) are all – so Anselm would say – either necessary truths or at least statements whose truth can be established. Clearly, then, (5) is the culprit; if so, then *reductio ad absurdum* allows us to negate it.

One way of negating a statement is simply to place the phrase 'it is false that' in front of it. Thus we can negate (5), the offending premise, by means of:

8. It is false that the GCB exists only in the mind.

We are now almost finished. We know by premise (1) that things can exist in only two ways, in the mind and in reality; we know by premise (3) that the GCB exists (at least) in the mind; and we know by premise (8) that it is false that the GCB exists only in the mind. Thus it follows that:

9. The GCB exists both in the mind and in reality,

which was what we were trying to prove.

III. GAUNILO'S CRITICISMS OF THE OA

Suppose we now consider some of the important ways in which the OA has been criticized. A good place to begin is with Gaunilo, a contemporary of Anselm, a monk from Marmoutier, who wrote a response to the *Proslogion* entitled, interestingly, *On Behalf of the Fool*.[12] This of course was a reference to the foolish atheist of Psalm 14 whom Anselm mentioned in *Proslogion* II. Gaunilo raised several criticisms of the OA; let me discuss three of them.

(1) *The 'boy scout' objection*

This is my name for a common objection to the OA that is not explicitly stated by Gaunilo but seems to lurk behind much of what he says. When I was about five or six years old, I remember clearly my deep puzzlement when one day my father told me that boy scouts could rub sticks together and produce fire. I did not doubt him, but with the knowledge of physics typically had by children of that age, I could not see how you could possibly take things like sticks, rub them together, and produce something so very different as fire. Similarly, the 'boy scout' objection to the OA argues against the very idea of an *a priori* existential argument. It denies that you can take mere ideas or definitions or concepts and produce, by rubbing them together intellectually, so to speak, the existence of something in reality. The OA illegitimately tries to move from the level of *in intellectu* to the level of *in re*, and (so the objection goes) you cannot do that. Thus Gaunilo says:

> If it should be said that a being which cannot even be conceived in terms of any fact, is in the understanding, I do not deny that this being is, accordingly, in my understanding. But since through this fact it can in no wise attain to real existence also, I do not yet concede to it that existence at all, until some certain proof of it shall be given.[13]

But in defense of Anselm it must be pointed out that we *can* use purely *a priori* procedures to show *some* things about reality, for example, that certain things do not exist in it. Note that by purely *a priori* procedures, that is, without empirically 'looking around', it can be shown that no married bachelors ('unmarried adult males who are married') or square circles ('plane four-sided geometrical figures all of whose points are equidistant from the centre') exist *in re*. Such arguments seem entirely innocuous – who would object to them?

Of course the 'boy scout' objector might then reply that we can use purely *a priori* procedures to show that certain things *do not* exist in reality, but not to show that certain other things *do*. But that move seems a bit forced, and involves special pleading. Why is it that we can go in one direction but not the other with *a priori* existential arguments? And surely we *can* go in the other direction. As Norman Malcolm asks, 'Is the Euclidean theorem in number theory, "There exists an infinite number of prime numbers," an "existential proposition"? Do we not want to say that *in some sense* it asserts the existence of something?'[14] Similarly, can we not prove by an *a priori* argument the truth of the statement 'There exists at least one prime number between six and ten'? Now it might be replied that numbers are not like God, and in terms of our earlier discussion, they do not enjoy the same sort of existence in reality that God (according to Anselm) does. That would be true. Still, haven't we cast doubt on the 'boy scout' claim that you can't rub together mere ideas or definitions and prove in some senses that something exists *in re*?

But the most important point is that it seems question-begging simply to insist against Anselm that 'you can't do that,' that is, that no *a priori* existential argument can possibly succeed. The OA itself will have to be examined to see whether it *does* succeed. If it does not, the precise reason that it fails will have to be shown.

(2) *Can we 'conceive of God'?*

Gaunilo also took exception to Anselm's implicit claim to be able to conceive of God. That Anselm did indeed claim this is clear because of his insistence on the point that the GCB 'exists *in intellectu*'. But it is a well-accepted item of the Christian theological tradition, shared by both Anselm and Gaunilo, that we humans are unable fully to comprehend God. Thus Gaunilo said:

> I, so far as actual knowledge of the object, either from its specific or general character, is concerned, am as little able to conceive of this being when I hear of it, or to have it in my understanding, as I am to conceive of or understand God himself . . . For I do not know that reality itself which God is.

A bit later, he added (speaking directly to Anselm):

> I am not able . . . to have that being of which you speak in concept or in understanding, when I hear the word *God* or the words, *a being*

greater than all other beings. For I can conceive of the man according to a fact that is real and familiar to me: but of God, or a being greater than all others, I could not conceive at all, except merely according to the word.[15]

Gaunilo was in effect saying that the OA cannot even get going, since we humans are quite unable to conceive of God.

I will discuss in more detail in Chapter 3 what I take to be Anselm's reply to this criticism. For now, let me simply point out a distinction that Anselm made in *Proslogion* IV and that seems relevant to the issue at hand. There he said: 'A thing may be conceived in two ways: (1) when the word signifying it is conceived; (2) when the thing itself is understood.'[16] Perhaps the thing for a defender of Anselm to do at this point is happily to admit that we are quite unable to 'conceive of God' in the second sense (understand the thing). The defender should then go on to insist on two further points – first, that we can 'conceive of the GCB' in the first sense (understand the words, that is, understand the meaning of the words, 'greatest conceivable being'); and, second, that this is all that is needed for the purposes of the OA. That is, in order for the OA to get going, the ontological arguer does not need to understand all about God but simply know the meaning of Anselm's definition of God. (Again, we will explore further the implications of Anselm's distinction between the two sorts of 'conceiving' in the next chapter.)

(3) *The lost island*

But Gaunilo's most famous objection was also his most ingenious. In effect he tried to reduce the OA itself to absurdity by showing that it proves too much. He wanted to take the exact logical form of Anselm's OA and create what we might call a 'parallel OA' by systematically removing all mentions of the term 'GCB' and replacing them with some other term, for example, 'the greatest conceivable lost island' (GCLI). If successful, Gaunilo's strategy does not tell us precisely *what* is wrong with the OA but does show that something *must* be wrong with it. Obviously, this is because we can use parallel OAs to 'prove' the existence of all sorts of bizarre things (for example, 'the greatest conceivable hangnail') – many of which we know good and well do not exist. Gaunilo made some minor mistakes in his statement of the 'lost island' objection,[17] but they are easy to correct. There *is* a serious problem for the OA here.

Gaunilo first defined his lost island and explained why he called it 'greatest'. It has 'an inestimable wealth of all manner of riches and delicacies in greater abundance than is told of the Islands of the

Blest',[18] etc. He then added that there is no problem in understanding the sentence 'The GCLI exists.' But, he said, suppose someone were to argue in the manner of *Proslogion* II that the GCLI actually exists ('it is more excellent for it to exist than for it not to exist; thus if it did not exist any existing island would be greater; thus the GCLI would not be the GCLI,' etc.). Gaunilo then acutely said:

> If a man should try to prove to me by such reasoning that this island truly exists, and that its existence should no longer be doubted, either I should believe that he was jesting, or I know not which I ought to regard as the greater fool; myself, supposing that I should allow this proof; or him, if he should suppose that he had established with any certainty the existence of this island.[19]

Anselm's response to Gaunilo's *On Behalf of the Fool* was a small book sometimes called *Reply to Gaunilo*. His response to the lost island objection was brief and seemingly rather flippant, but I will argue than it is more incisive than it might first appear:

> Now I promise confidently that if any man shall devise anything existing either in reality or in concept alone (except that than which a greater cannot be conceived) to which he can adapt the sequence of my reasoning, I will discover that thing, and will give him his lost island, not to be lost again.[20]

In other words, Anselm wanted to argue that the OA is a sound argument and that Gaunilo's parallel OA (containing the term GCLI) is unsound.

But Anselm seemed to follow a blind alley in trying to establish this point. He took great pains to show that the GCLI is not the same thing as, and is less great than, the GCB. This is surely true, but it need not bother Gaunilo. Gaunilo's 'lost island' objection does not depend on mistakenly identifying the GCB and the GCLI. His point was rather this – if the OA is sound, then so must be the parallel OA, because they follow the same logical structure. For surely – so Gaunilo might say – in any valid argument substitutions can be made for terms that appear in the argument; and if the substitutions are made carefully, the resulting argument will also be valid. Thus the argument:

10. All men are mortal
11. Aristotle is a man
12. Therefore, Aristotle is mortal,

is surely valid, just as is the traditional argument in which the term 'Socrates' appears.

How might Anselm argue, and not just claim, that his OA is a sound argument and that Gaunilo's parallel argument containing the term GCLI is not? Let's look again at the second premise of each argument. Anselm's says:

> 2. The GCB might have existed in reality, that is, is not an impossible being.

And Gaunilo's would say (let's add the letter 'a' to signify that we are talking about a parallel OA):

> 2a. The GCLI might have existed in reality, that is, is not an impossible being.

We have already argued that (2) is true. Some philosophers have tried to show that the notion of the GCB is contradictory or otherwise incoherent, but these arguments have never amounted to much. How then might Anselm argue that the notion of the GCLI is incoherent?

First, two definitions. Let us say that a 'necessary being' (NB) is a being that cannot not exist, and depends for its existence on no other being. A 'contingent being', let's say, is a being that can either exist or not exist (some contingent beings exist, and some do not), and if it exists, it depends for its existence on another being or other beings.

Suppose we decide to draw very wide limits of conceivability, contrary to our earlier decision to make conceivability equal to possibility. Suppose, that is, we say that we can conceive of impossible things like limited, contingent beings possessing unlimited perfections. Then the problem with the GCLI is that the greater we make it in conception, the less it will resemble an island. Recall that earlier we decided to interpret Anselm's notion of greatness as power, freedom of action, ability to do things. Notice also that in *Proslogion* III Anselm explicitly said that to be necessary is greater than to be contingent. Thus if any two beings, A and B, are equal in all their properties except that A is a necessary being and B is not, or except that A is omnipotent and B is not, it follows that A is greater than B.

So the GCB must be a necessary being, but the GCLI, if it is going to be an island, must be contingent – it must depend for its existence on the geological forces (or whatever) that created it. But notice that on the wide notion of conceivability the logic of the definition '*greatest conceivable* lost island' requires that this being be a necessary being. For any contingent island of which we can conceive, no matter how great, we can always conceive a greater one, namely, one that is necessary. Similar reasoning will push us toward the GCLI being omnipotent – being able, for example, to solve equations and manufacture shoes. An island that can do those things is surely greater than one that cannot. But of course no island can be omnipotent – islands are just islands, after all. Thus the very definition 'GCLI' is a contradictory notion.

But at this point Gaunilo might plead that we draw narrower limits of conceivability and return to our stipulation that conceivability equals possibility. If so, Gaunilo can argue that we conceive the GCLI in terms of great-making properties that are logically compatible with islandness. He can then argue that his parallel OA still refutes the OA because its premise (2a) is true. The term 'GCLI', he will say, describes a perfectly coherent, but obviously non-existent, being which is a contingent and limited being. It is the 'greatest conceivable' member of the set of lost islands because it possesses to the maximal degree all those great-making properties that islands can possibly have. These would presumably be properties like the beauty of the scenery, the temperature, the amount of sunlight, the taste of the coconuts, power to provide shade and shelter, power to nourish flora and fauna, etc.

This notion, however, also appears to be incoherent, but for a different reason. If we conceive of the GCLI in such terms, one problem is that we are talking about properties that contain no intrinsic criteria of greatness. How do we decide which temperature is 'greatest'? How do we decide that the scenery of a certain beautiful island is the 'greatest conceivable' scenery? Aren't some of these points matters of taste? How then would we decide? Would we vote? Who would be allowed to vote?

The other problem is closely related – these sorts of great-making properties have no intrinsic maximums or discernible limits. Take the notion 'tallest conceivable human'. This notion is not explicitly contradictory, but is still clearly incoherent. No matter how tall we imagine a certain human as being, we can always conceptually add another inch and thus show that it was not the 'tallest conceivable human'. Thus there logically *can be no* 'tallest conceivable human'. Similarly, there logically can be no GCLI because its greatness will be measured, like height for a human, in terms that have no intrinsic maximum. What exactly is the greatest conceivable degree of good taste for a coconut? What is the maximum degree of ability to nourish flora and fauna?

So it still appears that whichever way we decide to understand 'conceivability', premise (2a) of Gaunilo's parallel OA is false. The GCLI could not possibly exist in reality. Accordingly, Anselm was right in insisting that the term GCLI cannot be adapted to the sequence of his reasoning. The 'lost island' objection to the OA appears to fail.[21]

IV. KANT'S CRITICISM

Undoubtedly the most serious objection ever raised against the OA is Kant's criticism of it in his *Critique of Pure Reason,* especially his claim that the word 'exists' is not, as he said, a 'real predicate'.[22] The idea that Kant refuted the OA has attained something like the status of philosophical orthodoxy. Very many philosophers accept this notion, including such twentieth-century luminaries as Bertrand Russell,[23] Norman Malcolm,[24] and John Hick.[25] Let me first explain Kant's criticism, and then see whether the OA can be defended against it.

Explaining the criticism is not easy. The concepts are difficult, and Kant's exposition of his critique is not a model of clarity. In the sentence 'The horse is fast,' let's say that 'horse' is the subject of the sentence and 'is fast' is the predicate. In his critique of the OA, Kant made a distinction between what he called a *logical predicate* and a *real predicate.* Anything at all, Kant said, can be a logical predicate; the subject can even be predicated of itself. (In the sentence 'The horse is a horse,' the phrase 'is a horse' is a logical predicate.) So a logical predicate, let's say, is *any* word or phrase that appears in the predicate position of a sentence. What then is a real predicate? To use some of Kant's expressions, it is a predicate that 'determines a thing' or 'expands' or 'is added to' or 'enlarges' our concept of the subject. If I say, 'The horse is a horse,' or even, 'The horse is bbdsaf,' these logical predicates do not enlarge the concept of 'horse' that I already have. But if I say, 'The horse is fast,' then, since fastness is not part of the concept of horse (some horses are slow), I have succeeded in adding to your concept of the horse I am describing. I have used a real predicate.

Now what about the sentence 'The horse exists'? Kant's argument is that the word 'exists', which in this sentence is certainly a logical predicate, is not also a real predicate. This is because it fails to expand our concept of 'the horse'. 'By whatever and by however many predicates we may think a thing,' Kant insisted, 'we do not make the least addition to the thing when we further declare that this thing *is.*'[26] In other words, both concepts and objects have content. The content of an object, let's say, is its properties, and the content of a concept is the set of properties the object must have in order for it to fall under the concept.[27] And, said Kant, a given concept C can be the concept of a given object O only if the content of C and the content of O are identical – otherwise C is not a concept of O after all but of something else. Thus, the logical predicate in the sentence 'The horse exists' is not a real predicate; it does not enlarge our concept of 'the horse'.

Kant's claim that 'exists' is not a real predicate is extremely difficult to prove rigorously,[28] so most advocates try to convince us of its truth by giving examples. Kant himself said, 'A hundred real thalers [sometimes translated dollars] do not contain the least coin more than a hundred possible thalers.'[29] In other words, the number of dollars in the real one-hundred-dollar bill in my wallet and the number of dollars in my concept of it in my brain must be exactly the same. Malcolm says that the sentence 'My house will be a better house if it is insulated than if it is not' makes perfect sense; but the sentence 'My house will be a better house if it exists than if it does not' does not.[30] But the best example in the literature, in my opinion, is Malcolm's second example. He says:

> A king might desire that his next chancellor should have knowledge, wit, and resolution; but it is ludicrous to add that the king's desire is to have a chancellor who exists. Suppose that two royal councilors, A and B, were asked to draw up separately descriptions of the most perfect chancellor they could conceive, and that the descriptions they produced were identical except that A included existence in his list of attributes of a perfect chancellor and B did not. (I do not mean that B put nonexistence on his list.) One and the same person could satisfy both descriptions. More to the point, any person who satisfied A's description would *necessarily* satisfy B's description and *vice versa*![31]

Hick says that talk of certain things existing 'in the mind' and certain others existing both 'in the mind and in reality' is simply a pre-critical way of talking about certain concepts having instances in reality and certain others not having them. Once we understand Anselm's language in this way, he says, it follows that the OA is powerless to show that the concept 'GCB' is an instantiated concept as opposed to a noninstantiated concept. He says, 'The concept of the GCB is still a concept, and whether or not it is instantiated is a further factual question. This cannot be decided *a priori*, or by definition, but only *a posteriori*, by some kind of procedure of observation or experience.'[32]

Let's hold off for a moment on addressing the question of whether Kant is right in denying that 'exists' is a real predicate. Let's first ask what relevance this point has to the OA. I see Kant's argument as a critique of Anselm's claim that it is greater for something to exist *in intellectu* and *in re* than it is for it to exist *in intellectu* alone. Interpreting Anselm, we expressed this point by means of premise (4), which says:

4. Whatever exists only in the mind and might also have existed in reality might have been greater than it is.

Anselm was apparently claiming something like this: if two beings, A and B, are exactly alike in all their properties as much as possible, except that A exists in both modes and B exists just in the mind, then A is greater than B. In other words, the concept of a thing *does* (or at least can) change when you add that that thing exists – it changes in terms of the *greatness* of the thing. So Anselm did hold, and needed to hold, that 'exists' is or can be a real predicate. Thus, if Kant is correct that 'exists' is *not* a real predicate, it follows that premise (4) of the OA is false, and the OA fails.

Well then, is Kant correct? Let me present a brief argument in favour of the claim that 'exists' is, or at least can be in some circumstances, a real predicate. 'Exists' is certainly an unusual predicate, and in some contexts it appears that Kant is right that it does not 'enlarge' or 'add to' our concept of the subject. Notice the following dialogue:

> Do you own a pencil?
> Yes, I do.
> Is your pencil painted yellow?
> Yes.
> Is there an eraser on your pencil?
> Yes.
> Does your pencil write?
> Yes.
> But does your pencil exist?

The problem here is that the pencil's existence was apparently presupposed throughout the conversation; thus the oddness of the concluding question. If the reply were to be, 'Yes, of course, my pencil does indeed exist,' this would not (as Kant would say) change or expand our concept of the pencil. We were assuming an existing pencil all along. Here Kant is right.

But what about those linguistic contexts in which the existence of the thing being discussed is not necessarily presupposed? To say that the thing exists may well, in those cases, expand our concept of it. I am quite sure that my concept of the Loch Ness Monster would change if someone were to convince me that the creature exists, that there really is (let's say) a reproducing colony of plesiosaurs in the loch left over from the Cretaceous period. Here 'exists' *is* a real predicate.

Let us return to the examples given by Kant and Malcolm. Kant knew, of course, that there is a difference between a real hundred thalers and the mere concept of them,[33] but his point appears to be that the content of the two *concepts* must be identical. And it is obviously correct to claim that the two concepts do not differ in *number of thalers*. If the real hundred thalers contained a hundred thalers and the idea of them contained only ninety-nine, the one would not be the idea of the other. Fair enough. But that does not show that the concepts cannot differ in other ways. And surely they do.

Of the real hundred thalers, my concept of them includes the property of having-purchasing-power-in-the-real-world. My concept of the concept of a hundred thalers does not have that property.

Contrary to his linguistic intuitions, I think there are contexts in which Malcolm's sentence 'My house will be a better house if it exists than if it does not' can make perfect sense. But then what about Malcolm's claim that 'any person who satisfied A's description [of the most perfect chancellor] would *necessarily* satisfy B's description and *vice versa*'? This does not appear to be true. There might be a character in a Dostoyevsky novel who satisfies all the attributes on B's list (knowledge, wit, resolution, etc.) but who, since he does not exist *in re*, fails to satisfy all the attributes on A's list (since 'A included existence in his list of attributes'). Somebody who is dead – Charles De Gaulle, for instance – might satisfy all the requirements in B's list but not those in A's list. Accordingly, Malcolm is wrong – the lists *do* differ, and 'exists' can be a real predicate.

The deep issue raised by Hick concerns the legitimacy of talk about things existing 'in the mind.' But I see no fatal problem here; exactly why is it 'pre-critical'? (Such talk certainly would be illegitimate if the claim that something exists in the mind were covertly taken to entail some other, more substantial, species of existence, but it is not.) Nor do I agree that 'X exists in the mind' is just a different way of saying what we can more felicitously express by talk of uninstantiated concepts. If it were merely a matter of saying the same thing in more currently permissible words, then the OA could equally well be expressed in the terminology that Hick allows. But if Hick is right that it can't, it follows that there is a substantive metaphysical claim (perhaps something like 'There are no property-bearing non-existing things') buried in Hick's apparently merely linguistic claim.

So it makes perfectly good sense to speak, as I did earlier, of possibly existing things (that is, sets of compossible properties that might exist in reality) and to say that a possibly existing thing that exists in reality is greater, in the sense defined earlier, than that thing would be if it did not exist in reality. If I am right, Kant's argument does not refute the OA.

V. ROWE'S CRITICISM

Let us now consider an ingenious twentieth-century critique of the OA, one that succeeds in breaking new ground. It is a criticism by William Rowe, who holds that the OA commits the informal fallacy of 'begging the question.'[34]

Rowe recognises that there are several ways in which an argument might be guilty of begging the question. He is interested in what he calls 'the epistemological way' of begging the question. You commit this fallacy,

Rowe says, if one or another of the premises of your argument cannot be
known apart from knowledge of the conclusion. Thus in the argument

13. Whatever the Bible says is true;
14. The Bible says that God exists;
15. Therefore, God exists

premise (13) cannot be known independently of (15) (Rowe is thinking here
of the view that the Bible is inerrant because inspired by God); accordingly,
this argument begs the question. What does this have to do with the OA?
First let's look at an argument Rowe calls the 'Simple Ontological
Argument' (SOA). (This is not, of course, anything that we find in
Anselm.)

16. 'God' is defined as 'an existing, supremely perfect being';
17. Some possible object is God;
18. Therefore, God actually exists.

Rowe first wants to convince us that the SOA begs the question; then he
will turn to the question of whether the OA itself begs the question.

Premise (16), Rowe says, does not all by itself entail that God exists; but
it does entail something important, viz., a premise that we will call the
'preliminary conclusion' of the OA:

16a. No nonexisting thing is God.

Now normally when we allow that a given concept or definition is
coherent, all we mean to allow is that it is logically possible for the thing
defined to exist. Rowe wants us to notice, however, that in certain
contexts, including the context of the SOA, to allow as (17) does that a
given concept is coherent is in effect to allow that the thing actually exists.
This is because we have already learned via (16) that no non-existing thing
is God. But if no non-existing thing can be God, then either the concept of
God is incoherent or else God actually exists. Thus when we grant (17), we
grant much more than we thought. We thought we were merely granting
that either God is a possible thing that exists (like you or me) or a possible
thing that fails to exist (like my ninth daughter). Unbeknownst to us, we
were granting that God actually exists.

We learn two things from this exercise, Rowe says. First, it is not true
that every coherent concept is exemplified by some possible object. Take
the concept 'unicornex', which Rowe defines as 'an actually existing
unicorn'. Note that some possible object is a *unicorn*, but *since in fact no
unicorns exist*, no possible object is a unicornex. That is, unicornexes,
despite the coherence of their concept or definition, are not possible

things because no possible thing that does not in fact exist can possibly be a unicornex. Here then we have a coherent concept that fails to be exemplified by anything coherent. So the only way to know that unicornexes are possible is to know that unicornexes exist. Second, the SOA begs the question because we cannot know that (17) is true unless we know that (18), the conclusion, is true. This is because of the fact that if it happens that no existing thing is supremely perfect, (17) is false.

The same point can be made about the OA, Rowe claims. It is true that in the case of Anselm's argument we don't arrive at 'No non-existing thing can be the GCB' by definition, as we do with the SOA. In the case of the OA, we arrive at the preliminary conclusion via the definition of God plus premise (4). But it is still true, Rowe insists, that we cannot know premise (2) of the OA, that is,

> 2. The GCB can possibly exist in reality, that is, is not an impossible thing

without already knowing (9), the conclusion. The definition of God plus premise (4) of the OA lead to the preliminary conclusion 'No non-existing thing is God.' But, again, if no non-existing thing can be God, then either the concept of God is incoherent or else God actually exists. Then when we grant premise (2), we grant more than we wanted to grant. We cannot truly know premise (2) unless we know (9). So when we grant premise (2), we beg the question.

This is a clever argument, in my view the most original twentieth-century objection to the OA. But I do not think it succeeds.[35] Let us turn to the SOA and the OA. Here is the SOA:

> 16. 'God' is defined as an existing, supremely perfect being;
> 16a. No non-existing thing is God;
> 17. Some possible thing is God;
> 18. Therefore, God actually exists.

And here is the form of the OA against which Rowe is training his guns:

> 19. 'God' is defined as the GCB;
> 20. If something exists only in the understanding and might also have existed in reality, then it might have been greater than it is;
> 21. No non-existing thing is God;
> 22. Some possible thing is God;
> 23. Therefore, God exists.

Now Rowe believes that both these arguments beg the question, but his criterion of question-begging is relevant to the OA in this way: as regards things which are possible only if they exist (unincornexes, the GCB), we can only know that they are possible if we know that they exist. So we cannot know premise (22) of the OA unless we know the conclusion. Thus the OA begs the question.

Now my own view is that SOA begs the question and that the OA does not. Since (16a), (17), and (18) of the SOA are identical to (21), (22), and (23) of the OA, it is obvious (if I am right) that the reason the one argument is far more convincing than the other is to be found in the difference between (16) of the SOA and (19) and (20) of the OA. Or, to put it another way, the difference is to be found in the different ways the two arguments derive the premise 'No non-existing thing is God.'

I believe the SOA begs the question because it derives (16a) merely from an unacceptable definition of God. I believe that the OA does not beg the question because it derives (21) by valid entailment from a true premise ((20)) and an acceptable definition of God ((19)). Now it does seem that some propositions can be proved by definition. The following argument, for example, is convincing at least to me:

24. 'Bachelor' is defined as 'unmarried adult male';
25. Therefore, bachelors are unmarried.

No question-begging is going on here, in my opinion, because the definition is clearly acceptable; that is, all rational persons ought to accept (24). But suppose someone tried to prove in a similar way that all bachelors have green hair:

26. 'Bachelor' is defined as green-haired unmarried adult male;
27. Therefore, bachelors are green-haired.

That is, this person might say: '"Green-haired unmarried adult male" is just what I *mean* by the word "bachelor"; thus, bachelors have green hair.' This argument, I believe, proves nothing because it begs the question. Its definition is clearly unacceptable to most rational persons. The person who offers the argument may use the word 'bachelor' in the stipulated way, but nobody else does.

Now suppose that (26) and (27) are premises of a longer argument:

26. 'Bachelor' is defined as 'green-haired unmarried adult male';
27. Bachelors are green-haired;
28. If bachelors are green-haired, bachelors color their hair;
29. Therefore, bachelors colour their hair.

I believe that this argument too begs the question. (26), the guilty premise, does not directly entail the conclusion, but it does directly entail (27), which together with (28), entails the conclusion. So the argument still begs the question. Again, the person who offers the argument may use the term 'bachelor' in this way, and so perhaps there is a sense in which it is true that everything that falls under *this person's meaning* of the term 'bachelor' is a thing that colours its hair. But, again, this proves nothing about the grooming habits of (what the rest of us refer to when we use the word) bachelors.

The SOA is similar to the above argument. (16), the premise that I claim begs the question, does not directly entail the conclusion but rather (16a), the preliminary conclusion of the OA. But together with (17), (16a) does entail the conclusion, and so the SOA begs the question – there is no reason for anyone to accept (16) who does not already accept (18). (16) is problematical, then, because it offers a definition of God that would not be acceptable to the majority of rational persons who are not already convinced of the conclusion. Since God's existence is in doubt, it is cheating (they would say) to define God as an existing being.

But the OA, as it seems to me, does not beg the question, for its definition of God is a perfectly acceptable definition of the Judeo-Christian God. The words 'greatest conceivable being' capture well what theists mean by God – which is one reason Anselm used the term in the first place. Furthermore, this definition of God does not beg the issue at hand by defining God as existing. So the words 'greatest conceivable being' ought to be acceptable to theists and atheists alike. (It turns out, of course, that together with other assumptions, this definition logically entails that God exists, but that is another matter.)

Now some philosophers criticize the OA on the grounds that the words 'greatest conceivable being' subtly 'contain' the notion of existence – a notion that is smuggled into the argument at the point where God is defined and only comes into the open later. This seems to have been Schopenhauer's objection. But this is just not true, at least not of Anselm's *Proslogion* II OA. The definition 'greatest conceivable being' by *itself*, that is, apart from the other premises of the OA, entails nothing about the existence or non-existence of anything. And if it did, the OA would be informally invalid and not particularly interesting.

But the form of the OA that Rowe and I are discussing (that is, (19)–(23)) does not beg the question by positing an unacceptable definition. The OA offers a definition of God which could perfectly well be accepted by a rational person who does not accept the conclusion. That is, atheists too can agree that the words 'greatest conceivable being' constitute a good definition of God. Thus the OA does not beg the question in the way that I claim the SOA does.

But let us return to premise (22) of the OA,

22. Some possible thing is God,

for this is the point where Rowe claims that the OA begs the question. Rowe says that this premise begs the question because (22) cannot be known independently of

23. God exists.

In order to know (22) it is necessary to know (23), he says; there is no available way of knowing (22) without knowing (23). Are these claims correct? Is there no way to know (22) without knowing (23)? Let us first notice that the claim that (22) is true is logically equivalent to the claim that (23) is *possibly* true. So we can rephrase our question in this way: Do we have any way of knowing that (23) is possibly true?

This raises a vexing question: How can we prove or come to know of *any* proposition that it is possibly true? One sure way is to prove that the proposition is true (or necessarily true), for all true propositions (and all necessarily true propositions) are possibly true. But if the proposition in question (like (23)) is not known to be true, how can we prove that it is possibly true? The answer is that we have no hard-and-fast method of proof here: what we usually do is appeal to what might be called intuition. That is, we simply ask ourselves whether the proposition in question *seems* possibly true. As noted earlier, if we can detect some contradiction or incoherence in the proposition, we conclude that it is necessarily false, that is, not possibly true. Otherwise, we consider it possibly true. Thus, for example, it simply seems to us that the proposition 'There is life on Mars' is the sort of proposition that can be true, while the proposition 'There are square circles on Mars' cannot. So we do have a criterion for discovering that a proposition is possibly true apart from discovering that it is true.

Rowe recognises this, but he also claims that there are some coherent, non-contradictory concepts which do not describe possible objects. These are concepts which are only possible if they actually exist and which do not in fact exist, for example, unicornexes. The notion 'unicornex' (actually existing unicorn) is coherent, he claims, but no possible object is a unicornex because no real object is a unicorn. To know that things like unicornexes and the GCB possibly exist we must know more than that these concepts are coherent – we must know that such things actually exist.

But this is true of *all* concepts and propositions. We can only *know* that a concept describes a possible being if we know that it describes an actual being; we can only *know* that a proposition is possibly true if we know that it is true. If Rowe's term 'unicornex' did describe possible things (and if there were no other difficulties in the *a priori* existential arguments in which these terms appeared) we would have to admit that these beings actually exist. But these notions are not coherent – existence cannot be an essential property of a contingently non-existing thing like a unicorn. These beings cannot be necessarily existing beings and retain their status as unicorns – any more than can Gaunilo's lost island.

It is true that the proposition 'The GCB exists' is possibly true if and only if it is also true; that is, (22) is true if and only if (23) is true. But we can imagine someone accepting (22) without accepting (23) – many atheists and agnostics do this very thing, in fact. Perhaps if Anselm is right they are being inconsistent in doing so. Perhaps logically they should accept (23) too: but the mere fact that they should does not indicate that ontological arguers beg the question when they posit (22).

But is 'The GCB exists' possibly true? I believe it is: I can detect no contradiction or incoherence here, at any rate. I have never encountered an argument with even a fair degree of plausibility to the effect that (22) is not acceptable. This proposition, like any other proposition that might or might not appear as a premise in a deductive argument, must be judged acceptable or unacceptable apart from any other premises with which it might be conjoined in an argument. If a premise is acceptable before appearing in any version of the OA – as (22) is – then it is acceptable in the OA. I cannot *prove* (22); but there is good reason to accept it. And if the best judgement I can make about a proposition like (22) is that it is possibly true (remembering that like all propositions we can only know that it is possibly true if we know that it is – or was or will be – true), then I believe I must accept whatever philosophical consequences follow. In this case, I must admit that the GCB actually exists.

What then are we to say about such arguments as this:

30. 'Unicornex' is defined as 'existing unicorn';
31. No non-existing thing is a unicornex;
32. Unicornex is a possible thing;
33. Therefore, unicornex exists?

This would be a convincing argument, and we would have to accept the consequences and embrace (33), except that there are two serious problems with it: premise (30) begs the question and premise (32) is false. Rowe would agree that (32) is false – he would say that it can only be true if (33) is true, and (33) is false. This certainly can be said. I would prefer to say, however, that (32) is false just because unicorns cannot have existence as an essential property.

It is true that the OA boils down to this: if God is possible then God exists. This is because premise (22) of the OA is true if and only if the conclusion is true. So Rowe and I agree that the OA has these properties: first, it shows that if God is possible God exists; and second, the only way for a person to know that God is possible is to know that God exists. Rowe claims that this means it begs the question. I see no reason to say this. What we are talking about is a characteristic of the argument, not a fallacy in it. Thus I conclude that Rowe has not shown that the OA begs the question.

VI. TWO BRIEF 'REFUTATIONS' OF THE OA

More often than most TPs, the OA is subject to brief, back-of-the-hand 'refutations', sometimes from respected philosophers. These arguments then tend to be repeated by other philosophers, and to take on canonical status. Let me conclude this chapter with a brief discussion of two of them.

David Hume, through his character Cleanthes, famously said this about the OA:

> Nothing is demonstrable unless the contrary implies a contradiction. Nothing that is distinctly conceivable implies a contradiction. Whatever we conceive as existent, we can also conceive as non-existent. There is no being, therefore, whose non-existence implies a contradiction. Consequently there is no being whose existence is demonstrable.

Cleanthes then adds that he considers this argument 'as entirely decisive', and that he is 'willing to rest the whole controversy upon it'.[36]

But Hume's argument is altogether unimpressive; the first three statements in his refutation are all either false or misleading. It isn't true that 'Nothing is demonstrable unless the contrary implies a contradiction.' There are several ways in which propositions can be intellectually unacceptable besides being strictly logically contradictory. The statement 'There exists a tallest conceivable human being' is not strictly logically contradictory, but it is necessarily false; its contrary is demonstrable. Some statements are intellectually unacceptable because they are incoherent ('The "Not" negates itself non-negatively') without, so far as we can tell, being contradictory. And in at least some senses of the word 'demonstrable', some statements are demonstrable because their contraries are (not contradictory but) very highly improbable. (As we will see in Chapter 6, that is what some theistic provers think about the statement 'The universe was created by an intelligent designer.')

Next, Hume is wrong in saying, 'Nothing that is distinctly conceivable implies a contradiction.' As we have seen, there are several senses of the word 'conceive', and on some of them it is quite possible to conceive of contradictory states of affairs. Even Anselm argued that it is possible to word-conceive a statement that he considers contradictory, namely, 'The GCB does not exist.'

Finally, Hume misleads us when he says, 'Whatever we conceive as existent, we can also conceive as non-existent.' If what we have called word-conceiving were the only species of mental conceiving, Hume might be within his rights. But it isn't. As we have seen, there is also thing-conceiving. Just as a contradictory thing (for example, a square circle) cannot be thing-conceived as existing, so a necessary being (if there is such a thing) cannot be thing-conceived as not existing.

Richard Swinburne argues that if theism is true, that is, if God exists and is a logically necessary being, there can be no successful OA. He says:

> For such an argument proceeds from some general purported logically necessary principle and endeavors to show that it is a consequence of that principle that there is a God. It thus claims that it is because of something about God that – in virtue of that principle – he has to exist. The premises of such an ontological argument do not merely entail the existence of God, but provide a reason why he exists. The traditional version of the ontological argument is of this kind – it is, it claims, because the existent is more perfect than the non-existent that there must be a God. But God would seem less than totally supreme if he depended for his existence on something quite other than God – for instance, on such a general logically necessary principle . . . [T] he claim that there is logically sufficient reason why God exists would seem to make God in some way less ultimate than he would otherwise be.[37]

According to Swinburne, what you cannot have, if theism is true, is 'some other fact, e.g., a truth of logic, which makes it the case that there is a God . . . God is too ultimate for anything else (however necessary that thing) to provide a sufficient reason why there is a God.'[38]

But this argument is also unconvincing. Let's distinguish between *the existence of God* and *proving the existence of God*. It is true that the OA, an attempt to prove the existence of God, depends for its soundness on certain principles (like the premise that it is greater to exist *in intellectu* and *in re* than just to exist *in intellectu*). But why does it then follow that God's *existence* depends (in some theologically unacceptable way) on those principles?

These principles do not 'provide a sufficient reason why there is a God', not at least in the sense that God's existence depends on them. If the God of theism exists, God would still exist even if it were false (as indeed some philosophers have claimed) that it is greater to exist both *in intellectu* and *in re* than just *in intellectu*. It is easy to see this point when we are talking about an *a posteriori* proof of the existence of something.

Suppose I prove that x exists by pointing x out. Does my pointing x out constitute a 'logically sufficient reason' for x's existence? Of course not. Indeed, it's the other way round: I could not point x out unless x existed. But I would argue that a similar claim would be true if we were talking about an *a priori* proof. Suppose I prove, by an entirely *a priori* procedure, that there exists at least one prime number between five and ten. Would my proof, or any of its premises, then constitute a 'logically sufficient reason' for the existence of (say) the number seven? Of course not. It only proves that there is such a number. I could not prove that x exists unless x exists.

The OA does not supply a sufficient reason why God exists – it only proves that God exists. God's existence does not depend upon the OA.

NOTES

1. It is found in Chapters II–III of Anselm's *Proslogion*. See Saint Anselm, *Basic Writings* (LaSalle, Illinois: Open Court, 1962), pp. 7–11.
2. For a different reading of the *Proslogion* from mine, see Marilyn McCord Adams, 'Praying the *Proslogion*: Anselm's Theological Method,' in Thomas D. Senor (ed.), *The Rationality of Belief and the Plurality of Faith* (Ithaca, New York: Cornell University Press, 1995), pp. 13–39.
3. Anselm, *Basic Writings*, p. 7.
4. For a helpful explication of the concept, see Alvin Plantinga, *The Nature of Necessity* (Oxford: Clarendon Press, 1974), Ch. I.
5. Anselm occasionally uses the term *melius* ('better') instead of *maius* ('greater'). See also *Monologion II* and *Proslogion V* (where he says to God: 'Therefore, thou art just, truthful, blessed, and whatever it is better to be than not to be').
6. I am ignoring the various recent attempts to show that the theistic concept of God is incoherent–for example, that omniscience is incompatible with immutability, that omnipotence is incompatible with perfect goodness, that essential goodness is incompatible with moral freedom, that incorporeality is incompatible with agency and so on. All such attempts, in my opinion, have been shown to fail.
7. Tom Morris, 'The God of Abraham, Isaac, and Anselm,' *Faith and Philosophy*, Vol. 1, No. 2 (April, 1984), p. 180.
8. Anselm, *Basic Writings*, p. 7.
9. I add the clause about being a concrete thing that has causal properties because some philosophers hold that all abstract objects–propositions, numbers, sets, properties–exist in reality. But clearly the sort of existence that such things have (if these philosophers are correct) is not the sort of 'existence *in re*' that Anselm had in mind. He meant the kind of existence had by such things as physical objects and living persons, whether embodied (like human beings) or not (like angels and God).
10. My wife and I have two sons and no daughters.
11. Again, if those philosophers are correct who hold that all abstract objects like numbers and sets exist in reality, that entails that non-existent PETS like 'Davis's ninth daughter' and (if the fool is correct) 'God' exist in reality. But, as noted, this is not the sort of existence *in re* of which premise (4) speaks.
12. It is also found in Anselm, *Basic Writings*. See pp. 145–53.

13. Anselm, *Basic Writings*, pp. 149–50.
14. Norman Malcolm, 'Anselm's Ontological Arguments', in John Hick (ed.), *The Existence of God* (New York: Macmillan, 1964), p. 59.
15. Anselm, *Basic Writings*, pp. 148–49.
16. Anselm, *Basic Writings*, p. 9.
17. For example, he spoke of his lost island as if it were the most excellent of all *existing* islands, while he should have spoken of it as the most excellent of all *conceivable* islands.
18. Anselm, *Basic Writings*, p. 150.
19. Anselm, *Basic Writings*, p. 151.
20. Anselm, *Basic Writings*, p. 158.
21. Gaunilo might conceivably argue that we can play the same sorts of games with the notion of God or of the GCB. Exploring this point would take us beyond the bounds of the present book. Let me simply say that the great-making properties of God–necessary existence, omnipotence, omniscience, etc.–do appear to have intrinsic maximums. For further exploration of this and other points connected with the 'lost island' objection, see Stephen T. Davis, 'Anselm and Gaunilo on the "Lost Island"', *The Southern Journal of Philosophy*, Vol. XIII, No. 4 (Winter, 1975), pp. 435–48.
22. Immanuel Kant, *Critique of Pure Reason*, trans. by Norman Kemp Smith (New York: St. Martin's Press, 1965). See pp. 500–7.
23. See Bertrand Russell, 'Logical Atomism', in *Logic and Language* (London: Allen & Unwin, 1956), pp. 228ff; and *Introduction to Mathematical Philosophy* (London: Allen & Unwin, 1919), Ch. 16.
24. See Malcolm, 'Anselm's Ontological Arguments'.
25. See John Hick, 'Comment on Stephen Davis', in Linda J. Tessier (ed.), *Concepts of the Ultimate: Philosophical Perspectives on the Nature of the Divine* (London: Macmillan, 1989), pp. 32–3.
26. Kant, *Critique of Pure Reason*, p. 505.
27. I owe this way of putting Kant's point to Alvin Plantinga. See *God and Other Minds: A Study of the Rational Justification of Belief in God* (Ithaca, New York: Cornell University Press, 1967), p. 34.
28. Both Kant and Malcolm admit as much. Kant said: 'I should have hoped to put an end to these idle and fruitless disputations [i.e., about the OA] in a direct manner, by an accurate determination of the concept of existence, had I not found that the illusion which is caused by the confusion of a logical with a real predicate . . . is almost beyond correction' (*Critique of Pure Reason*, p. 504). And Malcolm admits: 'It would be desirable to have a rigorous refutation of the doctrine [that 'exists' is a real predicate] but I have not been able to provide one' ('Anselm's Ontological Arguments', p. 51.).
29. Kant, *Critique of Pure Reason*, p. 505.
30. Malcolm, 'Anselm's Ontological Arguments', p. 50
31. Malcolm, 'Anselm's Ontological Arguments', pp. 50–1.
32. Hick, 'Comment on Stephen Davis', pp. 32–3.
33. 'My financial position is, however, affected very differently by a hundred real thalers than it is by the mere concept of them (that is, of their possibility)' (Kant, *Critique of Pure Reason*, p. 505).
34. It is found in Rowe's 'The Ontological Argument', in Joel Feinberg (ed.), *Reason and Responsibility: Readings in Some Basic Problems of Philosophy*, 3rd ed. (Encino, California: Dickenson Publishing Co., 1973), pp. 8–17; in 'The Ontological Argument and Question-Begging', and in 'Comments on Professor Davis' "Does the Ontological Argument Beg the Question?"', both found in *International Journal for Philosophy of Religion*, Vol. VII, No 4 (1976), pp. 425–32, and 443–47. In explaining Rowe's argument, I am going to concentrate on his third and latest essay.
35. See Stephen T. Davis, 'Does the Ontological Argument Beg the Question?' and 'Anselm and Question-Begging: A Reply to William Rowe', *International Journal for Philosophy of Religion*, Vol. VII, No. 4 (1976), pp. 433–42, 448–57. I have one quibble with Rowe's definition of epistemological question-begging: I think it ought to be defined not in terms of *knowing* or *how one knows* a premise but rather in terms of the acceptability of premises that are not known. If a proposition is known, then no matter how it is known, it is acceptable. The arguer has every right to use it as a premise in an argument. I would say that an argument begs the question in the epistemological way if it employs a premise that will only be acceptable to those who already accept the conclusion.
36. David Hume, *Dialogues Concerning Natural Religion*, ed. by Henry D. Aiken (New York: Hafner Publishing Company, 1959), p. 58.
37. Richard Swinburne, *The Christian God* (Oxford: Oxford University Press, 1994), p. 145.
38. Swinburne, *The Christian God*, pp. 249–50.

3

Theistic Proofs and Religious Realism

I. RELIGIOUS NONREALISM

Religious nonrealism is the name of a movement that has arisen in theology in the second half of the twentieth century, although it has roots that go back before then. It is related to the brand of nonrealism that some philosophers now defend in metaphysics and epistemology. It is also related to the versions of nonrealism that have long existed in some non-western, especially Buddhist, religious traditions.[1]

The full relevance of religious nonrealism to the project of proving the existence of God will be clear by the end of the chapter. For now, suffice it to say that most scholars who consider themselves, or can arguably be considered, religious nonrealists do not affirm what Anselm would call the *in re* existence of God. Accordingly, they have no enthusiasm for theistic proofs, and sometimes offer caustic criticisms of them. Showing that those criticisms are unjustified is one of the aims of the present chapter.

It is enormously difficult to achieve clarity on the meaning of the term 'religious nonrealism'. But it seems to be used in three main ways. (1) Some seem to hold that religious nonrealism is the explicitly atheistic theory that *talk about God and some religious practices may or may not be worth preserving, but what we call 'God' has no existence independent of the human mind and in fact is a product or projection of the human mind.* Such views are associated with the great 'projection theorists' of the nineteenth and twentieth centuries, especially Feuerbach, Marx, and Freud. (2) Others seem to hold that religious nonrealism is the view that *talk about God and some religious practices are valid expressions of human emotions, hopes, aims, moral impulses, or spiritual ideals.* Talk about God, it is said, is a helpful way to focus and apply those ideals; it is an essential part of the theistic way of life. But no ontological commitments, one way or the other, are entailed by this notion on the existence of God. (3) Finally, some seem to hold that religious nonrealism is *the practice of accepting weakened, watered-down, revisionist, demythologised, rationalistic, or reductionist versions of traditional beliefs.* This use of 'religious nonrealism' is normally used by those who are critical of it.

The various contemporary versions of religious nonrealism seem to be tied together by two factors. The first is an acceptance, by religious nonrealists, of much of the force of the nineteenth- and twentieth-century positivistic critique of religion, a critique usually associated with but not limited to the 'projection theorists' mentioned above. The second is a commitment by those same people to the idea that at least some aspects of religion are worth retaining. In other words, if literal and ordinary belief in God can no longer be sustained, it is still true that some facets of the religious life can be valuable and even liberating to human beings. Religious nonrealists – to put it more bluntly than most of them would be inclined to do – want to go on being religious despite the fact that they no longer hold many of the crucial beliefs that once defined religion. In the case of many of them, this includes belief in God.

There are also several definitions of 'religious realism'. Oddly, the versions of religious realism that are discussed in the contemporary philosophical and theological literature are not symmetrically related to the versions of religious nonrealism that are discussed in the same places. The plethora of definitions of both terms causes confusion and is doubtless one of the reasons that debate between realists and nonrealists is so often fruitless, with scholars simply talking past each other. For example, I once attended an academic conference that was devoted to the topic of religious realism and nonrealism. Because I was confused about what these terms meant, I took it upon myself to write down all the ways in which the term 'religious realism' was either explicitly used or presupposed in the essays and discussions. Here are the six definitions I was able to locate. I do not claim that these are the only definitions currently in use. (It should be noted that some are definitions of religious realism that were given in order to be attacked by religious nonrealists.)

The first two definitions are ontological: (1) *Religious realism is the view that God's existence is completely independent of what any human being thinks or believes about God.* In other words, God might or might not exist, but human opinion about the matter – indeed, human praxis in general – has nothing to do with what is in fact the case. (2) *Religious realism is the view that God's existence is completely independent of what any human being thinks or believes about God and God exists.* This definition is explicitly theist, and contradicts 'projectionist' views of God like those typically attributed to people like Feuerbach, Marx, and Freud.

The next two definitions are linguistic. (3) *Religious realism is the view that some true statements about God have literal meaning.* Perhaps this definition ought to say, 'Some statements about God with positive theological content have literal meaning.' This is because almost everybody would agree that statements like 'God is not a horse', or 'God is mysterious' have literal meaning. (4) *Religious realism is the view that some true statements about God have transcultural meaning, that they are not culturally or historically conditioned.* Are there any contemporary philosophers of religion or theologians who defend religious realism as defined in this way? It is not easy to think of any, but views like this are vehemently criticised, so *somebody* must hold them.

The last two definitions are epistemological. (5) *Religious realism is the view that one's beliefs about God – or, alternatively, the beliefs of one's religious community – are mainly true.* We might call this moderate religious conservatism. (6) *Religious realism is the view that one's beliefs about God – or, alternatively, the beliefs of one's religious community – are all true.* People who accept (6) often in effect also hold that God is not mysterious to them; and that anybody who disagrees with their beliefs about God is mistaken. We might call this radical religious conservatism (or even fundamentalism).

The definition of religious realism that we will principally discuss in this chapter is (2) (which of course entails (1)). This is because the present book concerns theistic proofs. Now it may be that the very enterprise of offering a theistic proof commits one to something like definition (3). And it may be that some theistic provers were themselves committed to definition (5) or even (6). But it is clear that all the classic theistic proofs in the history of philosophy presuppose religious realism in the sense of definition (1), and all theistic provers are committed to religious realism in the sense of definition (2). What I want to do in this chapter is to see whether there is anything in Anselm's OA that is relevant to religious realism in the sense of definition (2) and thus (1).[2]

II. ANSELM ON 'CONCEIVING'

Let me now turn to Anselm. Attending to certain points in the early chapters of the *Proslogion* – points that we only briefly treated in Chapter 2 – may help us in our discussion of religious realism. At *Proslogion* IV, Anselm faced a problem. He thought that he had proved, in the two previous chapters, the existence and even necessary existence of God, understood as the Greatest Conceivable Being, by a purely *a priori* procedure (which later philosophy would call the ontological argument). Thus he believed he had proved that the non-existence of God is in some sense impossible or inconceivable. So then – he asked – how can the fool conceive or say in his heart (Anselm explicitly defines 'conceiving' as 'saying in one's heart'), 'There is no God'?

Let us suppose that it is possible to conceive of *things*, *properties*, *relations*, and of linguistic entities like *propositions* or *sentences*. Perhaps it even makes sense to talk of conceiving *ideas* or *conceptions*, or at least of having them. Anselm's answer to the problem he was addressing crucially involved his insight that there is more than one way in which a thing can be mentally conceived. He said: 'For, in one sense, an object is conceived, when the word signifying it is conceived; and in another, when the very entity, which the object is, is understood.'[3]

Let's call these two notions W-conceiving (for word-conceiving) and T-conceiving (for thing-conceiving), respectively. To W-conceive something, apparently, is to understand the meaning of the words used to describe or refer to it. Thus, in some sense, I W-conceive Bill Clinton when I recognize the referent of the name 'Bill Clinton' or when I understand the meaning and referent of words like 'The man who is President of the United States in May, 1996.' To T-conceive something, apparently, is to understand the thing itself – to know its properties and relations. Now only an omniscient being can *fully* T-conceive anything, whether that thing be a president or a tree. Those of us who are nonomniscient T-conceive Bill Clinton – so I think Anselm would say – when we understand enough of his properties and relations to be able to make generally true statements about him and distinguish him from other beings with whom he might be confused.

Anselm solved his problem, then, by suggesting that the words *God does not exist* can be W-conceived (those words can be understood) but not T-conceived. As he said, 'No one who understands what God is can conceive that God does not exist; although he says these words in his heart, either without any, or with some foreign signification.' T-conceiving, Anselm suggests, must be 'in accordance with the nature of the facts themselves.'[4] So any false statement (e.g. 'San Francisco is south of Los Angeles') can be W-conceived, but not T-conceived. Nobody can T-conceive a square circle (since the fact is that no square circles can possibly exist), but it is possible to W-conceive the definition 'four-sided plane geometrical figure all of whose points are equidistant from the center'.

Of course the two methods of conceiving appear to be related in ways that Anselm did not explore. You cannot understand (W-conceive) the meaning of a word for a property (say, red) without understanding something about the property itself, that is, without in some sense T-conceiving red. You cannot understand (W-conceive) the denotation of a name, e.g., 'Bill Clinton,' unless you know something about the thing named, that is, unless to some extent you T-conceive Bill Clinton. If you mistakenly think 'Bill Clinton' was the commander of the Army of the Potomac at the end of the Civil War, you aren't even W-conceiving 'Bill Clinton.' But despite these points, it seems that Anselm was correct in his main claim: there is a difference between these two ways of 'conceiving.'

We are now in a position to be able better to understand a point from *Proslogion* II that is crucial to the ontological argument, namely, Anselm's notion that there are two ways in which a thing might exist. The fool who talks about God or hears others talk about God must admit, Anselm says, that God exists at least *in intellectu*. What the fool wants to insist on is that God does not also exist *in re*. To claim that God or the GCB exists *in intellectu* is merely to claim that somebody – Anselm, the fool, anybody – W-conceives the word 'God' or the words 'Greatest Conceivable Being'. So we can imagine the fool saying (along with many contemporary atheists), 'Yes, I know what the word "God" means, I understand full well what people mean when they talk about God, I even think the statement "God exists" is possibly true; I just don't think it is true; I don't think God exists *in re*.'[5]

The fool's position, then, is that God exists *in intellectu* and only *in intellectu*. Talk about God is talk about a mere concept – like a unicorn or like Stephen Davis' ninth daughter – that does not correspond to anything that exists *in re*. God exists in people's minds, but nowhere else.

Now anybody who holds such a position is likely – or so we might think – to hold what we might call the normal atheist's view of religion. That is, we would expect such a person to be highly critical of religion, to speak against it, to dismiss it as superstition or weakness or silliness, to recommend against being religious. But suppose Anselm's fool took another tack. Suppose the fool continued to deny God's existence *in re* but also argued that talk about such a being (mistaken as it is) is religiously or morally or politically important. That is, suppose the fool held that people should continue to talk about God and practise the religious life. If so, then the position of the fool would be somewhat like views attributed to some of those late twentieth-century thinkers who are said to be religious nonrealists.

III. D. Z. PHILLIPS' POSITION

Why would anybody want to be a religious nonrealist in the sense of denying definition (2) of religious realism: *God's existential status is completely independent of what any human being thinks or believes about God and God exists?* Obviously, atheists (who deny the right hand conjunct of (2)) and agnostics (who suspend judgement on the matter) will do so. But in this chapter let us focus on objections to religious realism (understood in terms of definition (2)) that are, so to speak, internal to religion.

Here we find several arguments and claims to ponder – religious defences of religious nonrealism, if you will – that usually revolve around the claim that religious realism misunderstands what religion is all about. One's first temptation, in reading writings in this genre, is to dismiss them as the work of theological super-sophisticates whose views are to be politely noted but not taken seriously. 'What?' – one feels like asking – 'theistic religion does not essentially involve belief in the *in re* existence of God? Why then be religious at all? Why not just be a moral humanist?' But perhaps this is an unfair reaction, one that is explained in part by the fact that people who are likely to have it usually believe in the *in re* existence of God and consider that belief important for theistic religion.

Let me focus on just one of the scholars who is sometimes interpreted as a religious nonrealist, namely, D. Z. Phillips. He is doubtless the foremost contemporary philosopher of religion who has been strongly influenced by Wittgenstein.[6] Let us first note that several of the points that Phillips always insists on seem beyond reproach – that religious viewpoints can only fully be appreciated from the perspective of the 'form of life' in which they are imbedded; that religion accordingly is not reducible merely to metaphysical or theological beliefs; that truth can be conveyed in other ways than by empirical, factual statements; and that the cognitive and the affective aspects of the religious life are to be considered together. There are also several critical points often made by Phillips which I disagree with but will not dispute here, for example, the notion that criteria of truth and falsity are relative to language games.[7] We will focus only on those aspects of Phillips' theory that can be interpreted as disputing definition (2) of religious realism.

Although one suspects that Phillips is not particularly interested in arguing about definition (2), there are three aspects of his theory that certainly seem inconsistent with it, and they are closely related. (a) The first is his oft-repeated claim that 'God is not an object.' He says of the word 'God' that it 'is not the name of an individual; it does not refer to anything.'[8] If God were an object, Phillips says, then God would be like other objects and so would not be the God of religion. Obviously, only objects can be said to exist, so if God is not an object, then definition (2), which contains as its second conjunct the words 'God exists', is either false or incoherent. (b) The second is Phillips' denial that statements such as 'God exists' are claims or hypotheses.[9] The affirmation of God in religious experience, he insists, is not theoretical. The primary use of religious language is in the context of worship or praise of God, and in such contexts talk of God is anything but a hypothesis that stands in need of proof. The basic teachings about God – that God is a merciful and loving judge, for example – Phillips says, 'are not taught as beliefs which require further reasons to justify them. They are not opinions or hypotheses.'[10] (c) The third is Phillips' notion that the grammar of such terms as 'believe' and 'true' is different in religious contexts from how it is in empirical contexts. In the case of religious beliefs, Phillips says, 'the grammar of "belief" and "truth" is not the same as in the case of empirical propositions or the prediction of future events.'[11]

Phillips is not an easy writer to interpret. Many philosophers of religion who read him with interest and respect confess to puzzlement as to what his position actually is on the existence of God and allied issues. Would he accept a characterization of him as a religious nonrealist? Perhaps he would say that the Wittgensteinian critique of religion entails that *both* religious realism *and* religious nonrealism are products of conceptual confusion. So it would not be at all be surprising if he were to call my interpretation of him confused and Anselm's position on this issue incoherent. (Incoherent, confused, muddled, unintelligible – these are words that we find frequently in his writings.)

J. L. Mackie argues that Phillips is open to the following dilemma: either religious statements like 'God exists' are literal, fact-stating (or putative fact-stating) utterances, or else they are purely expressive or metaphorical utterances.[12] Phillips emphatically denies the first horn of the dilemma; to accept it, he would say, is to be guilty of superstition. Hume's criticisms of such views, he says, are entirely correct. But he also denies the second horn; he is at great pains to separate his views from reductive theories of religious language like those of R. M. Braithwaite.[13] But since there is no third possibility (so Mackie implies), Phillips' theory is in deep trouble.

But now Phillips has replied to this line of argument.[14] He rejects the dilemma, arguing that religious language is not contingently related to religious behaviour (as, e.g., a psychological aid *à la* Braithwaite). Rather, religious language is 'internally related' to religious behaviour in that 'it is in terms of this language that the believer's conduct is to be understood.'[15] 'God exists' is not to be understood as a factual, empirical statement. Metaphors can express truths, Phillips insists, although the 'truth' in religious language is not factual, empirical truth. What kind of truth it is, Phillips says, emerges in the primary uses of religious language, which as noted is the language of praise and worship. The God of religious experience is not 'an object among other objects.'[16] Indeed, according to Phillips, this is one of the main insights of Anselm. If God were an object among other objects, then God would be the sort of thing that comes to be and passes away. If God were an object among other objects, it would then be impossible to understand why you cannot miss if you try to spit in God's face.[17]

Let me now respond to each of Phillips' three points. (a) Is God an object?[18] Phillips claims that if God is an object among other objects, then God is the sort of thing that comes to be and passes away.[19] But what exactly is there that Phillips detects in the grammar of the word 'object' that requires that all objects be contingent? Why can't there be everlasting objects? One way to approach this question is to ask whether there are any generic nouns that satisfy these two criteria: (1) they cover or can refer to both God and contingent things, and (2) they do not rule out or lessen God's transcendence over all contingent things. Of course there are (or so it seems): terms like 'object', 'thing', or 'being' (Anselm's preferred term) will do nicely. I simply do not detect as Phillips does anything in the grammar of these terms that makes them applicable to contingent things but not to God. That is, I see no theological or philosophical danger in saying that God is an object, that God is a thing, or that God is a being.

But suppose Phillips is correct. Suppose God is neither an object, a thing, nor a being. What then? Well, then the religious realist would simply allow Phillips to use these three terms as he wishes and make up a new technical term ('sobject', let's say), defined so as to satisfy both of the above criteria. God, then, like me and like my computer, would be a sobject. And God's existence, like that of any existing sobject, could be proposed as a hypothesis, affirmed as a claim, accepted as a belief, or demonstrated in a proof. Another possibility: We'll simply make up a new term ('lobject') that is designed to cover or refer to anything that is both existent and noncontingent. I would not then be a lobject, and neither would my computer, but God would. And the statement 'God is a lobject' would be unobjectionable.[20]

One of the things we learn from *Proslogion* II-III is that God's existence is different from the existence of contingent things. They exist in such a way that their non-existence is quite T-conceivable or logically possible; God exists in such a way that God cannot be T-conceived not to exist. But how does it follow from this that God is not an object? It only follows if something in the sense of the word 'object' requires that all objects be contingent. But I certainly detect nothing like that in the sense of this word.

Phillips' denial that God is an object is closely related to his denial that the term 'God' refers. But when pressed on this point by religious realists, he is inclined to say that even if it is allowed that the term 'God' refers to something, no clarificatory work whatsoever has been done in showing what sort of thing the term refers to. How are we grammatically to distinguish the 'something' that the term 'God' refers to from other sorts of things (like physical objects)? We still do not know the grammar of the sentence 'God is an existing, transcendent thing.'[21]

There is certainly truth here. Religious realists who insist that the term 'God' refers must go on to explain God's nature. Still, something philosophically worthwhile has been accomplished by allowing that the term 'God' refers: emotivist, nonrealist and other nonreferential theories of religious language have been ruled out.

What does Phillips mean by his claim that if God were an object, it would then be impossible to understand why you cannot miss if you try to spit in God's face? This is surely metaphorical language; since God has neither body nor face, we cannot in any literal sense spit in God's face even if we try to do so. What Phillips perhaps means is that anyone who tries to insult or curse God cannot fail to succeed in doing so. But how is that related to the claim that God is not an object? Presumably the idea is something like this: anybody who tries to insult or curse 'an object among other objects' (an object like you or me, for example) might well fail to do so. The words of the curse might miss their intended target. But with God the words cannot miss: if you *intend* to curse God you *do* curse God. But even if we grant this much (and it is a lot to grant), what is to rule out the possibility that God is a special sort of object, the sort of object whom intended insults and curses cannot miss?

(b) Is the religious affirmation of God a *claim* or *hypothesis*? This is a subtle question. It is true, as Phillips claims, that the natural context of talk of God is worship (and, as I would add, religious instruction). It is also true that the epistemic state of most religious believers on the existence of God is not that of entertaining a hypothesis (in hopes, say, that evidence or proof will later emerge). But there is no reason why a deeply committed religious believer (one who does not for a moment doubt the reality of God) cannot, in contexts outside worship, prayer, or religious instruction, treat 'God exists' as a hypothesis or claim. This, indeed, was just what Anselm was doing in the *Proslogion*. For the purpose of the argument, he assumed that the existence of God was doubtful until the argument was complete. As he said to Gaunilo: 'I was attempting to prove what was still uncertain.'[22]

Here perhaps Phillips will reply that you can't yank religious language out of its natural context of praise and worship and use the terms in a quite different context. But why not? In both philosophy and science we are quite used to treating certainties as if they were doubtful and dubious claims as if they were certain. In both philosophy and science we are used to borrowing terms from one context and using them in another, and the usual result is that there is enough similarity of meaning to make successful communication possible.

(c) Is the grammar of such terms as 'believe' and 'true' different in religious contexts than in the context of empirical statements? I suspect Anselm would say no. The sense in which 'God exists' is *true* is the same sense in which 'Poodles exist' is *true*. Obviously, God is not a poodle, so (among other things) the ways in which we might try to verify or falsify the two propositions are quite different. Similarly, the truth of 'Black holes exist' is verified quite differently from the way in which the truth of 'Poodles exist' is, yet the notion of 'truth' is the same. Now Phillips will say that the very idea of trying to verify 'God exists' is deeply confused, shows that the sense of the statement has not been grasped. But why so? The ontological argument is an attempt to verify 'God exists', and it is hard to see any confusion in the attempt to do so. So at the very least it is hard to know what to make of Phillips' claim. It is worth noting that my point here is different from Mackie's rather strong criticism of Phillips that talk of different notions of 'true' only leads to evasion and doubletalk. My point is simply that I do not know what notion of 'true' Phillips intends, nor why he thinks the word 'true' must be used differently in empirical and religious contexts.

So it seems that Phillips still faces Mackie's dilemma. Religious language may well be internally related to religious behaviour in the way Phillips specifies, but this does not entail that the affirmation of the reality of God in the religious life is not factual or literal. Suppose we agree that religious behaviour is to be understood in terms of religious language, and that religious belief cannot be understood apart from religious practice. Even if we admit this much, we do not settle the question of the nature of religious language in favor of religious nonrealism. Indeed, the reverse seems to be true. The behaviour of typical theists reveals (so it seems) that they believe in the *in re* existence of God. It shows that their affirmations of the reality of God should be taken as factual. They behave very differently toward God from the way I behave toward, say, Paul Bunyan or toward my ninth daughter, both of whom I believe not to exist in reality. They ask things of God, they praise God for having done certain things, they expect God to do things in the future.

It might be helpful to ask this question: Who is the most authoritative interpreter of the nature of religious language? Specifically, who is in a

position authoritatively to decide whether factual truth claims, especially
ones about the existence of certain beings, are involved in religious
language? Do philosophers get to make the decision? If so, which one –
Aquinas or Braithwaite? Or do theologians get to decide? Again, which one
– Calvin or Cupitt? Or do ordinary believers get to decide?

In a qualified way, I would argue for the last option. Of course we would
not ask ordinary believers to settle abstruse debates in philosophical
theology. But I would argue that their views are at least relevant to the
issue at hand, and can helpfully be inquired after. Remember, we would
not be asking ordinary believers to settle the paradox of divine foreknow-
ledge and human freedom, or to calculate the date of the Big Bang, or to
solve Fermat's last theorem. We would be asking them: '*What do you
mean* when you say things like "God is to be thanked and praised" or
"God was in Christ"?' We must of course take seriously the arguments of
philosophers and theologians. But if the vast majority of ordinary believers
would claim (as they surely would) that such statements as these involve or
entail factual belief in the *in re* existence of God, we should only reject this
claim for very compelling reasons indeed. At the very least, the religious
nonrealist who offers a non-factual analysis of religious language owes us
an explanation of the fact that most ordinary believers interpret religious
language as implying the factual, *in re* existence of God.

The vast majority of ordinary theists would insist that the religious form
of life includes certain beliefs or statements taken as factually true about,
for example, the existence of God, the origin of the world, and survival of
death. That is, it includes beliefs about certain transcendent realities, about
certain facts about human beings and the world, and about certain future
states of affairs. Obviously, it is a mistake to hold that these beliefs exhaust
the religious form of life, but they are an essential part of the religious form
of life for typical believers.

IV. ANSELM AGAINST PHILLIPS

Phillips would surely resist any suggestion that his views constitute a denial
of the *in re* existence of God. And I agree: his position in the philosophy of
religion does not amount to a defense of atheism. Nevertheless, for others
than Phillips his theory would seem attractive primarily for those who are
either atheists or agnostics and who want to retain certain aspects of the
religious life. That is, it is an impressive version of religious nonrealism.
But apart from a prior commitment to atheism or agnosticism, it is not
clear why Phillips' theory should be an attractive option.

Phillips suggests his theory as a purely philosophical analysis of the
nature of religious language. And in one sense that is just what it is. But

who might be inclined to accept it? It is not difficult to see why Phillips' theory of religious language might be attractive to an atheist or agnostic religious nonrealist. So one challenge for Phillips is to show why his views ought to be attractive to *anybody*, even a believer in the *in re* existence of God. Such a theist (like Anselm) could well ask Phillips: 'Why should I accept your theory? When I say things like "God is to be thanked and praised" I mean these statements to imply the factual claim "God exists." Am I in error about the sense of my own language? Why?'

It may be true that God does not exist. The fool may be correct. It may even be true that God does not exist but that certain aspects of the religious life are worth retaining. But it is unconvincing to argue that religious nonrealism is preferable to religious realism for purely religious reasons. The only good reasons to opt for religious nonrealism presuppose a prior commitment to atheism or agnosticism. For if the fool is correct, that is, if God exists only in the minds of those who form conceptions of God, then religious realism as defined even by definition (1) is false. God's existence, such as it is (that is, *in intellectu* alone), *does* then depend on what human beings think or believe. This is because the only sorts of things that depend for their existence on what humans believe or think are things that do not exist *in re*, for example, things that are mythical, fictional, or imaginary.

We have learned from Anselm that there are at least two ways of 'conceiving' a thing, W-conceiving and T-conceiving. (I say 'at least' because there are surely other senses of the term than these.) We have also learned that there are two ways in which a thing can exist, *in intellectu* and *in re*. In this case, there are no other options, no other ways in which a thing can exist beside: (1) *in intellectu* alone; (2) *in re* alone; and (3) *in intellectu* and *in re*. Both Anselmian distinctions are legitimate and helpful.

So Anselm's 'Greatest Conceivable Being' (which is a fair definition or at least description of the God of theism), like every other conceivable thing, exists either *in intellectu* alone or *in intellectu* and *in re*. If God exists only *in intellectu*, as the fool and as some religious nonrealists suppose, then God's *in re* existence can be W-conceived but not T-conceived. If God exists *in intellectu* and *in re*, as Anselm claimed, then it is a fact that God exists *in intellectu* and *in re*. And if that much is true, then the *in re* existence of God is a 'matter of fact'. And if that much is true, then statements like 'God exists' are or at least can be factual statements. (Of course this sentence might well be used on some occasions non-factually as well.) Furthermore, if God exists *in re*, and if we can W-conceive of God, then definition (2) of religious realism is true.

In this chapter I have been defending religious realism, especially in terms of definition (2): *God's existential status is completely independent*

of what any human being thinks or believes about God and God exists.
Naturally, I cannot claim to have proved (2), since I have not tried to prove
that God exists. I do hope, however, to have made a good case for the truth
of religious realism by answering some of Phillips' implicit objections to it.
If I have done so, then for theists like Anselm (that is, those who already
accept the right hand conjunct of (2)), I have also made a good case for
acceptance of (2).

V. CONCLUSION

The final point I wish to make is not meant to be directed at Phillips at all.
It is about what might be called the essence or core of religion. One of the
most intriguing aspects of the position of some religious nonrealists (and
one that is puzzling to many laypersons) is that they insist on the value of
practising the religious life, or at least some aspects of it, despite having
given up on such items as belief in God. For some of those religious
nonrealists, it seems that the core value in religion is a kind of spirituality
that transcends all religious beliefs and symbols. For others it is a sort of
praxis, a way of living one's life in the world.

And it does seem true that if spirituality – understood as a certain sort of
psychological state – is the goal and heart of religion, then, obviously, one
can be a nonrealist and even an atheist and still be religious. Indeed, I know
a practising Zen Buddhist who is an atheist, and his level of spirituality is,
so far as I can tell, very high indeed. It even seems true that if a certain sort
of praxis – say, working for justice and peace among people – is the goal
and heart of religion, then, obviously, one can be a nonrealist and even an
atheist and still be religious.

It would be difficult in any way strictly to disprove the contention that
spirituality or praxis precede doctrine and that one or the other (or both)
constitutes what really matters in religion. It is possible, however, to place
on the table the views of Anselm, Aquinas, and other theistic provers. They
would strongly deny the claim that the essence of Christian faith at least
(one branch of theism) is a kind of spirituality, or a certain sort of praxis, to
which God is logically and causally and (so to speak) teleologically
dispensable. It rather concerns a call from God that we respond appro-
priately to the love of God as it is revealed pre-eminently in Christ. 'Man's
chief end', as the Westminster Shorter Catechism of 1643 beautifully says,
'is to glorify God and to enjoy him forever.' So it seems that God – by
which I mean a being whose existence is independent of anybody's views
about God – is essential to Christian faith (and surely to the other theistic
faiths as well).

The point is that the basic issue here turns out to be the topic of this book, namely, the existence of God. So anybody who wants to evaluate religious nonrealism must begin by asking: Did God create us or did we create God? Those who believe that we created God and that accordingly there is little point in our being religious will be atheists. Those who believe that we created God but that there is still value in religion will follow the path of religious nonrealism. Those who believe that God created us and that accordingly we owe God certain religious obligations, will be religious realists.

NOTES

1. In this chapter, as well as elsewhere in the book, I will limit myself to talk of realism and nonrealism concerning *God*, that is, the ultimate reality of Western monotheism. Conversations about religious realism and nonrealism could be carried on about the divine beings or ultimate realities, personal or impersonal, of other religious traditions.
2. Given the many definitions of religious realism and nonrealism, it is quite possible for some religious nonrealists to be quite unaffected by the Anselmian argument to follow. They can with justification point out that the type of religious realism Anselm's argument supports is consistent with the type of religious nonrealism they espouse.
3. Anselm, *Basic Writings* (LaSalle, Illinois: Open Court, 1962), pp. 9–10.
4. Anselm, *Basic Writings*, p. 10.
5. Presumably some atheists will not grant that the concept of God is coherent, and so will deny that 'God exists' is possibly true. But undoubtedly others will grant this much.
6. See D. Z. Phillips, *Religion Without Explanation* (Oxford: Basil Blackwell, 1976), especially Chapters 9, 10 and 11, and D. Z. Phillips, *Faith After Foundationalism* (London: Routledge, 1988), especially Chapter 22.
7. This claim of Phillips is carefully analysed and criticized in Joseph Runzo's *Reason, Relativism, and God* (New York: St. Martin's Press, 1986), pp. 175–94.
8. *Religion Without Explanation*, p. 148.
9. *Ibid.*, p. 181, and *passim*.
10. *Ibid.*, p. 164.
11. *Ibid.*, p. 142.
12. This dilemma is raised as a criticism of Phillips by J. L. Mackie in *The Miracle of Theism* (Oxford: The Clarendon Press, 1982), pp. 222–9.
13. R.M. Braithwaite, 'An Empiricist's View of the Nature of Religious Belief', in B. Mitchell (ed.), *The Philosophy of Religion* (Oxford: Oxford University Press, 1971).
14. See *Faith After Foundationalism*, pp. 317–25.
15. *Ibid.*, p. 320.
16. *Ibid.*, p. 321.
17. *Ibid.*, p. 324.
18. I agree with Phillips that 'God' is not 'the name of an individual,' although for quite a different reason. The word 'God' can be used as a name, of course, as can virtually any expression, but I think it best to think of 'Yahweh' as the name of the individual who is God and 'God' as a title-term.
19. *Faith After Foundationalism*, p. 321.
20. Don't ask me for the grammar of the terms *sobject* and *lobject*. These are technical terms that I've just invented in order to make a point: they don't *have* a grammar, a context, a use in ordinary language.
21. See, *inter alia*, Phillips' lecture, 'At the Mercy of Method' (Claremont, California: Claremont Graduate School, 1993), pp. 7–8.
22. Anselm *Basic Writings*, p. 164 (*Reply*, VI).

4

The Cosmological Argument

I. INTRODUCTION: AQUINAS' VERSIONS OF THE CA

The cosmological argument (CA) is actually a whole cluster of related arguments that has had a long history. Probably the CA's first appearance as a theistic proof is in Plato's dialogue *Laws*.[1] Since then it has been both defended and attacked throughout the history of philosophy, with important discussions of it found in the ancient, medieval, modern, and contemporary periods.[2] It is important to note that there are many varieties of cosmological arguments for the existence of God. All, however, are *a posteriori* arguments; that is, they attempt to argue for the existence of God based on things that we know from experience, things that we have learned through the senses.

Let us focus on three versions of the CA that are found in the *Summa Theologica* of the medieval philosopher Thomas Aquinas (AD 1225–74). In a noted passage in that book, Aquinas suggests 'Five Ways' of arguing for the existence of God, the first three of which are versions of the cosmological argument.[3] All five of the arguments are brief, even terse; but they are models of the clarity and power of argumentation that we expect from Aquinas, whom many consider the greatest philosopher of religion.

Here is Aquinas' statement of the First Way, which concerns motion:

> The first and more manifest way is the argument from motion. It is certain, and evident to our senses, that in the world some things are in motion. Now whatever is moved is moved by another, for nothing

can be moved except it is in potentiality to that towards which it is moved; whereas a thing moves inasmuch as it is in act. For motion is nothing else than the reduction of something from potentiality to actuality. But nothing can be reduced from potentiality to actuality, except by something in a state of actuality. Thus that which is actually hot, as fire, makes wood, which is potentially hot, to be actually hot, and thereby moves and changes it. Now it is not possible that the same thing should be at once in actuality and potentiality in the same respect, but only in different respects. For what is actually hot cannot simultaneously be potentially hot; but it is simultaneously potentially cold. It is therefore impossible that in the same respect and in the same way a thing should be both mover and moved, i.e., that it should move itself. Therefore, whatever is moved must be moved by another. If that by which it is moved be itself moved, then this also must needs be moved by another, and that by another again. But this cannot go on to infinity, because then there would be no first mover, and, consequently, no other mover, seeing that subsequent movers move only inasmuch as they are moved by the first mover; as the staff moves only because it is moved by the hand. Therefore it is necessary to arrive at a first mover, moved by no other; and this everyone understands to be God.[4]

Let me summarise the argument as follows:

1. Everything that is in motion is moved by something else.
2. Infinite regress is impossible.
3. Therefore, there must be a first mover.

The second 'Way' concerns cause, and is parallel to the first. Here is Aquinas' statement of it:

The second way is from the nature of efficient cause. In the world of sensible things we find there is an order of efficient causes. There is no case known (neither is it, indeed, possible) in which a thing is found to be the efficient cause of itself; for so it would be prior to itself, which is impossible. Now in efficient causes it is not possible to go on to infinity, because in all efficient causes following in order, the first is the cause of the intermediate cause, and the intermediate is the cause of the ultimate cause, whether the intermediate cause be several, or one only. Now to take away the cause is to take away the effect. Therefore, if there be no first cause among efficient causes, there will be no ultimate, nor any intermediate, cause. But if in efficient causes it is possible to go on to infinity, there will be no first efficient cause, neither will there be an ultimate effect, nor any intermediate efficient causes; all of which is plainly false. Therefore it is necessary to admit a first efficient cause, to which everyone gives the name of God.[5]

Let me summarise this argument as follows:

4. Every effect has a cause.
5. Infinite regress is impossible.
6. Therefore, there must be a first cause.

The two initial premises, that is, (1) and (4), are the *a posteriori* premises. Aquinas thinks that these claims are so obviously true that anyone ought to accept them. The identical second premise in each argument, that is, (2) and (5), is the crucial one, and will require discussion.

First a point about the sort of causation that Aquinas has in mind. One natural way of reading these arguments is to take them as attempts to rule out the possibility of an infinitely long series of movers and things moved or causes and their effects, stretching back into the past, with each cause existing temporally prior to its effect. However, this is clearly not what Aquinas intended. He suggested in another place that an infinitely long temporal regress of causes and effects is quite possible.[6] Authoritative interpreters of Aquinas stress that what he had in mind was an infinitely long causal series in which the causes and effects exist simultaneously, and in which causes exist 'prior to' their effects in a logical rather than temporal sense.[7] *That* kind of series, Aquinas says, can only be finite in length.

Let us stipulate that 'x is the *linear* cause of y' means that x causes y to exist in such a way that y can continue to exist even if x ceases to exist or ceases its causal activity. Clearly there are causal relationships like this, for example 'The carpenter makes (that is, causes to exist) the chair.' Here the causal relationship between the carpenter and the chair is such that the chair can perfectly well go on existing even if the carpenter ceases all chair-making activity or even dies. Let us stipulate that 'x is the *hierarchical* cause of y' means that x causes y to exist in such a way that y cannot continue to exist unless x continues x's causal activity. That is, y depends here and now on x. Clearly there are causal relationships like this too, for example 'The minstrel makes the music.'[8] Here the causal relationship between the minstrel and the music is such that if the minstrel dies or even stops playing, the music ceases; the existence of the music depends here and now on the minstrel.[9]

Now it is easy to understand why Aquinas thought that the causal relationship between God and the world is hierarchical rather than linear.

Like virtually all Christian theologians, he held to the doctrine that the world depends for its existence not just on God's initial act of creation long ago but on God's continual *sustaining* activity. If God were to cease sustaining the world in existence, the world would no longer exist. This much, I think, is clear.

But there is still something puzzling here. How are we to understand the purely logical claim of Aquinas that infinite regress is possible in a linear series but not in a hierarchical series? Precisely why is it that the first two Ways can successfully rule out infinite regress when we are talking about hierarchical causation (or, with the First Way, the hierarchical moving of one thing by another) but not when we are talking about linear causation? This question is not answered in Aquinas' statements of the first two Ways.[10]

One possible explanation comes to mind. Aquinas was opposed to the idea that any actual infinites could exist.[11] In the real world there can be no such thing as a set with an infinite number of members; it is impossible for there to be, say, an infinite number of trees or molecules or baseballs in existence. (We will discuss actual infinites and their relation to the CA in much more detail in Chapter 8, so I will not argue for the point here.) Now if there were an infinite number of *linear* causal ancestors of some presently existing thing – some human being, say – those ancestors would not all have to be existing right now. That is part of what we mean by the notion of a linear cause. Most of them would presumably be dead and gone. No actual infinite would be required to exist all at once.

But suppose we are talking about *hierarchical* causation, where the continued existence of the effect depends on the continued causal activity (and thus existence) of the cause. In this case, the effect cannot exist unless all its hierarchical causes simultaneously exist. So if there were an existing human being who had an infinite number of hierarchical causes, that would require the existence all at once, here and now, of every one of them – an actual infinite. We can now understand Aquinas' claim (premises (2) and (5)) that infinite regress in hierarchical causes is impossible. (In Section III of this chapter, we will return to this point and offer what I take to be a stronger argument on Aquinas' behalf.)

In any case, Aquinas' argument is this: Suppose we have a large system of movers and motions or causes and effects (let's combine the two and simply speak of *changes*), where each change depends on a (logically) prior one. Think, for example, of a watch that has a great many gears, and where the movement of each gear is caused by the motion of the (in this case temporally as well as logically) prior gear.[12] Now clearly the whole system itself requires something to begin the process of change. Even if the watch had an infinite number of gears, they would not move apart from the causal activity of a spring, which initiates the movement. If this thing be itself changed by a prior changer, it is obviously not the *initiator* of the change. So the initiator of all change in the universe must be itself unchanged, that is, it must be outside the system (like the fact that the spring is not itself a gear). This initiator, then, is what confers the power of change on all the members of the system. Now if infinite regress is allowed, Aquinas reasons, that is, if there were an infinite number of movers and things moved, there would be no initiator of the change (first mover or first cause) and thus no change here and now. Since we know *a posteriori* that there is change here and now, there must have been a first mover and a first cause.

Aquinas' argument to the effect that 'If there is an infinite number of movers there is no first mover' is beyond reproach. But his argument that 'If there is no first mover there would be no motion here and now' has seemed to many philosophers to be question-begging.[13] Why does there have to be a *first* mover in any series of movers and things moved? Why cannot each member of an infinitely long series genuinely be the cause of the motion of the next member? What we need is an argument why every such series must have a first mover, and we do not find such an argument in Aquinas' statements of the first three Ways. However, as I will note below in our discussion of the Third Way, it is now customary to interpret Aquinas' three versions of the CA as claiming that in an infinitely long series of movers and things moved (or of causes and effects, or of contingent beings) there will be no proper *explanation* of present motion (or of present effects, or of presently existing contingent beings). And this claim does seem to supply an argument against infinite regress. Whether it is a cogent argument we will consider then.

II. THE THIRD WAY

Let us now move to Aquinas' Third Way. It is an argument about contingent and necessary existence. Here is the heart of the Third Way:

> The third way is taken from possibility and necessity, and runs thus. We find in nature things that are possible to be and not to be, since they are found to be generated, and to corrupt, and consequently, they are possible to be and not to be. But it is impossible for these always to exist, for that which is possible not to be at some time is not. Therefore, if everything is possible not to be, then at one time there could have been nothing in existence, because that which does not exist only begins to exist by something already existing.

Therefore, if at one time nothing was in existence, it would have been impossible for anything to have begun to exist; and thus even now nothing would be in existence – which is absurd. Therefore, not all beings are merely possible, but there must exist something the existence of which is necessary . . . This all men speak of as God.[14]

There are several preliminary points that must be made before we ask whether this is a good argument. First, Aquinas uses the words 'things' and 'beings', and they should be taken as synonymous. 'Being' does not mean human being; a being (like a thing or entity) is anything that can possess properties or that has an identity and is thus distinct from everything else. These terms are meant to have as wide a reference as possible. Anything of which you can think is a being and a thing.

Second, we need to notice that despite what we said earlier about Aquinas' emphasis on hierarchical causation (which continues in the Third Way), this argument makes explicit reference to the past. If everything were contingent, then at one (past) time, Aquinas says, 'there *could have been* nothing in existence'. He also claims that something which comes into existence does so by 'something *already* existing'.[15] Furthermore, as interpreters of Aquinas point out, in the Third Way Aquinas assumes for the sake of argument the thesis of the eternity of the world, i.e., that time is of infinite duration.[16]

Third, another point about terminology. Some things or beings are (as philosophers say) 'contingent'. A contingent being is something that can either exist or not exist. I am contingent because I exist and it is quite possible for me not to exist. We know this because I did not exist a hundred years ago, and it is possible that at some future point I will no longer exist. Some contingent things exist (you, me, the computer on which I type this sentence) and some contingent things do not exist (sabre-tooth tigers, John F. Kennedy, my ninth daughter). Now contingent things that do not exist can possibly exist; there is nothing illogical or incoherent about the idea of their existing. And contingent things that do exist depend for their existence, while they exist, on another being or other beings. Let us say that when Aquinas uses the expression 'things that are possible to be and not to be', he means 'things that are contingent'.

How do we know that some existing thing is contingent? Because it comes into being at a certain time (this is what Aquinas means by saying that it is 'found to be generated') and it ceases to exist at a certain later time (this is what he means by saying that it is 'found . . . to corrupt'). It follows, then, that contingent beings (or at least those that do in fact exist at some time or other) have finite lifespans – they come into existence, exist for a certain finite number of seconds, years, or centuries, and then cease to exist.

One last definition – let us say that a 'necessary being' (NB) is a being that (1) exists at all moments in time, and (2) depends for its existence on no other being or beings. Let us assume that this is what Aquinas means by 'something the existence of which is necessary.'[17] Of course we do not yet know whether there *are* in fact any NBs. Indeed, Aquinas' Third Way is an attempt to prove that not all things can be contingent; that is, at least one NB must exist.

We are now in a position to consider Aquinas' argument. Let us break it down into premises and a conclusion. I will again translate the argument into the form of a syllogism, which simply means a three-step argument (two premises and a conclusion). We can begin with the *a posteriori* premise:

>   7. Some contingent beings exist.

Aquinas thinks the truth of this premise ought to be obvious to all sensible people. It is perfectly clear that contingent things exist, things like you and me and my computer and the North American continent and the Milky Way galaxy. This obviousness is important because, like any argument, the strength of the CA will depend in part on the truth of its premises. You can refute the CA – or any other argument – if you can find a good reason to deny the truth of any of its premises. But so far as premise (7) is concerned, it seems that Aquinas can be quite confident that no such reason will be found.

The rest of the argument can be stated in this way:

>   8. If any contingent beings exist, a necessary being exists.
>   9. Therefore, a necessary being exists.

Now the argument that we are considering – that is, (7), (8), and (9) – corresponds to a long-recognised argument form called *modus ponens*, and is accordingly formally valid. It is impossible for (7) and (8) to be true and (9) false. That is, *if* (7) and (8) are true, then (9) must be true; a NB must exist. Now as noted, we know that (7) is true, so the crucial question before us is whether (8) is true. Whether we think the CA is a sound argument will depend in large part on whether we think (8) is true. Let us accordingly consider the case that Aquinas makes for the truth of (8).

Notice Aquinas' claim in the Third Way, 'that which is possible not to be at some time is not'. This amounts to the claim noted above that all contingent beings have finite lifespans. That is, no contingent being is everlasting. Now there exists a certain very large but finite number of contingent beings. Let's be as generous as possible (to the potential critic of the CA) and say that there are what mathematicians call a 'googol' of contingent beings that have existed, exist, or will ever exist. The number called a googol is written as 10^{100}, that is, as 1 followed by 100 zeros. We are being generous here because there are in fact nowhere near that many contingent beings; even if we count every atom, electron, photon, and quark in the universe, the number will be far less.[18]

But let's just suppose that there are a googol number of contingent beings. Notice that they all (as noted) have finite lifespans. Some such beings (for example, fruit flies) exist for short periods of time – say, a few days. Some (for example, humans) exist for moderate periods of time – at most, say eighty or ninety years. Others (for example, our Solar System) exist for very long periods of time – say, five billion years. Now of course many of these lifespans overlap – you are existing at the same time as the Solar System, and at the same time as countless fruit flies. But let's ignore that fact. Again for the sake of generosity toward the critic of the CA (that is, to come up with as much past time as possible), let's pretend that this googol of contingent beings exists one at a time. No lifespans overlap; first one contingent being exists, and another comes to exist only when it ceases to exist.

Suppose we were somehow able to add up all the seconds, days, or years during which each of our googol number of contingent beings existed (again assuming they exist only one at a time). Again being as generous as possible to the critic of the CA, let's suppose that this amounts to what mathematicians call a googolplex number of years. The number called a googolplex is written as $10^{10^{100}}$, that is, 1 with a googol number of zeros following it. This is exceedingly generous because cosmologists estimate that the Big Bang, which was certainly the beginning of the existence of any contingent beings of which we know, occurred somewhere in the neighbourhood of 15 billion years ago – far, far less than a googolplex number of years ago.

Now let's make two final assumptions. First, let's assume as Aquinas does (at least in the context of the Third Way) that there was no first moment of time, that time is infinite. (Actually, all he needs is that there be more than a googolplex number of past years.) Second, let's assume the negation of what we are trying to prove, namely, that all existing beings are contingent, that is, that there are no necessary beings. Now even if we generously allow that contingent beings have existed for a googolplex number of years, there must have been a point in the far distant past – say, a googolplex plus one number of years ago – when nothing at all existed. After all, a googolplex number of years, large a number as it is, is not an infinite number of years. Now if there ever was a time when nothing at all existed, then nothing would exist today. As Aquinas says, 'that which does not exist only begins to exist by something already existing'. It was an axiom of ancient and medieval philosophy that *ex nihilo nihil fit* ('out of nothing nothing can come').

Despite the opposition of some philosophers,[19] the principle that nothing can come out of nothing seems eminently plausible. J. L. Mackie argues that it is at least conceivable that a thing could pop into existence out of nothing, for no reason at all, that there is no *a priori* reason why this could not occur. Now it is in general difficult to argue successfully that some imagined event or thing is or is not conceivable or is or is not possible. For one thing (as we saw in Chapter 2), the two relevant terms ('conceivable' and 'possible') can be used in a great variety of ways and are not always synonymous. For another, if an event or thing is not known to be actual, the only way to argue that it is or is not conceivable or possible is by an appeal to what we might call intuition, to what simply seems to one to be conceivable or possible. And such arguments are often less than probative.

It can sensibly be said, however, that there is a significant burden of proof issue here. For there seem to be powerful reasons to doubt Mackie's claim. In one sense, he is of course right that something popping into existence for no reason at all is 'conceivable'. I can conceive of a kangaroo popping into existence right now in my office without any cause at all. But my ability to do so proves little. There are lots of reasons why some given event simply cannot occur beside the reason that it is literally inconceivable.

As with anyone who wants to convince us of the possibility of something that seems initially impossible, Mackie owes us an argument. He needs to provide an explanation or give an analogy or tell a story or supply a model (or *something* of the sort) to help us see that he is right, to help us grasp how it is possible that something could come into existence out of nothing. In the absence of such an account (and Mackie does not provide one in *The Miracle of Theism*), we are within our intellectual rights in rejecting his claim. We are within our rights in continuing to affirm *ex nihilo nihil fit*.

If at one time nothing existed, Aquinas says, then 'it would have been impossible for anything to have begun to exist, and even now nothing would be in existence'. But we know that this is absurd because we know that

    7. Some contingent beings exist.

It follows that our assumption that all beings are contingent must be false. As noted in Chapter 2, *reductio ad absurdum* (reduction to absurdity) is a well-recognised and honoured logical device wherein one proves the truth of a proposition by showing that its negation is contradictory or absurd or otherwise logically illicit. The assumption that all existing beings are contingent was the assumption that produced the result that nothing would exist now; since that result is absurd, we are allowed by *reductio ad absurdum* to negate it. It accordingly follows that at least one NB must exist, and (as Aquinas says) 'this all men speak of as God'. He could have added (as medieval logicians often did at the end of their arguments) the expression, QED. These letters stand for *Quod erat demonstrandum* ('which was what we were trying to prove'); they amount to a kind of medieval logician's 'high five'. 'I've done it'; 'I've proved it' – QED in effect says.

Let me now introduce an additional point that I mentioned earlier; it applies to all three Thomistic versions of the CA. Although the notion of *explanation* is not explicitly mentioned by Aquinas, his three versions of the CA have frequently been interpreted as presupposing the Principle of Sufficient Reason (PSR). And there seems to be a consensus among philosophers of religion that the Thomistic arguments are rendered stronger if they are interpreted in terms of the PSR,[20] as later versions of the CA almost always explicitly are.[21] And perhaps Aquinas himself was presupposing something like the PSR; he does hold that something can only be changed from a state of being potentially S (where 'S' is some state like 'being hot' or 'being alive') to being actually S by something else that is itself actually S.[22] There are many versions of the PSR, but they all revolve around something like this claim: *Everything that exists has a reason for its existence.* That is, if something x exists, there must be a reason or explanation why x exists.

Defenders of the PSR usually point out that it cannot be proven, since it constitutes one of the basic axioms of rational thought against which all others claims are measured. But the Principle is, they claim, presupposed in all our rational thinking. Richard Taylor says that you cannot argue for it without assuming it; he calls the PSR 'a presupposition of reason itself'.[23] We encounter thousands of existing things daily, and our assumption always is that there is some reason or explanation why they exist. Suppose one day you were to encounter an unusual automobile, or a rare animal, or a new building. You would dismiss as absurd any such statement as 'There is no reason why it exists; it's just there – that's all.' That is, your commitment to the PSR would make you reject out of hand any suggestion that the existence of the thing is entirely accidental or random.

How does this relate to the CA? The point is that we have no proper explanation for the existence of x (or of the occurrence of some motion or some effect) if x has an infinite number of causal antecedents. The explanation (in this case, of x's existence) is never given but is only indefinitely postponed. No sufficient reason is ever given why it exists. Thus the PSR is only satisfied if there is a first motion, first cause, or necessary being that initiated the state of affairs or thing that we are trying to explain and that itself had no causal ancestors.[24]

Critics of the PSR, and of versions of the CA that depend on it, will in reply ask such questions as: Is the PSR true? If y causes x to exist, why does this not count as a valid explanation of x's existence (thus satisfying the PSR) even if y itself was caused to exist by some other being? Why does an explanation have to be total or comprehensive, that is, leave nothing unexplained, in order truly to count as an explanation? (Since we will discuss these very points in Chapter 8, we will drop them for now.)

III. WHY IS INFINITE REGRESS IMPOSSIBLE IN A HIERARCHICAL SERIES?

Let us return to Aquinas' claim that infinite regress is possible when we are talking about a linear causal series but impossible when we are talking about a hierarchical causal series. As noted above, it is not hard to see important theological reasons why Aquinas preferred to speak of God's causal relation to the world in hierarchical terms. What is not so easy to grasp is his purely logical claim just mentioned.

But it is possible to show that Aquinas was correct. Let me now try to do so. I will offer a long version of the Third Way (any eighteen-step proof counts as long!). I will make some assumptions that Aquinas did not make, for example, that hierarchical causes must exist some finite amount of time prior to their effects (as well as, of course, at the same time as their effects), so I do not claim that I am giving *Aquinas'* reasons for the claim that infinite regress can be ruled out only for those causal series that are hierarchical.

The argument begins with five assumptions; let me now state and explain them. ('NB' means necessary being; 'CB' means contingent being; and 'HC' means hierarchical cause.)

10. Every existing being is either a NB or a CB.

As noted earlier, a CB is a being that might or might not exist, and if it exists, it depends for its existence on another being or beings that existed before it. A NB is a being that cannot fail to exist and does not depend for its existence on any other being. Accordingly, premise (10) is necessarily true. It is a substitution-instance of one of the laws of logic, the law of excluded middle, which says that every proposition is either true or, if not true, then false. (10) simply says that every existing thing either is contingent or else is not contingent.

Premise (11) would be difficult strictly to prove, but it does seem highly plausible.

11. All existing CBs have HCs.

All the existing CBs of which I can think, at any rate, seem to depend, here and now, on other beings for their existence.

12. All CBs are such that they exist at any given time t only if all their HCs also exist at t.

The truth of (12) follows from the definitions of the terms 'CB' and 'HC'. Note that the relationship of 'being the hierarchical cause of' is transitive, that is, if x is a HC of y and if y is a HC of z, then x is a HC of z.

13. All CBs are such that at some time they fail to exist, and one of the times they fail to exist is before they exist.

In other words, all CBs have finite lifespans; they fail to exist, and then they exist, and then they cease to exist.

14. There is no first moment of time.

This final assumption entails that prior to the existence of any CB, an infinite amount of time has already elapsed.

Two more premises must be stated before proceeding to the logical outworking of the assumptions. The first is a premise that the argument endeavours to disprove by reducing it to absurdity. The second is a premise which is known *a posteriori*.

15. All existing beings are CBs.
16. A given CB, namely, x, exists now.

Let me now state the remaining steps in the argument. After each step I will list in parentheses the premises above it that entail it.

17. All of x's HCs exist now. (12, 16)
18. A given HC of x, namely, y, has existed for an *infinite time*. (11, 12, 14, 17)

The derivation of premise (18) requires explanation. One's initial reaction is to ask what rules out the possibility that the causal chain leading to x began with a certain being z that came into existence at some point in time – say, in the year 1940. But what rules out this notion is the fact that any hierarchical cause of x that began to exist at some past point in time is by premise (15) itself a CB which by premise (11) requires a HC. Thus, given that all existing beings are CBs that require HCs; given that all CBs (including x) have HCs that preceded them temporally; given that since x exists now all of x's HCs exist now; and given that time is infinitely long; it follows that at least one HC of x (namely, y) has existed for an infinitely long time.

19. y is a CB. (15)
20. All CBs begin to exist at some point in time. (13, 14)
21. At some past point in time y began to exist. (19, 20)
22. At some past point in time y did not exist. (21, 14)
23. y has not existed for an infinite time (22)
24. y has both existed for an infinite time and has not existed for an infinite time. (18, 23)
25. (19) and thus (15) are false. (19, 15, 24, RAA)
26. Therefore, y is a NB. (10, 25)
27. Therefore, at least one NB exists. (26)

It should be noted that the deduction of the incoherent premise (24) does not automatically point to (15) as the premise which by *reductio ad absurdum* we are allowed to negate. Strictly speaking, what the deduction of (24) entitles us to do is search the assumptions above it for the culprit premise, the one that is responsible for the contradiction. This normally means searching for the least plausible of the assumptions. Since I am not here suggesting that the (10)–(27) argument is a successful theistic proof – we have not even yet come to the criticisms of the CA – I will only suggest here that defenders of the CA will surely focus on (15) as the premise that is to be negated.

What I do want to claim is that the argument we have been discussing helps us see that Aquinas was importantly right in his claim that infinite regress can be ruled out in a hierarchical causal series but not in a linear causal series. How does it show this? Notice that the (10)–(27) argument is obviously invalid if we substitute the expression 'LC' (linear cause) in place of HC in it. Premises (12) and (17) will be simply false, and (18) will not follow from the premises above it.

Why is it, then, that infinite regress is possible in a linear causal series but not in a hierarchical causal series? The crucial difference is that x's hierarchical causes must exist (and exercise causal power) as long as x exists, while this is not true of linear causes. Thus, a series of linear causes of x need not necessarily have begun; it is quite possible that the series never began, with all of infinite past time filled up with an infinite number of its members. But a series of hierarchical causes of *x* is quite different – since one of its members has always existed, the series must have begun with it.[25]

As noted earlier, it is doubtful that Aquinas would approve of this method of defending him. There are several reasons for this, but the most important is that Aquinas was a defender of divine timelessness – God is outside of time, he thought; God has no temporal location or temporal extension. So Aquinas would deny any claim to the effect that the eternity of God has to do with duration or existence for an infinitely long time. So just because God is the hierarchical cause of the universe, it does not follow (so Aquinas would say) that God must exist temporally prior to the universe.

It follows that I have not been giving *Aquinas'* reasons for affirming the possibility of an infinitely long chain of linear causes and denying the possibility of an infinitely long chain of hierarchical causes. Nevertheless, our argument shows that Aquinas was aware of something important of which cosmological arguers and philosophers of religion ought to be aware. No hierarchical causal series can regress infinitely; it must have a beginning.

IV. CRITICISMS OF THE CA

Are these versions of the cosmological argument good arguments? Ought they to convince us that God exists? Let's look at three objections that might be brought to bear against them.[26]

(1) *Who made God?* Some critics of the CA suggest that if we are allowed to ask, 'Who made the world?', we can equally well ask, 'Who made God?' That is, if it is puzzling why the world exists – and it is true that the question, 'Why is there anything instead of nothing?' is the question that is at the heart of all versions of the CA – then why is it not equally puzzling that God exists? Indeed, it seems that cosmological arguers are committed to the causal principle – the principle that every effect has a cause – until they get back to God. Thus Schopenhauer, in his criticism of the CA, claims that defenders of the CA treat the causal principle 'like a hired cab, which we dismiss when we have reached our destination.'[27]

But this criticism is hardly decisive against the CA. It is true that when we are talking about any contingent being *x*, the question, 'What made *x*?', is a legitimate question. In fact, if the PSR is true, the question *must* have an answer. But if we are talking about a necessary being *y*, this implies (1) that *y* always exists; and (2) that *y* depends for *y*'s existence on no other being. Thus such questions as:

What made *y*?
Where did *y* come from?
What is the explanation for *y*'s existence?

do not even make sense. Some philosophers accordingly interpret the PSR as saying, 'Everything *contingent* that exists has a reason for its existence.' This entails that necessary beings need no explanation of their existence. Or if we want to preserve the earlier and stronger version of the PSR – 'Everything that exists has a reason for its existence' – it follows that of any necessary being *y*, the reason for its existence is simply the fact that it is a necessary being.

(2) *The CA commits the fallacy of composition.* This line of argument against the CA began with Kant. Suppose we grant, he said, the principle that says that every effect in the world must have a cause. It does not follow from this that the huge aggregate that we call the world, that is, the sum total of all the things that have ever existed or events that have ever occurred, must itself be an effect that requires a cause. Kant says of the causal principle that it 'is applicable only in the sensible world [that is, the world that we experience with our senses]; outside that world it has no meaning whatsoever'.[28]

The fallacy of composition is the fallacy of assuming that anything that is true of all the members of a set must be true of the set itself. Every single human being has a mother; therefore, the human race has a mother. The version of this fallacy which the cosmological arguer is said to commit is this: Every single existing thing (or existing contingent thing) has a cause for its existence; therefore, the world (the set of all existing things) has a cause for its existence.[29] Now it is certainly true that if you have explained the existence of all the members of a set, there is nothing called 'the set' that is left to explain. If we can give a plausible explanation of the existence of all the contingent things that have ever existed, there is nothing called 'the world' (the set of all the contingent beings) that is left unexplained and that accordingly requires the existence of a necessary being outside the set to explain it.

But the claim that apart from any necessary being we can give a plausible explanation of the existence of all the contingent beings that have ever existed is precisely what the cosmological arguer is denying. Indeed, it seems a necessary truth that you *cannot* do so. Let's imagine a very simple universe consisting of just five existing things (all of them contingent), namely, A, B, C, D and E. Suppose we can explain the existence of E because E was created by D. And suppose we can explain the existence of D and C because both were created by B. And suppose we can explain the existence of B because it was created by A. What, then, is the explanation of the existence of A? It seems that this very problem will exist no matter what what sort of universe we envision, no matter how many contingent beings it contains. *Something* – the temporally or logically first member of the set – will remain unexplained.

Furthermore (as Richard Taylor argues),[30] the world has all the ear-marks of a contingent thing. It is true that the world's contingency does not follow merely from the fact that everything in the world is contingent. (But inferences of this sort are sometimes valid – 'All the tiles of this mosaic are blue; therefore, the whole mosaic is blue.') Whether or not it follows in this case, it is at least a significant fact that everything in the world is contingent. There is nothing about the world that implies or even suggests that it is a necessary being. Notice further there is no absurdity in the notion that the world never existed, that is, that there never was anything at all. (We would not be here to notice such a state of affairs, of course, but that does not rule out the possibility.)

Thus the cosmological arguer need not be guilty of the committing the fallacy of composition. The arguer's point is not the absurd claim that there remains something unexplained even if everything has been ex-plained. The point is that if everything is contingent, it is simply not true that everything can be explained. But since the PSR says that every existing thing *can* be explained, there must be a necessary being to provide the missing explanation.[31]

(3) *Can there exist an everlasting contingent being?* As we have noted, Aquinas argues that all contingent beings have finite lifespans ('that which is possible not to be at some time is not'). Indeed, this point is crucial to the Third Way. Without it, a critic could simply suggest that all of infinite past time is filled up, so to speak, with the existence of an everlasting contingent being. And thus the conclusion that there must have been a time when nothing existed (and thus that nothing would exist now) would not follow. Now I do not know whether it is sensible to believe that there *actually exists* a contingent being that has never not existed. Some say physical matter satisfies this description. But the deepest question is whether the existence of such a being is logically possible. For if it is, then Aquinas' strategy in the Third Way appears to fail.

Now earlier we defined a contingent being (among other properties) as a being which, if it exists, has a finite lifespan. But of course we cannot settle the substantive issue here (Can there be an everlasting contingent being?) simply by definition. So the question can be put as follows: Can there be a being that is both everlasting and contingent *in the sense that it is possible for it both to exist and not exist* (or, as Aquinas says, it 'can not-be')?

It is not difficult to think of one way in which such a being might exist: suppose that God exists, is a NB, and is so enamoured of a certain contingent being (a certain incredibly beautiful rose, let's say) that God ensures that there is no moment of time at which this rose does not exist. The rose is contingent because (1) it *can* fail to exist (if God were to tire of it, for example); and (2) as long as it exists it depends for its existence on something else (namely, God). It is everlasting because God ensures that it always exists.

But of course this scenario supports the position of Aquinas rather than the position of the critic of the CA, since the scenario explicitly includes the existence of God. So the deepest question that we can ask here is this: In the absence of any God or necessary being to provide ontological support, is it possible for a contingent being to be everlasting? And I must confess that so far as I can see, the answer is no. I cannot imagine a possible scenario in which there exists no necessary being and there does exist an everlasting contingent being. Aquinas appears to be correct.

NOTES

1. Edith Hamilton and Huntington Cairns (eds), *The Collected Dialogues of Plato* (New York: Pantheon, 1961), pp. 1,455–79 (894A–899C).
2. See, for example, the essays collected in Part I of Donald R. Burrill (ed.), *The Cosmological Arguments* (Garden City, New York: Anchor Books, 1967). See also William Craig, *The Cosmological Argument from Plato to Leibniz* (New York: Barnes and Noble, 1980).
3. Thomas Aquinas, *Summa Theologica* (New York: Benzinger Brothers, 1947), I, 2, 3 (pp. 13–14). This passage, usually called the 'Five Ways,' is only a small part of the case Aquinas makes for the existence of God in this *Summa*. Indeed, to be fair to Aquinas, one should consider together all of the First Part, Questions 2–11.
4. *Summa Theologica*, I, 2, 3.
5. *Summa Theologica*, I, 2, 3.
6. *Summa Theologica*, I, 46, 2.
7. See, for example, Frederick C. Copleston, *Aquinas* (Baltimore, Maryland: Penguin Books, 1961), pp. 118–20.
8. This example is used by P. T. Geach. See his 'Commentary on Aquinas', in Donald Burrill (ed.), *The Cosmological Arguments*, p. 60.
9. The distinction between hierarchical and linear causes is often made using different terminology. What I (following Copleston) am calling hierarchical causes are sometimes called essential or *per se* causes or causes *in esse*, and what I am calling linear causes are sometimes called accidental or *per accidens* causes or causes *in fieri*.
10. Nor, in my opinion, do we find a satisfactory answer elsewhere in Aquinas. For argumentation, see Stephen T. Davis, 'Hierarchical Causes in the Cosmological Argument', *International Journal for Philosophy of Religion*, Vol. 31, No. 1 (February, 1992), pp. 13–27.
11. See, for example, *Summa Theologica* I, 7, 4; and I, 46, 2ad 7. See also *Summa Contra Gentiles*, trans. by Anton C. Pegis (Notre Dame, Indiana: University of Notre Dame Press, 1955), II, 38.
12. I owe this example to William L. Craig.
13. See William L. Rowe, *The Cosmological Argument* (Princeton, New Jersey: Princeton University Press, 1975), pp. 18–19.
14. Thomas Aquinas, *Summa Theologica*, I, 2, 3. There are many interpretations of Aquinas' Third Way, and I make no exegetical claim that the argument I find there is precisely the argument he intended. For example, I am going to ignore a distinction Aquinas makes, toward the end of the Third Way in a section that I have omitted, between a necessary being that owes its existence to another being and a necessary being (for example, God) that owes its existence to no other being.

For a quite different interpretation of the Third Way, see Anthony Kenny, *The Five Ways* (London: Routledge and Kegan Paul, 1969), pp. 46–69.

15. The italics in these two quotations were added by me.
16. See, for example, Etienne Gilson, *The Christian Philosophy of St. Thomas Aquinas* (New York: Random House, 1956), p. 70.
17. More precisely, Aquinas' view is that a necessary being is a being that has no capacity for generation or corruption, but I will take the two notions as being similar enough for our purposes.
18. According to Alan Guth and Paul Steinhart, there are some 10^{80} elementary particles in the universe. See their 'The Inflationary Universe', in Paul Davies (ed.), *The New Physics* (Cambridge: Cambridge University Press, 1989). Notice that the CA is sometimes criticised on the grounds that if there have existed an infinite number of contingent beings, their lifespans, when added together, could fill up all of infinite past time. But of course the defender of the CA can reply that there is no good reason to believe that there have existed an infinite number of contingent beings.
19. See, for example, J. L. Mackie, *The Miracle of Theism* (Oxford: Clarendon Press, 1982), pp. 89, 94.
20. Rowe, *The Cosmological Argument*, pp. 32, 38–9.
21. I refer specifically to the eighteenth-century versions of the CA, especially those of Leibniz and Clarke. See Gottfried Leibniz's essay 'On the Ultimate Origin of Things', in Philip P. Wiener (ed.), *Leibniz: Selections* (New York: Charles Scribner's Sons, 1951), pp. 345–55; for Clarke, see the selections from Samuel Clarke, *A Demonstration of the Being and Attributes of God* quoted in D. D. Raphael (ed.), *British Moralists 1650–1800* (Oxford: Oxford University Press, 1969).
22. This point is argued by Scott McDonald in his 'Aquinas' Parasitic Cosmological Argument', *Medieval Philosophy and Theology*, Vol. I (1991), p. 129.
23. Richard Taylor, *Metaphysics*, 4th edition (Englewood Cliffs, New Jersey: Prentice-Hall, 1992), p. 101.
24. Again, this is not quite Aquinas' point. His notion was not that in an infinitely long hierarchical causal chain motion would be unexplained but rather that there would be no motion at all.
25. For further discussion of these points, see Davis, 'Hierarchical Causes'.
26. Two other important criticisms will be discussed later. The CA is sometimes said to 'beg the question', and we will consider that objection in Chapter 8. The CA also is commonly criticised on the grounds that the being that is 'proved' to exist, even if the CA is entirely successful, is not the God of theism. We will discuss that point in Chapter 10.
27. Arthur Schopenhauer, *On the Fourfold Root of the Principle of Sufficient Reason and on the Will in Nature*, trans. by K. Hillebrand (London: 1888), pp. 42–3.
28. Immanuel Kant, *Critique of Pure Reason*, trans. by Norman Kemp Smith (New York: St. Martin's Press, 1965), p. 511.
29. This criticism is developed with considerable power by Paul Edwards. See his 'The Cosmological Argument,' in Donald R. Burrill, *The Cosmological Arguments*, pp. 113–14.
30. Taylor, *Metaphysics*, pp. 105–7.
31. Furthermore, Thomistic versions of the CA seem particularly immune to the 'fallacy of composition' criticism. Aquinas would argue that a necessary being must exist if even *one* contingent being exists. He was not arguing from part to whole.

5

Theistic Proofs and Foundationalism

I. INTRODUCTION

In this chapter, we will consider the somewhat complicated relationship between TPs and a theory known as foundationalism. We will define foundationalism soon enough, but for now let's just say that it is an epistemological theory with a long history that seemed so obviously true to so many people that it was not even recognised as a theory, or at least not one that needed defending, until fairly recently. This could hardly be less true today – one can scarcely pick up a book or article in epistemology, theology, or even popular intellectual culture, without encountering confident declarations of the death of foundationalism.

Let us begin by noting a certain fact about the historical setting of TPs in the philosophy of religion. The fact is that that setting seems radically to have changed. In the classic period of medieval TPs – roughly the eleventh, twelfth, and thirteenth centuries – arguments for the existence of God were located in a certain setting and played a certain role that seems very different from the setting and role of TPs (even some of the same TPs) in the eighteenth, nineteenth and twentieth centuries.

In the medieval period, theistic provers were aware of the fact that there were people who did not share their beliefs about God. In his argument in *Proslogion* II, Anselm pointedly referred to the 'fool' of the Psalms, who said 'There is no God.' And it is often said (whether it is true I do not know) that Aquinas intended his *Summa Contra Gentiles* as a handbook to be used by Christian missionaries in Muslim nations. Still, the TPs that these and other medieval thinkers offered sound like intellectual efforts that are largely internal to faith. The central aim was not to convince atheists and religious sceptics that God exists, nor even to convince them that Christians are rational in asserting that God exists. Yes, objections from outside faith were being addressed; still, one does not get the impression that Anselm, Aquinas, Duns Scotus, or William of Occam felt in any sense *responsible* to outsiders. Their TPs read like attempts from within the ambit of faith to answer objections brought to it from the outside. The purpose of medieval TPs was not to *convince people* that God exists but to show that 'God exists' can, via conclusive demonstrative proofs, be *known*. And whether a given TP constitutes a successful argument is to be decided by those who are members of the community of faith, not by outsiders.[1]

But by the time we arrive at people like Paley and Clarke (and other theistic provers of the modern period like Descartes, Locke, Leibniz, Malebranche, Berkeley, and Kant), let alone their nineteenth- and twentieth-century colleagues, the intellectual situation is quite different. Pretty much the same TPs are given (albeit in new versions) in the modern period as were given in the medieval period, but the setting has changed. As D. Z. Phillips says, 'in Enlightenment thought, what is demanded of the proofs is very different. Instead of being defenses from within an existing Faith, that Faith itself is said to depend on them. They become foundations of the Faith. The religious category is no longer decisive. It now stands in need of external justification.'[2]

In short, by the time we reach the Enlightenment, it seems that theistic provers feel somehow responsible to atheists and religious sceptics; it seems that the main job that theistic provers accept for themselves is to produce arguments that would or should be convincing to those same sceptics. If sceptics cannot be convinced that God exists, the fall-back position is at least to convince them that theists are rational in asserting that God exists. But whether a given TP is a successful argument will be decided by the sceptics at whom it is directed, not by believers.

What happened between the medieval period and the modern period to bring about these changes in the context and purpose of TPs? Three things – the Enlightenment, classical foundationalism, and the evidentialist objection to religious faith.

The Enlightenment was a period in the history of European thought that began in the seventeenth century and hit its stride in the eighteenth. Some of its central themes were: (1) mistrust of religion and of authority in general; (2) emphasis on human experience and reason as the only reliable guides to truth; (3) the emergence of certain political ideals, especially secular, democratic, and liberal ones; and (4) optimism about the prospect of human problems being overcome through education, the use of reason, and a roughly utilitarian approach to social and moral issues.

Obviously, points (1) and (2) are crucial for the new role of TPs. Enlightenment thinkers (and those influenced by them) would never accept a claim on *any* subject merely because the church or the Bible or the church Fathers endorsed it. It is *only* rational to believe a statement if that statement can be proved or rendered probable by human reason. Human reason is the final – indeed, the only – arbiter of what can be rationally believed.

What is *classical foundationalism*? Let me follow Alvin Plantinga's analysis of it.[3] Let's say that my *noetic structure* is all the beliefs that I have together with the logical and epistemic relations among those beliefs (for example, some beliefs may be entailed by or made probable by others). Some beliefs, of course, I hold more firmly than others, and some are much more crucial to the coherence of my entire noetic structure than others. Now some of the beliefs in my noetic structure are foundational to it or (as we might say) are located in its foundation. These are beliefs that are held not on the basis of any other beliefs. Perhaps they are known immediately (that is, not through the mediation of any other beliefs) or perhaps they are self-evident. We'll call them *basic beliefs*. All other beliefs are non-foundational or non-basic, that is, they are held on the basis of other beliefs.

Now some people are rational and some are not; and so some noetic structures are rational and some are not. The basic epistemological intuition of foundationalism is this: *in order to be rational, beliefs must be based on good evidence*. So a belief is rational if and only if it either is a foundational belief that is *properly basic*, or else is a non-foundational belief that is based on or supported by a properly basic belief. In the case of any basic belief (again, this is one that is located in the foundations of my noetic structure), how can we tell whether it is properly basic?

Here Plantinga distinguishes between ancient and medieval foundationalism, on the one hand, and modern foundationalism, on the other. For people in the first group (of whom Aquinas is a good example), a basic belief is properly basic if it is either self-evident (that is, to understand it is to see that it is true) or else evident with respect to the senses (that is, it is something that we know directly through the senses). For modern foundationalists like Descartes and Hume, a belief is properly basic if it is either self-evident or incorrigible. An incorrigible belief is a belief about which the believer cannot possibly be mistaken, like 'I am now in pain' or 'I now seem to be seeing a green apple'.

What is *the evidentialist objection*? It is an objection to belief in God, and it is based upon classical foundationalism. Notice that belief in the existence of God does not fit any of classical foundationalism's categories for rational belief. A rational belief, for classical foundationalism, must be either a basic belief that is properly basic, or else a non-basic belief that is entailed by or in some other strong sense based upon a properly basic belief. But note that belief in God cannot be properly basic because it is neither self-evident, evident with respect to the senses, nor incorrigible. So the only way that belief in God can be rational for a person is that it must be entailed by, or made probable with respect to, or in some epistemic sense *supported by* beliefs that are themselves properly basic.

The evidentialist objection to belief in God in effect says that theists are in trouble because this is not true. Their belief is neither properly basic nor is it based upon beliefs that are properly basic. It is an irrational belief. Again, in order to be rational, all non-basic beliefs must be based on evidence. They must be grounded in *certitude*. Classical foundationalists were convinced that firm epistemic standards like these were absolutely necessary. To loosen the strictures would encourage two great epistemic evils – first, it would allow for virtually anything to be believed by anybody, that is, people could believe things that are *not* based on evidence or even that are *contrary to* the evidence; second, it would allow for dogmatism, that is, the holding of one's beliefs with a degree of certainty stronger than the evidence allows. Belief in the existence of God is not rational. To believe in God is accordingly gullible, credulous, soft-headed, dogmatic.

II. REFORMED EPISTEMOLOGY

There are several approaches theists can take in response to the evidentialist objection. One is to admit that religious belief is irrational, at least in some senses, but to recommend it anyway. A related response is to continue to hold to religious belief, but deny that it is subject to adjudication by reason (this view is often called fideism). Another would be simply to evade the force of the evidentialist objection by defending religious faith in only a practical or voluntarist way, as Blaise Pascal and William James did (see Chapter 8, where such arguments are discussed). Another is to argue that religious belief may not be – so to speak – *demanded* by the evidence but is *allowed* or *permitted* by it (in other words, although atheism can be a rational position, theism can be rational too).[4]

But clearly the most popular response to the evidentialist objection is to try to answer it, show that it is wrong, offer arguments to the effect that belief in God is rational after all. The most common way of doing that is in effect the topic of this book – to offer arguments for the existence of God.

How are TPs related to foundationalism? The answer is that they are normally allied to foundationalism, and in two important ways. The first point, which I am not going to discuss in detail, is that for centuries the TPs were used foundationally in both Catholic and (to a lesser extent) Protestant theological circles. That is, theologians considered that the first task of theology was to establish the existence of God (as a theological foundation, if you will) by human reason alone; once that was done, the rest of theology could be brought in.

The Roman Catholic notion of 'fundamental theology', as traditionally understood, worked in just that way. Its initial job was to establish, through the categories of Thomistic philosophy, the existence of God; then other topics such as the possibility of revelation and the authority of the church could be approached. The existence of God was considered, then, a prolegomenon to or foundation for all other theology. Indeed, the TPs themselves were foundational to faith.[5]

The second point has to do not so much with the theological role of TPs in the church as with their internal methodology, which, in the vast majority of cases, seems to be foundationalist. The usual strategy is to begin with some proposition about which the theistic prover thinks we can be certain. Perhaps we can be certain because the proposition is, so to speak, an item of consciousness, like 'I have an idea of God' or 'I have had certain experiences that I interpret in terms of divine forgiveness' or 'I have a strong sense of guilt whenever I tell a lie' or 'I understand the words "Greatest Conceivable Being".' Or perhaps we can be certain because the proposition is an empirical fact that is obviously true, like 'Some things move' or 'Some things seem to be designed' or 'Some things cause other things' or 'Some things exist for a time and then cease to exist.' The idea, then, is to ensure that one's TP be grounded in certainty by beginning with something that is axiomatic, known to all, obviously true, self-evident, necessarily true, or something of that sort. Then, of course, the idea is to introduce a piece of reasoning that assumes what is certain and which is itself logically impeccable, which entails in the conclusion 'God exists.'[6]

The clear assumption of the whole procedure is that belief in the existence of God is itself *not* foundational or basic or self-evident or axiomatic or anything like that. The existence of God is *uncertain* (because, obviously, many intelligent people deny or doubt it), and if one is rationally to believe it, the belief must be grounded in what is certain. That is, it needs to be *proved*. And if the belief isn't proved, it follows (via the evidentialist objection) that belief in God is irrational.

There is a group of contemporary philosophers of religion, all of whom are Christian philosophers, who get off the bus at just this point. They are called Reformed Epistemologists – this is because of the affinity of their position for certain opinions held by John Calvin and other 'Reformed' theologians.[7] Reformed Epistemology is a loosely-defined group of thinkers – Alvin Plantinga, William Alston and Nicholas Wolterstorff are the central figures – that is following something like a common research programme. It is too early to assess the results of that programme, especially since it is only about twenty years old, and the work is continuing.

But at one point their programme intersects with the topic of this volume: the Reformed Epistemologists are united in denying that belief in God must first be rationally approved by sceptics, or rationally established by arguments from natural theology, before it is rational. Accordingly, they are not enthusiastic advocates of arguments for the existence of God. Why think – they ask – that you need a convincing TP in order to be rational in believing in God? What needs justification, what is at fault – they say – is not belief in God but rather unbelief.

Let's return to Plantinga's argument.[8] One of his central claims is that classical foundationalism (CF) is an incoherent position. Notice, Plantinga says, that CF is crucially based upon this proposition:

1. A proposition p is properly basic for a person S if and only if p is either self-evident to S or is incorrigible for S or evident to the senses for S.[9]

But notice further, Plantinga says, that proposition (1) is neither self-evident nor incorrigible nor evident to the senses. Thus (1) is not properly basic. Nor does there seem any sensible hope of (1) being self-evidently entailed by any proposition that *is* properly basic. Thus classical foundationalism is, as Plantinga says, self-referentially incoherent; that is, it is a position that refutes itself (like, say, the position of the person who writes, 'I cannot write a single sentence of English').

Furthermore, Plantinga says, there are lots of things that we rationally believe without any argument at all. My belief that the past is real is not based on any convincing or non-circular argument. Nor is my belief that there is a world external to my consciousness. Nor is my belief that other minds exist in the world besides mine. Nor is my belief that my cognitive faculties are generally reliable. In none of these cases have philosophers been able to come up with convincing, non-circular arguments that refute the views of sceptics. Probably there simply *are* no such arguments. Still, we are rational in believing that the past is real, that the external world exists, that there are other minds (things that think and feel and remember and formulate intentions) besides mine, and that my cognitive faculties are generally reliable. Indeed, it seems that in these cases it is the doubter and not the believer who is the irrational one.

Notice proposition (2):

2. I had lunch today at noon.

This is, Plantinga says, a basic proposition to the person (in this case, me) who sincerely says it. That is, I do not believe (2) on the basis of other propositions – I just believe it. It is basic to my noetic structure. Notice also that (2) satisfies none of the criteria listed in (1). It is neither self-evident to me, evident to the senses to me, nor incorrigible to me. Thus, by criterion (1), if (2) is a basic belief to me it is *improperly* basic; it *should not* be basic to me. But nothing could be further from the truth, Plantinga says. I am entirely rational in taking (2) as basic.

But what then about the belief that

3. God exists?

Plantinga argues that it too can be properly basic for some people although it need not be based on argument or evidence. Like my acceptance of (2), for those people belief in God is one of the propositions with which they begin; believing in God is as natural to them as my believing that I lunch today at noon is to me. Now this way of making the point may not be quite correct, Plantinga admits. For most theists, it may not be true to say that (3) itself is properly basic; the more accurate way to make the point would be to say that (3) is self-evidently entailed by certain other propositions that *are* properly basic for many theists, propositions like: 'God has spoken to me,' or 'God has created all this,' or 'God is to be thanked and praised.'

Suppose there is somewhere a 14-year-old farm boy who is being raised in a Christian home and environment. He has never studied any philosophy or theology; he has never heard of Aquinas or Kant or Hume or Bertrand Russell. He finds it natural to believe in God; indeed, belief in God is basic to his noetic structure. Plantinga's point is that this boy's belief in God, despite the evidentialist objection, is not only basic but properly basic. It can even be said that he *knows* that God exists.

The Reformed Epistemologists, all of whom as noted are Christian philosophers, believe that God created us in a certain way and with certain things in mind. One aspect of that notion is the idea that God created us with a natural sense of God, a natural belief in God. This sense has been sullied, stained, and almost (but not quite) eradicated by the pandemic effects of sin in our lives. In any case, the point is that belief in God is for many people not only a basic belief but a properly basic belief. Like proposition (2), it can rationally be believed quite apart from argument. Certain experiences may serve as *grounds* for belief in God, but positive apologetic arguments such as we find in natural theology do not count as evidence for it.

We were created, Plantinga says, with a 'design plan', a set of epistemic inclinations and dispositions which is designed to work in a certain way. It is also designed to work in a certain context, that is, the environment of our epistemic situation as human persons in this world. The plan is the way that God intended our epistemic faculties to function. Some people misuse their epistemic equipment; on some occasions that equipment malfunctions. That is when human beings formulate beliefs that have little or no warrant.

But those who come to believe in God are following the divine design plan; their epistemic equipment is functioning properly. If *warrant* is that which when added to true belief produces knowledge, Plantinga argues that any true belief is warranted when it is produced by our epistemic faculties functioning properly in a proper context. Those who believe in God are not only rational in their belief that God exists – they can legitimately be said to *know* that God exists.

As noted, Reformed Epistemologists are not enthusiastic supporters of TPs or of natural theology in general. As we will see in a moment, they *are* advocates of what we might call negative apologetics, that is, responding to objections to theism or Christianity that are raised by critics. But providing arguments or evidence *in favour of* belief in God (what we might call positive apologetics) – as if belief in God were to be justified by those arguments or that evidence – is not something they favour.

Plantinga seems to give four arguments against natural theology. First, for most believers, TPs have nothing to do with their having come to believe in God; they do not constitute the true source of that belief. Second, TPs are not in any sense required for those beliefs to be warranted; as we have seen, Plantinga thinks that belief in God can be properly basic without any argument at all. Third, the project of natural theology has not succeeded up to this point. Fourth, if any believers do base their belief in God on TPs, that will constitute an improper source because the faith that will be produced will be unstable (always dependent on what objections might be raised in the philosophical journals or elsewhere).[10]

III. ANALYSING PLANTINGA'S ARGUMENT

Is Plantinga's argument convincing? This is not the place for a full critique of his epistemological theory, nor am I the one to give it.[11] But it is important that we consider those aspects of Plantinga's theory that are relevant to the project of offering proofs for the existence of God. Before raising some critical points of my own, let me make three preliminary points.

First, Plantinga does not reject foundationalism *in toto*; he does reject classical foundationalism, but his own proposal is foundationalist in its own way. Indeed, he specifically argues that all noetic structures have foundations, and that such beliefs as 'God exists' (or beliefs that self-evidently entail it) are properly basic for theists. His main criticism of classical foundationalism concerns not the appropriateness of foundationalism but the sorts of beliefs that can properly be said to be foundational.

Second, Plantinga and other Reformed Epistemologists, while not emphasising positive apologetics (natural theological arguments in favor of theism), are strong advocates of negative apologetics. They are skilled at answering objections to theistic or Christian beliefs that are raised by secular philosophers. Thus Plantinga himself has responded with extended reviews of such religiously sceptical books as J. L. Mackie's *The Miracle of Theism*[12] and Daniel Dennett, *Darwin's Dangerous Idea.*[13] On other occasions he has attacked such anti-theist viewpoints or arguments as verificationism, naturalism, the problem of evil, the grand evolutionary hypothesis, etc.

Third, Plantinga does not totally reject the tradition of offering TPs. He has sympathetically discussed several of them in his writings over the years, and he sees no problem with the idea of believers' conviction that God exists being strengthened by a TP.[14] A given believer's warrant for her belief in God could even be increased by a TP. His main criticism is aimed at the assumption behind the evidentialist objection to religious belief, namely, that if your belief in God is not based on convincing rational argument, it is unwarranted and irrational.

Let me raise three points. (I hesitate to call them objections because I actually think Plantinga would or at least could agree with each of them.) First, Plantinga is absolutely right that, for many and maybe most theists, natural theology is not necessary to provide warrant for their belief in God. There certainly are people like the teenage farm boy whose belief in God is not only basic to their noetic structure but properly basic. The farm boy does not have to be able to meet all the objections to belief in God that have been raised by Bertrand Russell, Antony Flew, Kai Nielsen *et al.* before his belief is rational. Natural theology should not be the ground of belief in God.

Still, it seems that *somebody* in the community of believers in God had better be conversant with and able to respond to any objections that might be raised. Indeed, somebody in the community had better be ready with arguments and evidence *in favour of* belief in God, in case that is called for. If there are objections to theism – raised by Bertrand Russell or anybody else – that remain unanswered, then theism (to borrow Stephen Wykstra's memorable phrase) is 'in big doxastic trouble'.[15]

Does this mean, then, that the rationality of my belief in God is dependent on whatever anti-theistic arguments Flew or Nielsen or any other philosopher might publish in the next issue of the *Journal of Philosophy*? Well, yes and no. The answer is no, in the sense that I have already argued that there are many members of the theistic community who – like the farm boy – remain quite doxastically unaffected by the comings and goings of philosophy. But the answer is yes, in the sense that the theistic community would be in trouble if certain unanswerable objections to theism were raised. So somebody in the theistic community had better digest whatever objections to theism emerge and see what can be said in response to them.

Second, the 'Great Pumpkin' objection has been around since the early days of Reformed Epistemology. There are aspects of it on which I will not comment, but it does raise issues that are relevant to our concerns. The objection is that Reformed Epistemology allows too much epistemic latitude. If theists can claim that belief in God is properly basic, why cannot believers in the Great Pumpkin hold that their beliefs (the Great Pumpkin returns every Halloween, etc.) are properly basic too? Indeed, why cannot *any* community, no matter how absurd its crucial beliefs, claim that those beliefs are properly basic, and thus rational, for its members?

Plantinga's reply is that Reformed Epistemologists are not committed to allowing that the crucial beliefs of Great Pumpkin believers (or the crucial beliefs of any other group) are properly basic. Reformed Epistemologists claim that: (1) belief in God is properly basic; (2) not every belief is properly basic; (3) belief in the Great Pumpkin is a fine example of a belief that is *not* properly basic; and (4) there is no infallible criterion that would be acceptable to everyone for determining which basic beliefs are properly basic and which are not. But why is that so bad, Plantinga asks? Each group is responsible for arriving at its own set of criteria for proper basicality, and not every group will agree. Presumably atheists have their own criteria of proper basicality, but theists will refuse to be bound by those criteria. Christians simply find belief in God to be one of the paradigm examples of properly basic belief, especially since they hold that a tendency to believe in God has been implanted in us by God; and they find belief in the Great Pumpkin to be a paradigm case of an improperly basic belief.

We appear to be at an impasse. Plantinga is surely correct in what I have just quoted him as saying: nothing in Reformed Epistemology requires its defenders to allow that Great Pumpkin belief is properly basic. But the impasse is this: apologists for Great Pumpkin belief can insist that they are responsible to their own criteria of proper basicality, not to the criteria proposed by Christians or even theists. They can even claim that there is a natural human tendency to formulate belief in the Great Pumpkin. Where do we go from here?

Well, it seems that TPs, or natural theology in general, constitute a way of trying to advance beyond our impasse. In one sense, it just isn't true that every community is responsible *only* to its own set of criteria of proper basicality. There are times where the thriving of the theistic community may well depend on some member of it understanding and answering the objections of atheist philosophers, objections written within the context of atheistic criteria of proper basicality. We aren't talking about two incommensurate world views whose members can simply brush each other off. There will be times when certain theists will be tempted and troubled by arguments that arise from the atheistic camp, and other times when certain atheists will be tempted to start believing in God. Natural theology is perhaps the only tool available in such cases. For example, it might be possible for theists to expose as absurd – on the basis of criteria accepted by Great Pumpkin believers – belief in the Great Pumpkin. It might even be possible for natural theology to show that atheism is absurd. That is one reason why natural theology remains necessary.

In general, natural theology will always remain as one possible route in which relief might be found for any theist who has discovered reason to doubt theism. Perhaps the teenage farm boy will eventually go to college. There he might take a class in biology from a teacher who ridicules theism. Or he might be troubled by the discovery that theists are in a distinct minority in his university community. Or he might find his theism sorely tempted by the fact of human suffering in the world – triggered, let's say, by the premature death of a childhood friend of his from cancer. Natural theology – both positive and negative apologetic arguments – might be able to restore the boy's belief in God and provide it with significantly more warrant than it had.[16]

The same point can emerge in a slightly different context. It is true that most theists will be inclined to accept beliefs that are common to theistic communities, especially if those beliefs have been confirmed by the theist's own experiences. Very many theists will claim to have experienced the grace or the guidance or the forgiveness of God in their own lives. But theists who are educated or who travel widely or who are simply aware of the world in which they live will also know that many other members of various non-theistic communities will claim to have experienced the reality of some non-theistic god or ultimate reality. This too can constitute a sort of defeater of one's own views: Can I believe my own religious experiences when other people have different experiences?

As William Hasker says (making a different point from mine), 'the religious believer is rational in affirming that experientially grounded religious beliefs are warranted if and only if she is rational in affirming a *reliability thesis* to the effect that the processes generating such beliefs are epistemologically reliable'.[17] Again my suggestion would be that natural theology may well be able to play some of the role that Hasker sees as necessary here. It may be that TPs or other rational arguments might be able to show that the processes generating beliefs from certain sorts of experiences are likely to be reliable, and others not. If for example the OA is a successful argument, any purported religious experience of a religious ultimate less great than the GCB will be under suspicion.

Third, what about Plantinga's four criticisms of natural theology cited earlier? The first and second points are quite innocuous, I would think, and ought to be agreed on by all sides. For most believers, it is certainly true that TPs are not the source of their belief in God. (As noted in the Introduction to this book, the quaint story that Bertrand Russell tells about his own youthful flirtations with the OA is a case where belief in God – in Russell's case, very fleeting belief in God – was produced by cogitating about a TP. But clearly such cases are unusual.) Moreover, I entirely agree with Plantinga that belief in God can be fully warranted for some theists (maybe the vast majority of them) apart from any TPs at all. Plantinga's third point – that the project of natural theology has not succeeded to date and perhaps cannot succeed – also seems easily acceptable, depending of course on what that project is taken to be. If the project is to convince all rational folk that God exists (or something of that sort), Plantinga is surely right.

The fourth point – that TPs are a poor source of religious beliefs because they will produce a faith that is wavering – is also one that I can accept. I would be surprised if any of the TPs discussed in this book, even any of them that I defend, constituted the only or even main source of some theist's belief in God. That is certainly not the role that I would envision for TPs in the lives of theists.

Still, I see nothing wrong, and a lot that is right, with trying to buttress propositions that I accept but other people consider uncertain or even false by showing that they can be derived from propositions about which everybody is certain. It might even be helpful to show that certain theological propositions can be shown to be derivable from certain non-theological ones. It might be true both (1) that some theist's belief in God is fully justified, and (2) that it will be helpful to that theist (or to others) to *show* that it is justified.[18] Perhaps that can be done by natural theology.

Furthermore, natural theology might well be able to convince a theist whose belief in God is based on the testimony of family or friends, or even on her own religious experiences, that the 'God' she believes in is identical to the 'Greatest Conceivable Being' of Anselm or the 'necessary being' of Aquinas or the 'designer of the universe' of Paley. In short, natural theology might be able to supply theists with the meaning and overall theological and philosophical context of the belief in God that they find themselves having.

IV. CRITICISMS OF FOUNDATIONALISM

We have already discussed Plantinga's critique of classical foundationalism, but we also noted that he has not rejected foundationalism entirely; indeed, his programme is still foundationalist. But we also noted at the outset of this chapter that many scholars today reject foundationalism *tout court*. Now this is not a book on epistemology or even religious epistemology; so I do not propose to engage in a thorough analysis of foundationalism or of the reasons that are given for rejecting it. (That would be a topic for a separate book.) Still, as we also noted, there is a close connection in the history of theism between foundationalism and the project of offering TPs. So we need to consider those aspects of the contemporary critique of foundationalism that are relevant to that project.

It is not always easy to determine which theories or arguments are committed to or presuppose foundationalism and which are not. Nevertheless, foundationalism in the theory of knowledge is characterised by two central traits: first, the attempt to discover claims that are absolutely certain and are designed to form the foundation of one's theory or argument. (Arguments or chains of arguments that justify propositions cannot be circular or question-begging, so they have to stop somewhere; and in foundationalism they stop at the point where a completely certain claim is reached.) Second, reasoning moves in one direction only, namely, from the more certain toward the less certain, or from the foundations toward the non-foundations.

We can illustrate this second point from Descartes.[19] Three claims (at least) are foundational in Descartes' system: (1) that he, Descartes, exists each time he thinks; (2) that all clear and distinct ideas are true; and (3) that a good, non-deceiving God exists. (There are also certain principles that Descartes says follow from the 'natural light' or 'the light of reason'.) Now suppose Descartes seems to himself at one point to be perceiving an apple on a table before him. The claim 'I am now perceiving an apple' is a perfect example of something Descartes would consider non-foundational. Now my point is this: Descartes would be perfectly comfortable with the project of trying to provide warrant for the claim 'I am now perceiving an apple' by showing that it follows from or is based upon claims that he considers foundational. (Indeed, that is how he *does* proceed: if the claim is clear and distinct, we can be sure that it has warrant; no good God would deceive us into thinking that a clear and distinct idea is true when it is not.) But notice that it would never enter Descartes' head to try to provide warrant for (1), (2), or (3) by showing that they follow from, or are in some sense based upon, 'I am now perceiving an apple.' That is why I say that for a classical foundationalist, justificatory reasoning can only go in one direction.

According to those contemporary thinkers who reject all forms of foundationalism, what are the main problems with that theory? Four criticisms are often given. (Obviously, not all anti-foundationalists will agree on all four points.)

First, it is claimed that there is no direct access to the world (that is, access that by-passes our own conceptual equipment). Since all facts and all data are theory-laden, there is no way to compare our ideas (for example, of an apple) with reality itself (the apple). Furthermore, what is indubitable varies from person to person. For example, Descartes thought that it was certain that 'there must be at least as much reality in the efficient and total cause as in its effect'.[20] Indeed, this principle constitutes a crucial step in one of his proofs for the existence of God. But hardly anybody else in philosophy has ever agreed with him that this point is certain. It is not even clear what it means.

Second, it is claimed that there are no absolutely certain foundations for knowledge (any claim can be denied), and no way in any case to justify what is uncertain via what is certain. No foundationalist has ever found an undeniable procedure for making non-foundational beliefs or statements certain by showing that they are 'based upon' absolutely certain statements or beliefs. Indeed, the locution 'is based upon' is little more than an empty metaphor. Another way of making the point is to say that there is a trade-off between indubitability and usefulness in beliefs. As Nancey Murphy puts it: 'Whenever one finds suitably indubitable beliefs to serve as a foundation, they will always turn out to be useless for justifying any interesting claims; beliefs that are useful for justifying other claims will always turn out not to be indubitable, and in fact will be found to be dependent upon the structure they are intended to justify.'[21]

Third, it is claimed that many contradictory theories, viewpoints, and statements can be equally well founded, and that there is no way that conflicts between them can be rationally settled. That is, there is no non-arbitrary way to establish that one set of foundational beliefs is superior to another. As Hugo Meynell says: 'If one is to set out a view of how judgments may be well founded, presumably that view has itself to consist in a series of judgments. But how can these judgments themselves be anything but arbitrary?'[22]

Fourth, it is claimed that knowledge is more like a web than a building. In foundationalism, noetic structures are like buildings; they have foundations, the foundations need to be solid, and all the rest of the building is built on the supporting foundation. But anti-foundationalists, following W. V. Quine,[23] argue that noetic structures are more like webs or nets. The whole web must be coherent, but there is no foundation, because any belief in a noetic structure can be revised or even given up if one is willing to pay the price of making the necessary adjustments elsewhere. Rather, the various beliefs all support each other in a mutually interlocking way. Beliefs are justified in terms of their relations with neighbouring beliefs and, ultimately, to the whole web. Some beliefs are of course closer to the core of the web than others, but nothing is absolutely indubitable.

Furthermore, reasoning can go in any direction. Beliefs nearer the outer limits of the web can be said to support the beliefs at the core of the web just as much as the other way around. We do occasionally change our beliefs, and when changes have to be made in a web of beliefs, the subject (or perhaps the community of those who share the web) decides which beliefs are least closely related to the beliefs that there is no reason to give up or revise; those are then changed, with as little damage to the coherence of the whole of the web as possible.

There are two issues here that we need to discuss. One is the purely epistemological question of whether the critique of foundationalism that we have just explained is compelling, and whether anti-foundationalists have anything better to offer. The second is whether the critique of foundationalism also constitutes a critique of the classic TPs, or of the whole programme of offering TPs. Let me make two comments on the first issue.

First, do we have 'direct access' to the world (to reality, to facts)? In one important sense, surely not. There is no way to by-pass our own conceptual equipment in order to compare our ideas with reality as such. Doing the comparing would obviously involve using our conceptual equipment. But surely it does not follow from this that we are irrevocably cut off from the world. Let's ask a different question: Can we *know* things (that is, certain facts) about the world? Of course we can (and do). (What *can* we know except the world?) Even enemies of foundationalism suppose as much. Aren't their dicta 'We have no direct contact with the world,' and 'All data are theory-laden' supposed to be facts?[24]

Nor is it easy to see why foundationalism must be more guilty than other epistemological theories of ignoring the fact that all data are theory-laden. What is indubitable may well vary from person to person, but there are also common human doxastic practices. It is possible to reach agreement among all normally gifted and non-insane adult human beings on the truth of the propositions expressed by statements like 'All bachelors are unmarried' and even 'San Francisco is north of Los Angeles.' Are there good theories or informed persons for whom these statements are false?

Second, the search for absolutely certain statements from which one can (through an absolutely reliable method) warrant statements that were uncertain has indeed thus far proved to be a will-o'-the-wisp. The prospects for Cartesian foundationalism or Lockean foundationalism do not look particularly promising. But perhaps there are versions of foundationalism that are not so easily refuted as these specimens. It is possible to begin not with absolutely certain statements but with commonly shared doxastic practices.[25]

I will not dispute the anti-foundationalist claim that knowledge is more like a web than a building. Although (as I noted earlier) it continues to be a valid epistemological strategy to try to ground the uncertain in the certain, it is also true that reasoning can go both from the core of a noetic structure to the edges and vice versa.

But the biggest problem with anti-foundationalism arises when we ask what the alternative is to foundationalism. What have been suggested so far are various versions of coherentism, pragmatism, or 'holism' that raise worries at least as alarming as the problems in foundationalism. My own major concern is that if we abandon foundationalism, then 'anything goes' in epistemology.[26] That is, people will be able impregnably to defend all sorts of preposterous claims and theories by showing either that they are consistent with everything else in the proposer's noetic structure (web), or by showing that belief in them tends to produce helpful practical consequences. In other words, the rejection of foundationalism leads to some version of relativism. If there are various webs, all of them self-consistent and in some sense workable, is there any rational, non-arbitrary way to choose one web over another?

Earlier in this chapter we noted some important differences between the programme of offering TPs in the medieval period and that same programme in the modern period. Let me now suggest a point on which theistic provers of all periods would agree: epistemological relativism is false. Some claims are true and others are false, quite apart from what any human being or human community holds to be true; some statements can be known and others cannot be known, quite apart from what any human being or human community claims to know. Indeed, if 'anything goes' in epistemology, if some interesting version of epistemological relativism is true, theistic proofs are not needed. Anybody can rationally believe in God, and perhaps can even *know* that God exists, by simply sincerely believing that God exists, or perhaps by being part of a community that sincerely believes that God exists. And other people equally could know that God does *not* exist.

There are some questions where relativism makes sense. Which tastes better, chocolate ice cream or vanilla? This seems to be what Kant would call a matter of taste, not judgement. One person could plump for chocolate and the other for vanilla and they could both be correct. They would not even be disagreeing. Both would simply be reporting their own preferences. But whether 'San Francisco is north of Los Angeles' is not a question like this. It is a matter of judgement, not taste. Two people could indeed disagree about it, but then it would follow that they cannot both be correct. Surely the question whether God exists is more like the second case than the first.

If that much is true (the existence of God is not relative to who you are or what you think), it follows that questions of evidence, rationality, and warrant are still relevant. Since it remains true that our beliefs ought to be based on evidence, and that their rationality depends on the degree to which they are based on evidence, the question whether there is evidence, or convincing evidence, for the existence of God remains an important question.

One final point. The TPs do not have to be interpreted as being committed to egregious versions of foundationalism. Even Thomas Aquinas' Five Ways can be interpreted as beginning not with claims that are supposed to be absolutely certain (some things move, etc.) but with claims that rational people accept. The proofs, then, can be seen as exercises in rational persuasion, of showing people that the existence of God follows from claims they already accept.

NOTES

1. Note, for example, Aquinas' rather negative evaluation of what we now call the OA. See Thomas Aquinas, *Summa Theologica* (New York: Benzinger Brothers, 1947), I, 2, 1.
2. D. Z. Phillips, 'Authority and Revelation,' *Archivo Di Filosofia*, Vol. LXII, Nos 1–3 (1994), p. 682.
3. Plantinga discusses this point in several of his writings, and more is expected from him in the future. I will mainly follow the analysis in his 'Reason and Belief in God', in Alvin Plantinga and Nicholas Wolterstorff (eds), *Faith and Rationality: Reason and Belief in God* (Notre Dame, Indiana: University of Notre Dame Press, 1983), pp. 16–93. Other sources: 'The Reformed Objection to Natural Theology', *Proceedings of the American Catholic Philosophical Association*,

Vol. 54 (1980), pp. 49–62, and 'Positive Epistemic Status and Proper Function', *Philosophical Perspectives*, Vol. 2 (1988).

4. Throughout his career, roughly this approach has characterised John Hick's writings on religious epistemology.

5. For a look at Catholic fundamental theology today, see Gerald O'Collins SJ, *Retrieving Fundamental Theology: The Three Styles of Contemporary Theology* (New York: Paulist Press, 1993).

6. The Design Argument is a possible exception. Although it can be stated in a foundationalist way (and was, for example, by Aquinas and others), it does not need to be. Instead of beginning with some one obviously true or completely certain statement on which the rest of the argument is to be erected, the DA can begin (as we will see in Chapter 6) with a whole series of claims which together are designed to make a cumulative case, and no one of which is claimed to be an absolutely certain foundation for the rest of the argument.

7. In his *Faith and Understanding* (Edinburgh: Edinburgh University Press, 1997), Paul Helm discusses Plantinga's relation to Calvin in the context of faith seeking understanding. See especially Chapter 8.

8. I am not going to try to explain all of it (for one thing, it is still in progress as Plantinga thinks and writes further). I will focus on certain aspects of it that seem related to the central concerns of the present book.

9. Plantinga, 'Reason and Belief in God,' p. 59.

10. See the excellent analysis in Laura L. Garcia, 'Natural Theology and the Reformed Objection,' in C. Stephen Evans and Merold Westphal (eds.), *Christian Perspectives on Religious Knowledge* (Grand Rapids, Michigan: Wm. B. Eerdmans, 1993), pp. 112–33.

11. But see William Hasker, 'Proper Function, Reliabilism, and Religious Knowledge', in *Christian Perspectives on Religious Knowledge*, pp. 66–86. See also Philip L. Quinn, 'In Search of the Foundations of Theism,' *Faith and Philosophy*, Vol. 2, No. 4 (October, 1985), pp. 468–86, and Philip L. Quinn, 'The Foundations of Theism Again: A Rejoinder to Plantinga' in Linda Zagzebski (ed.), *Rational Faith: Catholic Responses to Reformed Epistemology* (Notre Dame, Indiana: University of Notre Dame Press, 1993), pp. 14–47.

12. See Alvin Plantinga, 'Is Theism Really a Miracle?', *Faith and Philosophy*, Vol. 3 No. 2 (April, 1986), pp. 109–34.

13. See Alvin Plantinga, 'Dennett's Dangerous Idea', *Books and Culture: A Christian Review*, Vol. 2, No. 3 (May–June, 1996), pp. 16–18, 35.

14. See his essay 'The Prospects for Natural Theology', in James E. Tomberlin (ed.), *Philosophical Perspectives*, 5th ed. (Atascadero, California: Ridgeview Publishing Co., 1991), pp. 311–12.

15. Stephen Wykstra, 'Toward a Sensible Evidentialism: On the Notion of "Needing Evidence"', in William Rowe and William Wainwright (eds), *Philosophy of Religion: Selected Readings*, 2nd ed. (New York: Harcourt Brace Jovanovich, 1989), pp. 426–37. See also Stephen Wykstra, 'Externalism, Proper Inferentiality and Sensible Evidentialism,' *Topoi*, Vol. 14 (1995), pp. 107–21.

16. Indeed, John Greco argues that natural theology is about the *only* thing that could do so. See his 'Is Natural Theology Necessary for Theistic Knowledge?', in Zagzebski, *Rational Faith*, p. 191.

17. Hasker, 'Proper Function, Reliabilism, and Religious Knowledge', p. 83.

18. Several of the points in this and the next paragraph were made in a helpful article by John Zeis, entitled 'Natural Theology: Reformed?', in Zagzebski, *Rational Faith*, p. 68.

19. See Descartes' *Meditations*, especially Meditations I, II, and III. René Descartes, *The Philosophical Works of Descartes*, by E. Haldane and G.R.T. Ross, Vol. I (Cambridge: Cambridge University Press, 1970), pp. 131–71.

20. Meditation III.

21. Nancey Murphy, *Beyond Liberalism and Fundamentalism: How Modern and Postmodern Philosophy Set The Theological Agenda* (Valley Forge, Pennsylvania: Trinity Press International, 1996), p. 90.

22. Hugo Meynell, 'Faith, Foundationalism, and Nicholas Wolterstorff', in Zagzebski, *Rational Faith*, p. 86.

23. Among Quine's other writings, see W. V. Quine and J. S. Ullian, *The Web of Belief*, 2nd edn (New York: Random House, 1978).

24. Notice this argument: 'Justifying the knowledge that "a is F" by maintaining that it is a fact that a is F presupposes the hardly tenable doctrine of the transparency of nature, i.e., the availability of immediate access to the object scrutinized.' (Dirk-Martin Grube, 'Religious Experience After the Demise of Foundationalism', *Religious Studies*, Vol. 31, No. 1 (March, 1995), p. 39). Of course this

sweeping claim makes one wonder what happens if 'a is F' is the claim that 'Nature is non-transparent.'
25. As does William Alston. Among his many writings in epistemology, see *Perceiving God: The Epistemology of Religious Experience* (Ithaca, New York: Cornell University Press, 1991) and *A Realist Conception of Truth* (Ithaca, New York: Cornell University Press, 1996).
26. Hugo Meynell, 'Faith, Foundationalism, and Nicholas Wolterstorff,' p. 92.

6

The Design Argument

Like the CA, the design argument (DA) is an *a posteriori* argument. That is, it is based upon certain facts that we learn by experience, through the senses. Also like the CA, the DA appears in many forms. It has evolved in interesting ways in its history, and we will look at certain key moments in that history in this chapter. The DA is undoubtedly the most popular of the theistic proofs. If you ask ordinary theists for an argument in support of their belief in God, it is usually a nascent form of the DA that you will hear. 'How could the world have turned out with this sort of intricate harmony and sublime beauty unless it were designed by God?', you will probably be asked. The DA is also often called the teleological argument. The Greek word *telos* means end or goal or aim, and the basic idea of the DA is that nature seems to have been constructed with an end or goal in mind.

It will be helpful to point out two differences between the CA and the DA. First, the *a posteriori* facts about the world that the CA is based upon (some things move; all effects have causes; some things live and then die, etc.) are fairly simple claims that many people would take to be obviously true. But the purported *a posteriori* facts upon which the DA is based are far more complex, controversial, and difficult to establish. We will discuss many such purported facts in this chapter. Second, the DA is an inductive argument, i.e., it is an argument whose premises (if true) tend to render support for its conclusion, or make it more probable than it was, rather than deductively entail it. Also, the DA (unlike the CA) is often stated as an analogical argument, that is, one which asks the reader to notice a certain similarity between two distinct things, for example, between the universe and a watch.[1]

Let us say that the DA, in all its forms, does two things. First, it argues for the truth of certain claims about the world, all of which have the effect of pointing to apparent order brought about by an intelligent designer. Notice that the world has properties *a*, *b*, and *c*, the design arguer says. Second, the DA presents the reader with a dilemma. In the light of *a*, *b*, and *c*, it asks, which of the following two alternatives is the more plausible? *Alternative 1*: The world turned out in this way completely naturalistically, apart from any intelligent designer, entirely by scientifically describable forces; the world, quite blindly and accidentally, just happened to turn out this way. *Alternative 2*: The world was created this way by an intelligent and purposeful designer.

II. PALEY'S VERSION OF THE DA

The earliest version of the DA that we find in Western philosophy is found in Book X of Plato's *Laws*.[2] Thomas Aquinas' Fifth Way of arguing for the existence of God in the *Summa Theologica* is also a version of the DA.[3] Anticipating some of the themes that we find in later versions of the DA, he said:

> We see that things which lack intelligence, such as natural bodies, act for an end, and this is evident from their acting always, or nearly always, in the same way, so as to obtain the best result. Hence it is plain that not fortuitously, but designedly, do they achieve their end. Now whatever lacks intelligence cannot move towards an end, unless it be directed by some being endowed with knowledge and intelligence; as the arrow is shot to its mark by the archer. Therefore some intelligent being exists by whom all natural things are directed to their end; and this being we call God.

Terse as it is, the argument leaves us with lots of questions. It might have helped had Aquinas given a few examples of things without intelligence acting 'so as to obtain the best result'. Did Aquinas think that all 'natural bodies' act this way, or just some of them? And what exactly did he mean by 'the best result' – was it simply the survival of the organism, or some higher end? It is also apparent that there are serious objections that can be raised against this argument. For example, many people now think that Darwin's theory of evolution gives us a way naturalistically to explain the apparently intelligent behaviour that is exhibited by things that 'lack intelligence'. But let us hold that point till later.

One of the most famous design arguers was theologian and churchman

William Paley (1743–1805). In his book *Natural Theology* (1803), he offered a famous and influential version of the DA. Suppose you are crossing a heath, he said, and encounter a watch lying on the ground. If you picked it up and examined it thoroughly, you would notice how 'its several parts are framed and put together for a purpose',[4] viz. the purpose of telling time. Your conclusion would of course be that the watch must have had an intelligent and skilled maker who designed it to do what it does. You would not give up this idea if you discovered parts of the watch whose function you did not understand. You would not give it up even if the watch occasionally went wrong. The watch would have, in short, all the earmarks of design. No entirely naturalistic explanation of the existence of the watch – that is, an explanation that made no reference to intelligent design – would be acceptable.

But when we turn to nature, Paley said, we find far more intricacy, harmony, complexity, curiosity, and evidence of design than we do with the watch. Not only are there far more instances of it, but the degree of complexity is much greater. The evidence of design is greater, according to Paley, 'in a degree that exceeds all computation'. Paley seemed particularly impressed by complexity of anatomical structures – facts about how the various parts of animal bodies are minutely adjusted to each other, for example. Like many eighteenth-century design arguers, he particularly emphasised the delicacy and efficacy of the human eye. The motions of the planets and other heavenly bodies were also, according to Paley and others, indicative of design.

Paley accepted the general principle that 'there cannot be design without a designer; contrivance without a contriver; order without choice; arrangement, without anything capable of arranging; subserviency and relation to a purpose, without that which could intend a purpose.' The evidences of design that we see in nature, he accordingly said, 'imply the presence of intelligence and mind'. It follows, then, that nature must have had an intelligent designer.

Paley's theistic proof is clearly an argument from analogy. He argued that the similar effects that we see in watches and (say) the human eye indicate similar causes, namely, intelligent design. Obviously, arguments from analogy can be weak. Notice this one: Jet airplanes and race horses are both fast; therefore, jet airplanes and race horses have similar causes. What is lacking in this argument is a reason to think that the causes must or might well be similar. The question is whether there is any other, more plausible explanation of the similar effects. Arguments from analogy are at their strongest where there is some reason to think that this is the case, some reason to think that alternative explanations will not wash. Thus, as we will see later in this chapter, good arguments from analogy usually involve subarguments about which of the available explanations (in this case, of similar effects) is the *best* explanation.

III. HUME'S OBJECTIONS

Let us call versions of the DA that appeared prior to 1859 'older versions' of the DA or older DAs. Later versions we will call newer DAs. There were two great intellectual shocks to the older DAs. The first was the posthumous publication of David Hume's *Dialogues Concerning Natural Religion* (1779), which some philosophers consider the most devastating critique of the DA ever written. Some of his objections do not apply to the newer DAs, but some still have force today. The second was the appearance of the first edition of Darwin's *Origin of Species* eighty years later. Many philosophers are of the opinion that the theory of evolution ruined all the older versions of the DA, especially those that were based on cases of adaptation of living organisms to their environments.

Let us look first at the arguments that Hume brought to bear against the DA. Hume's *Dialogues* were published some twenty-three years before Paley's *Natural Theology*, but, oddly, Paley's work made no reference to Hume's arguments. Students can easily get the impression that Paley wrote first, and then later Hume criticised Paley-type arguments, but that is not the case. (The oddness is compounded by the fact that Paley's other work in the philosophy of religion, *A View of the Evidences of Christianity* (1794), did explicitly respond to Hume's argument against miracles in the *Enquiry Concerning Human Understanding* (1748).)

In the *Dialogues*, Hume first presented a powerful version of the DA through the mouth of his character Cleanthes:

> Look round the world, contemplate the whole and every part of it: you will find it to be nothing but one great machine, subdivided into an infinite number of lesser machines, which again admit of subdivisions to a degree beyond what human senses and faculties can trace and explain. All these various machines, and even their most minute parts, are adjusted to each other with an accuracy which ravishes into admiration all men who have ever contemplated them. The curious adapting of means to ends, throughout all nature, resembles exactly, though it much exceeds, the productions of human contrivance – of human design, thought, wisdom, and intelligence.

These are the facts, Cleanthes says. Next comes his argument from analogy:

Since therefore the effects resemble each other, we are led to infer, by all the rules of analogy, that the causes also resemble, and that the Author of nature is somewhat similar to the mind of man, though possessed of much larger faculties, proportioned to the grandeur of the work which he has executed.[5]

But then Hume went on, through his character Philo, to present a famous and brilliant critique of the DA. I will explain and discuss five of Hume's arguments.

(1) *What caused the designer of the universe?*

If the cause of the universe is the mind of some sort of intelligent designer, Hume said, then why can't we ask who or what caused that mind? What licenses design arguers to stop the regress once they get to the designer? Doesn't the order exhibited in minds require explanation as much as the order that we see in the universe? Thus Hume asked: how 'shall we satisfy ourselves concerning the cause of that Being whom you suppose the Author of nature . . . ? Have we not the same reason to trace [the regress past the Designer to] a new intelligent principle? But if we stop and go no farther, why go so far? why not stop at the material world? How can we satisfy ourselves without going on *in infinitum*?'[6] In other words, if your principle is that all order requires explanation, then if you fail to ask about the order exhibited by mind, you have dismissed the principle (to borrow Schopenhauer's jibe against the CA discussed in Chapter 2) 'like a hired cab'.

Now when Schopenhauer and others raise this same objection to the CA, defenders of that argument, as we saw in Chapter 2, have a clear answer: the regress stops once we arrive at a necessary being. This is because the question 'Who made *x*?' (where *x* is a necessary being) makes no sense. But there is no such appeal available to the design arguer, and Hume was surely right that there is no deductively compelling way to argue that the regress must stop at the designer. For all we can tell *from the DA alone*, the designer of the universe might well have had a maker.

But this is not the end of the matter. For one thing, it should be pointed out that explanations in terms of mind or intention or agency seem to be particularly intellectually satisfying in cases such as these. The question 'Who made the watch?' can be answered quite satisfactorily in terms of an intelligent watchmaker without that answer demanding an answer to the question, 'Who made the watchmaker?' (Hume himself made this very point.) So in cases where we are trying to account for apparent order, explanations in terms of the intentions of an intelligent agent typically constitute acceptable stopping points.

(2) *Any coherent universe will seem designed*

That is, Hume argued that any universe will look designed to its denizens, whether it is or not. Thus Hume said:

> Every event, every experience, is equally difficult and incomprehensible; and every event, after experience, is equally easy and intelligible . . . Whenever matter is so poised, arranged, and adjusted, as to continue in perpetual motion, and yet preserve a constancy in the forms, its situation must, of necessity, have all the same appearance of art and contrivance which we observe at present . . . It is vain, therefore, to insist upon the uses of the parts in animals or vegetables, and their curious adjustment to each other. I would fain know how an animal could subsist unless its parts were so adjusted?[7]

There are fascinating thoughts here. It is quite true that any universe that is regular and orderly enough to produce living organisms, especially living organisms intelligent enough to formulate thoughts like 'Our world was designed by a Designer', must seem designed to those intelligent organisms. But that admission gives Hume's point away, because the very fact being noted by the design arguer is the existence of a world of sufficient stability and order to produce such organisms in the first place. Although no one would be there to observe it, the world could easily have been far more irregular and unstable than it in fact is. We can easily imagine worlds far less regular and law-like than ours. And so it is a significant fact that our world is so regular as to produce intelligent organisms who can notice that fact. (We will return to this point later in the chapter when we discuss the anthropic principle.)

(3) *The DA, even if sound, is not a proof of God*

Hume's point here was that even if the DA is an entirely successful theistic proof, the designer whose existence will have been proved is far from the God of theism. For if your view of the designer is formed simply by the argument itself, there is no reason to hold that the designer is *unique*, that is, that there is but one designer. There is no reason to hold that the designer is *infinite* or *perfect*. There is no reason to hold that the designer is *incorporeal*. There is no reason to hold that the designer is *everlasting* or even still exists today. The designer must be very powerful and knowledgeable, of course, but why *omnipotent* or *omniscient*? Indeed, the world itself might strike some design arguers as being (as Hume said) 'very faulty and imperfect'. Such a person might well conclude that the world 'was only the first rude essay of some infant deity who afterwards abandoned it, ashamed of his lame performance.'[8]

Much of what Hume says here is correct. If one is doing natural theology alone, that is, if one argues simply from the analogy on which the DA is based and eschews revealed theology, the God of theism surely need not emerge at the end of the DA. There is nothing in a sound DA that is *inconsistent* with the God of theism, of course, but the proved designer or designers of the world need not be God. If one is looking for a proof of *God*, one can certainly use the DA, but must look to other arguments or evidence as well.

But suppose the DA *is* entirely successful. Suppose that we have proved the existence of a very powerful, very intelligent designer of the universe, or several of them. That would be a philosophically and theologically highly significant conclusion. The atheists will have been proved mistaken. Naturalism will have been proved wrong.

But a bit more even than this can be said in response to Hume's objection. If a designer of the universe were proved to exist, it would then be natural to ask about its properties. For example, we could ask: Is the designer corporeal? On this point it is possible to support the idea that the designer is like the God of theism. As Peter Payne says: 'Physically embodied designers would seem to be dependent upon the fundamental laws of physics and hence could hardly be invoked to explain them.'[9]

We could also ask: Is the designer unique, or are there more than one of them? Richard Swinburne argues on grounds of simplicity that *one* designer is superior to a plurality.[10] He also argues that considerations of simplicity support the postulate that the designer is infinite in power, knowledge, and freedom. If there is more than one designer, exactly how many are there? And why do they cooperate? Those questions do not need to be asked if there is but one designer. I will not stop to evaluate Swinburne's arguments, but the main point I want to make is that nothing prevents a successful design arguer from turning to other arguments to try to prove that the designer is God. Those arguments, of course, may or may not be successful. The DA would then become an important part of a cumulative case for theism.

(4) *The existence of evil in the world makes the DA unable to prove a morally perfect designer*

Similarly, Hume argued that if one practises pure natural theology and reaches conclusions about the designer only on the basis of the DA, the existence of evil and suffering in the world ruins the DA as an argument for the existence of a morally good designer. The evidence for design plus the evil that we see do not together suggest the existence of an all-powerful and morally good designer. For if the designer were omnipotent, it would have the *power* to create a world devoid of useless and undeserved suffering; and if it were morally perfect, it would surely *want* to create such a world. Why then is there so much suffering? Hume's character Demea at one point in the *Dialogues* suggested a theodicy based on the idea of ultimate rectification. God will insure in the end that all pain will be repaid, all ills will be healed, and all injustice will be rectified. But neither this theodicy nor any other, Hume said, follows from the evidence of design itself. 'A mere possible compatibility [between the misery in the world and divine goodness]', Hume said, 'is not sufficient. You must *prove* these pure, unmixt, and uncontrollable attributes from the present mixed and confused phenomena [that is, from the evidence of design that we observe in the world], and from these alone.'[11] The mere possibility that the problem of evil can be solved cannot by itself *establish* the claim that the world's designer is good.

Again Hume seems to have been essentially correct in his main contention. Arguing from the evidence of design that we see in the universe does not by itself produce a solution to the problem of evil. The most sensible conclusion probably is that we do not know the moral properties of the world's designer, and that other arguments and evidence must be appealed to in hopes of solving that problem. Now solving the problem of evil is not the aim of this chapter, or even of this book, so I do not plan to discuss the point. Suffice it to say that nothing prevents a successful design arguer from trying to argue, on other grounds, that the designer of the world is both all-powerful and perfectly good.[12]

(5) *The DA is based on a weak analogy*

The DA, at least the older versions of it, are all based upon an analogy. The universe is like a watch in certain crucial ways, it is said; therefore, the universe, like the watch, was probably designed. Hume's fifth argument is essentially the point that the analogy is too weak to support the inference to a designer. The universe is not like a watch. Of course *all* arguments from analogy presuppose dissimilarities; watches surely *are* quite different from the universe. But that fact by itself does not ruin the DA. More to the point, in places Hume suggested that the universe is more like an organism (say, a plant or animal) than a machine. Furthermore, Hume said, the universe is an absolutely unique thing; nothing else is like it. So no arguments based on comparing the universe to something else can be convincing. Finally, we observe only a tiny spatio-temporal speck of the universe. How can we infer the need of a designer from that kind of sample?[13]

Here is a way of clarifying Hume's point: The DA might be a good argument if we had experience of, say, 100 universes, all of which seemed designed in the same ways as ours does, and if we knew that 99 of them *were* designed by a designer. Then it would be appropriate to infer by analogy that our universe (the one about which we do not know whether it was designed) was in fact designed. But of course the expression 'the universe' is meant to include everything real, experienced or unexperienced by humans, and so the very idea of there being '100 universes' is incoherent. There are certainly other *possible* universes and I have no objection to talking, in modal contexts, of 'possible worlds'. But there is only one actual universe. Since then we have nothing analogous to the universe with which to compare it, the DA is based upon a weak analogy and accordingly fails.

Now some of Hume's points here are correct, but for reasons that I will give, they do not constitute a refutation of the DA. The fact is that *all* arguments from analogy are inherently unstable and person-relative. Probably any x is similar to any y in certain ways, and dissimilar in others. I might think that x and y are analogous, and even analogous enough to support a certain inference, and you might not. If I base an argument upon the analogy that I see between x and y, the danger is that you may with good reason reject my argument because you simply do not see the analogy, or enough of one. Presumably the reason Hume (through Philo) suggested that the universe is more like an organism than a watch or house is because we know that watches and houses were designed but we do not know this with organisms.

But several of Hume's points are simply false. The universe may be a unique thing, but not all of its members, properties, or processes are. Some events and things in the universe are quite similar to other events and things in the universe. Moreover, we certainly can argue to conclusions about the entire universe and its origins, whether it is absolutely unique or not. Cosmologists do this very thing as a crucial part of their science. Big Bang theory, as well as its competing hypotheses, would be ruled out of court if Hume were correct. Scientists would be quite unable to reach rational inferences about the age or size or rate of expansion of the universe. As Richard Swinburne points out, since the human race is apparently unique, physical anthropologists would be unable to reach rational conclusions about its origin and development.[14]

Furthermore, *everything* is unique in some ways. Presumably Bill Clinton is unique in lots of ways – for example, he is the only former governor of Arkansas to be elected President of the United States between 1990 and 1995 – but it would be odd to suggest that no argument from analogy could accordingly reach any proper inferences about him. This is obviously because even unique things have properties in common with other things.

And while it is true that we experience only a small part of the universe, it is quite mistaken to suggest, as Hume did, that we cannot argue from parts to the whole. The fundamental laws governing the parts of the universe with which we are familiar also (so far as we can tell) govern the whole. Notice that we've only experienced a small part of the matter of which the universe consists; but since all the matter we've experienced consists of molecules, we have no hesitation in concluding that *all* the matter in the universe consists of molecules.

Is the universe like a watch? In some ways it surely is. But is it *enough* like a watch to support the inference that it, like a watch, must have been designed by a mind? Is it more like a watch than it is like an organism? These are difficult and complicated questions. Hume's fifth argument is often taken as his most crucial objection to the DA. I do not think it refutes the DA, but perhaps that is because I am one of those persons who sees significant similarities between the universe and a watch. To those who do not see those similarities, older DAs will not be convincing.

IV. EVOLUTION AS A CRITICISM OF THE DA

Let us now turn to Darwin's theory of evolution. As noted above, in 1859 Darwin published *The Origin of Species* expounding his theory of biological evolution. It had an immediate and powerful impact upon both theology and the philosophy of religion. One aspect of this impact was that many people concluded that the DA was no longer viable. The reason was that Darwin provided a way of explaining apparent design and complexity in organisms that involved no reference to intelligent design.

Three central aspects of Darwin's theory were: (1) random genetic change (these changes occur mainly through mutations; sometimes by random genetic drift); (2) natural selection (in competition for scarce resources, those species and organisms that are the fittest will survive); and (3) self-replication (genetic structures are passed on to offspring; and because of natural selection, genetic structures that provide competitive advantages survive). These three factors, Darwin said – together of course with the natural laws and regularities in the universe – have produced, over long periods of time, complex and sophisticated organisms.

If Darwin is right, it is possible for the universe to produce apparently designed biological systems blindly, that is, without an intelligent designer or any sort of teleology. Darwin's great gift to enemies of the DA is that he provided a *theory* which allowed as much. By now Darwin's theory is well developed and, to most people, persuasive. It is an entirely naturalistic theory; it does not mention God or any intelligent designer. The importance of this result for the DA and belief in a designer of the universe is well captured by Richard Dawkins, a contemporary scientist and defender of Darwin: 'Although atheism might have been intellectually tenable before Darwin, Darwin made it possible to be an intellectually fulfilled atheist.'[15]

In the early aftermath of Darwin's theory, the DA had few intellectually first-rate defenders. But it is quite mistaken to think that evolution refutes the DA. This was shown, among others, by the work of British theologian F. R. Tennant (1866–1957), whose 'wider teleological argument' was the first important version of what I am calling newer DAs, and whose argument presupposes evolution.[16] For reasons of space, I will not explore Tennant's argument here. Let me simply note that like all newer DAs, it stressed not specific cases of adaptedness (which evolution can explain) but the general order of nature and the fitness of the inorganic environment (which cannot evolve) for life.

V. NEWER VERSIONS OF THE DA

It is time to look at what I have been calling newer DAs. Here I will not focus on any one thinker, but will draw together a variety of arguments that are in wide use among contemporary design arguers. Most of the arguments fall under the heading of what is called 'fine-tuning'. The central idea is that the basic regularities or laws of nature and cosmological constants are minutely adjusted to allow for life and even intelligent life. Some newer DAs (like Tennant's) presuppose evolution; some reject it entirely; some accept parts of the theory but not others (for example, by suggesting divine guidance of the process of evolution at various points); and some by-pass evolution entirely. All argue, however, for the existence of an intelligent designer of the universe.

Like early DAs, the contemporary versions are probabilistic as opposed to deductive. That is, the premises are designed to provide support for the conclusion, or make it more probable, rather than strictly entail it. The main differences are (1) (as noted) the newer DAs appeal to general examples of fine-tuning or overall order rather than to specific cases of biological complexity or adaptedness; (2) they primarily emphasise facts in physics, astronomy and chemistry rather than facts in the life sciences (which might be susceptible to Darwinian explanation); (3) they make little appeal to specific purposes ('the eye was designed for the purpose of seeing,' etc.) but rather emphasise only the general purpose of producing life or intelligent life; and (4) they are not primarily arguments from analogy but rather inferences to the best explanation.

Very many points are made by contemporary design arguers, and in several different areas of science. It is only possible to mention a few. Indeed, the *many* items that look to be fine-tuned for life – so far as I can tell, there are over fifty such items that are discussed in the literature – constitutes one of the great strengths of newer DAs. There is an impressive cumulative case that can be built up.

Most newer DAs emphasise the cosmic constants, or the fundamental constants of physics. These are items like the gravitational constant, the speed of light, the strong force, the weak force, the basic properties of elementary particles (for example, mass, charge, spin), Planck's constant, etc. The general point is that all these constants, the values of which could easily have been quite different from what they are, and which in most cases are causally quite unrelated to each other, must have values that fall within a very narrow range if life is to be possible. If any one of them were changed, even slightly, life (as least as we know it) would not have emerged.[17]

(1) *The rate of expansion of the Big Bang*

The speed at which bits of matter flew apart from other bits of matter soon after the Big Bang (it took time for individual particles to form) seems to be finely tuned in relation to the density of the universe, that is, the exact amount of matter that exists. Galaxies (and thus stars, and thus planets) would have been impossible had the expansion rate and the total mass of the universe not been finely tuned to each other. Too rapid a rate of expansion relative to the total mass would have overpowered the gravitational attraction of the various bits of matter to each other, and no gases could have been formed, let alone the galaxies that the gases later became. Too slow a rate of expansion relative to the total mass would have caused too much gravitational attraction, and the universe would have collapsed back into itself billions of years ago. The expansion rate lies perilously close to the borderline between recollapse into a crunch and total dispersal of all matter. Philosopher of science J. P. Moreland summarises the point as follows: 'A reduction by one part in a million million would have led to collapse before the temperature could fall below ten thousand degrees. An early increase by one part in a million would have prevented the growth of galaxies, stars, and planets.'[18] Design arguers take this fine-tuning as evidence of an intelligent designer who had the aim of producing life in mind.[19]

(2) *The strong force*

The strong nuclear force is what binds together the various elementary particles (for example, the quarks in neutrons and protons, and the neutrons and protons themselves) in the nuclei of atoms. It appears that either a 1 per cent increase or a 1 per cent decrease in the power of the strong force would have made impossible the stellar nucleosynthesis of carbon. A slight increase would have led to all the carbon being burned into oxygen; a slight decrease would have led to a universe consisting only of hydrogen. And of course carbon is necessary to life.[20]

(3) *The weak force*

The weak nuclear force is what is responsible for such nuclear processes as radioactive decay, fission and fusion; this includes energy from the sun. Very many points have been made about fine-tuning in relation to the weak force. I will mention just one. Just after the Big Bang, the universe had a brief period of nuclear fusion during which helium was formed. It appears that had the weak force been stronger, the burning produced by the Big Bang would have, as Leslie says, 'proceeded past helium and all the way to iron. Fusion-powered stars would then be impossible'.[21] That is, there would have been no hydrogen for them to burn. But had the weak force been much weaker, then the universe would consist entirely of helium.[22]

(4) *Isotropy*

Isotropy means smoothness or evenness in all directions; here it refers to the surprising and puzzling fact that the background temperature in the universe varies only slighly from region to region, something like only one part in a hundred thousand. The puzzle is how to account for this fact, since the various regions are far too distant from each other to have any causal influence on each other. Even at the early stages of the Big Bang, the regions were separating from each other at too high a rate for there to have been causal influence.

In addition, the matter that exists is amazingly isotropic in its distribution throughout the universe. The universe looks pretty much the same no matter which direction we look from the earth. On a smaller scale there are exceptions to this point; for example, astronomers are aware of immense bubbles in space which contain galaxies at their edges but little matter in their interiors. Still, the universe must have been amazingly isotropic at its early stage; this is evident from the uniform 'background radiation' that bathes the entire universe and is an artifact of the Big Bang. The uniformity is not exact – there are slight variations from region to region – but some such anisotropy is needed for the formation of galaxies.

But the main point is that slight variations either in background temperature or in distribution of matter would make life impossible. If the early universe were significantly anisotropic – which surely seems possible – the matter of the universe would have collapsed into black holes. If it were almost completely isotropic, it would have been destroyed by the heat resulting from the smoothing out of anisotropic regions. The problem is how to explain the fact that the universe has precisely the highly improbable delicate balance necessary for the formation of the universe as we know it. Paul Davies places 'the odds against a starry cosmos' at 'one followed by a thousand billion billion zeroes, at least.'[23]

(5) *The thermal properties of the earth*

The earth has certain properties, many of them causally unrelated to each other, which make it thermally hospitable to life. Changing any of them, even slightly, would have made life impossible. Let me mention just three. The earth is just the right distance from the sun to ensure that the temperatures on its surface will be right for life. Michael Hart performed some admittedly incomplete computer simulations (not all the relevant factors are yet known), which nevertheless produced the conclusion that if the earth were either 5 per cent closer or 1 per cent farther from the the sun, life would not be possible on it.[24] The earth also possesses an atmosphere which protects it from ultra-violet radiation and other dangers such as extreme temperatures. It also contains vast oceans over much of its surface, which serve as a thermostat for the earth, also shielding it from extreme temperatures.

(6) *Water*

The existence of water, essential as it is to carbon-based life, is another example of the fine-tuning which design arguers take to be evidence of intelligent design. There are other elements that are necessary to life, for example carbon dioxide, carbolic acid, and chlorophyll, but the unique properties of water make it a special case. Water has a very high melting point, boiling point, and vapourising point (this last property makes water an excellent coolant by evaporation, which many living creatures take advantage of through perspiration). Ice floats because (very unusually, compared to other substances) in its solid stage water is less dense than it is in its liquid phase. This causes ice to serve as a protective skin on the surface of bodies of water (if ice were denser than water it would sink to the bottom of the lakes and oceans and eventually freeze them). Water can store heat efficiently because it has a high specific heat, and this (as noted) serves to stabilise temperatures. Since living bodies consist mainly of water, its high specific heat keeps chemical reactions in them fairly stable (a low specific heat would mean that living bodies would die by 'boiling over' very readily).[25]

Again, we could mention many more such points, but this is enough to provide a sense of what design arguers mean by 'fine-tuning'. While all these points (and as noted, many others) are mentioned by newer design arguers, there seems to be a consensus that items that have to do with general laws of nature and basic cosmological constants are stronger evidences of design that the items than have to do with the physical conditions necessary to life.

But the general conclusion that newer design arguers draw from all these points is that if the initial conditions or fundamental constants in the universe were even slightly different than they in fact are, it is most unlikely that life or anything like it would have emerged. Note also that unless some 'Theory of Everything' (TOE) that says otherwise is proposed and gains acceptance, the values of most of the constants that we have discussed are quite independent of each other. We are talking, then, not just about each of many different constants falling within a certain narrow range (which in itself powerfully points to a designer), but about precise and narrow ratios of interactions between the various forces – all of which are necessary to life.

William L. Craig likens the emergence of life in the universe apart from intellent guidance not to a roulette wheel yielding a certain number, but to all the roulette wheels in Monte Carlo, quite unrelated to each other, simultaneously yielding numbers within narrow limits and bearing certain precise mathematical relations among them.[26] In other words, a universe without life, or at least carbon-based life, is far, far more probable than one with it. Design arguers accordingly conclude that what we have here is either a grand coincidence, so mathematically improbable as to be virtually impossible, or else evidence of fine-tuning by an intelligent designer whose aim was the emergence of life, perhaps even intelligent, conscious, morally aware life.

VI. CRITICISMS OF NEWER DAS

Now most of the items of fine-tuning that design arguers emphasise are points that will have been discovered or reported by scientists. Most of the scientists who write about such matters have found the case for fine-tuning to be impressive. But not all of them believe in God, let alone a designer of the universe, and very many philosophers are atheists as well. So naturally the question emerges: How do those folk who refuse to accept the existence of a designer respond to the case for fine-tuning? What is the atheist's counter-attack to the newer DAs?

The answer is that there are several such responses. Some deny that there is any problem here to be explained – the numbers are wrong; the laws could be different; life is possible under many conditions. But the idea that there is nothing unusual here is refuted by the simple fact that atheists feel a strong need to come up with an argument that responds to all the apparent fine-tuning. The *appearance*, at least, of cosmic teleology is pretty obvious. Others suggest (as Hume did) that the universe is in some sense self-organising (and thus far this is only a vague and unsupported suggestion). But I will focus on the two most popular responses, the anthropic principle and the idea of many universes.

(1) *The anthropic principle*

There are several versions of 'the anthropic principle'. Let us focus simply on what is called the weak version (WAP). Here is Barrow and Tipler's version of it:

> WAP: The observed values of all physical and cosmological quantities are not equally probable, but they take on values restricted by the requirement that there exist sites where carbon-based life can evolve and by the requirement that the Universe be old enough for it to have already done so.[27]

In other words, given our presence in the universe as observers, it necessarily follows that the requisite conditions for intelligent life are met. We should accordingly expect *only* to observe values that are compatible with our existence; our existence is a selection effect in assessing the various laws and constants.

The upshot of this argument is as follows: *We should not be surprised that we observe a universe with laws and constants that allow for intelligent life*. In other words, no explanation for apparent design is required or should be expected, for if the universe were other than it is, we would not be here. Since we *are* here, we must expect the universe to be much as it is.

Is this a good argument? Hardly; indeed, it is not difficult to refute. It is surely true that if the universe is observed by observers who exist in it, then it must have whatever properties are necessary for the existence of those observers. But this trivial observation does nothing to negate the idea that there is apparent design, nor does it explain the apparent design that we see. If our existence depends on certain basic conditions being met, then, since we *do* exist, we should not be surprised that those conditions are met. True enough. But this does nothing to rule out the need for an explanation of the fact that the conditions are met.

Several philosophers have pointed out the error at work here through stories like the following from Richard Swinburne:

Suppose that a madman kidnaps a victim and shuts him in a room with a card-shuffling machine. The machine shuffles ten packs of cards simultaneously and then draws a card from each pack and exhibits simultaneously the ten cards. The kidnapper tells the victim that he will shortly set the machine to work and it will exhibit its first draw, but that unless the draw consists of an ace of hearts from each pack, the machine will simultaneously set off an explosion which will kill the victim, in consequence of which he will not see which cards the machine drew. The machine is set to work, and to the amazement and relief of the victim the machine exhibits an ace of hearts drawn from each pack.[28]

Suppose the victim were to respond, 'No explanation is required why the ten aces of hearts appeared, since if they hadn't appeared, I would not be here.' This would obviously be an inadequate response. It is not true that the cards came up as they did *because* the victim survived. So clearly something puzzling remains to be explained – why the machine drew the ten aces of hearts (thus allowing the victim to live) in the first place.

Similarly, the problem of explaining why the universe shows the fine-tuning that it does remains. It is true that we should not be surprised that we do not observe conditions in the universe which allow no life to emerge. That is, we should not be surprised that we do not observe a universe that is incompatible with our existence. But we *should* be surprised that we *do* observe that we as living and intelligent creatures exist. What is surprising, and what still requires explanation is this: the fact that the extremely improbable conditions for life were all in fact satisfied.

(2) *Many universes*

The other main position taken by those who grant fine-tuning but deny the existence of a fine-tuner is the hypothesis of many universes, or the 'World Ensemble', as it is sometimes called. (The hypothesis is sometimes combined with the WAP.) The idea is that our observable universe is only one of many – maybe even an infinite number of – possible or actual universes. Now there is a terminological issue here, having to do with the term 'universe', but it can easily be sidestepped. As noted earlier, most people think of the universe as everything real, everything that there is. And if we accept that usage then by definition there cannot be 'other universes'. However, many physicists are comfortable with talk about other universes, for reasons that we will see, and so they use the term 'universe' in different ways. Perhaps it would refer to the reality that follows from any particular Big Bang, or to whatever exists in any one observable area, or to whatever exists in any one of many parallel realities. So the issue cannot be settled against these theories merely by definition.

There are several ways in which the World Ensemble thesis can be developed. We will consider three (there are others).

(a) It might be said that the universe is oscillating and that there have been many big bangs and ensuing universes, and that each cycle emerges with a new set of laws and constants. (b) It might be said that there are many causally unrelated regions of the present universe where the laws and constants are different from the way they are in our region. (c) Or the 'many worlds' interpretation of quantum physics might be adopted. In any quantum interaction, it is said, all possible states are actualised in some universe or other, with universes constantly splitting off into new universes.[29] The various parallel universes have no contact with each other; each observer observes but one universe. All universes are as equally real as all the others. Davies summarises the theory as follows:

> We must envision every atom in every galaxy as continually engaging in this type of scattering activity, thereby splitting the world again and again into a stupendous number of near-carbon-copies of itself. The universe must therefore be likened to a tree, which branches and rebranches. Nearby branches differ little from each other, perhaps distinguished only by the arrangements of a few individual atoms. However, amid the infinite array of parallel worlds will be examples representing all possible physical universes.[30]

The crucial point, in the case of each theory, is that all or many possible combinations of natural laws and cosmic constants are actualised somewhere; most of them do not produce intelligent life; but it is not surprising that some few of them do (including our universe).

There are problems with each of these views. All three, for example, face the objection that there is virtually no evidence for them apart from fine-tuning, the existence of intelligent life, and the desire to avoid a cosmic designer. Accordingly, they have an air of desperation about them.

(a) With the oscillating universe, it is not clear that there is enough density in the universe to overcome the initial impetus of the Big Bang and cause a 'Big Crunch.' Moreover, even if there does exist enough such matter, it is not clear that an implosion would produce a subsequent Big Bang. Craig says that 'there is no known physics which would cause the universe to oscillate'.[31] And how do we know that the basic laws and constants will be reshuffled each time (which of course is required if this theory is to constitute a viable alternative to theistic interpretations of fine tuning)?[32] And since time supposedly began with the Big Bang, how are the various universes that follow their own Big Bangs related temporally? The physics here are murky, to say the least.

(b) There are indeed causally unrelated regions of space in the existing universe, but there is no evidence at all that the basic physical laws and constants differ from region to region. And that is what is needed if this theory is to constitute a viable atheistic interpretation of fine-tuning. Only if there are innumerably many such regions, each with its own laws and constants, will it no longer be surprising that in *some* regions (including ours) the laws and constants allow for life. But, in fact, the reverse is the case; all the evidence supports the claim that the basic laws and constants are the same throughout the universe. The discipline of astrophysics is based upon that assumption.

(c) The many-worlds interpretation is favoured by a minority of physicists. It seems fanciful and speculative to many, especially since there is no known causal mechanism that could cause the splitting. And is there supposed to be a kind of timeless superspace in which all the parallel universes exist? If so, what is it? What are its properties? Moreover, the theory also seems to violate respected philosophical principles like parsimony (if two theories are equal in explanatory power, accept the simpler of the two) and Ockham's razor (do not posit the existence of more entities than are strictly necessary).[33]

VII. CONCLUSION

Recall that early in the chapter I noted that the DA does two things. First, it presents evidence of apparent intelligent design. Second, it asks, in the light of the evidence presented, which is the more sensible conclusion: Alternative 1 or Alternative 2. *Alternative 1* says that the world is fine-tuned as it is due to entirely blind forces and natural causes, apart from any intelligent designer. *Alternative 2* says that the world is as it is because it was designed this way by an intelligent designer.

Design arguers will claim that Alternative 2 is by far the most sensible of the two, especially given the severe weakness of the arguments based on the anthropic principle and of the World Ensemble models. Accordingly, design arguers will insist that the hypothesis of a designer of the universe is much stronger, relative to either naturalism or supernaturalism, given the evidence of fine-tuning, than it is apart from that evidence.

Finally, a point that is more related to the CA than the DA. Alternative 2 can answer questions like 'Why is there a universe at all?' and 'Why is there anything instead of nothing?' None of the theories that fit under Alternative 1 can do so. The existence of a reality at all must be, from the point of view of the friends of Alternative 1, an unexplained brute fact.

VIII. SWINBURNE AND BAYES' THEOREM

Richard Swinburne is one of the foremost contemporary proponents of theistic proofs; we have discussed arguments of his at various points in this book. One item that we have not mentioned, however, is his use of Bayes' Theorem. Now, Swinburne uses the theorem in relation to the entire cumulative case that he makes for the existence of the God in his book *The Existence of God* (and not just in relation to the Design Argument); still, this is a convenient place for us briefly to discuss the point. (As noted in the Introduction, I have tried to avoid undue technicality in this book, and have eschewed extensive use of symbols, helpful as they are in logic. The present discussion might seem formidable to some readers, however, and can be skipped over without endangering a grasp of anything that follows.)

Bayes' Theorem is one of the most important theorems of probability theory, and is named after its inventor Thomas Bayes (1702–61).[34] The aspect of it that is crucial to Swinburne is the insight that a given hypothesis *h* is probable if the evidence that we encounter is what we would expect to encounter if *h* were true. In evaluating any hypothesis, we have certain items of general background knowledge (let's call our background knowledge *k*). On the basis of *k, h* will have a certain prior probability, that is, probability *before* we investigate the available evidence that is relevant to its truth or falsity. Let's call the evidence *e*; typically it will consist of the phenomena that we are trying to explain by means of *h*.

There are different ways of dividing *k* and *e*. One is to include in *e* only the recently observed evidence that is relevant to *h*, in which case *k* will include lots of other items of contingent background knowledge. Another is to include in *e* all the contingent evidence that has ever been observed, in which case *k* will only include what is called 'tautological background knowledge.' Or perhaps there simply is no contingent background knowledge that is relevant to *h*. In such cases, prior probability becomes 'intrinsic probability,' i.e., the probability of *h* based on the tautological evidence alone. Swinburne is clear on the point that it does not matter to his overall argument how we divide *k* and *e*, i.e., which route we choose to follow. It is important to note, however, that every hypothesis must have an intrinsic probability if it is to have a probability based on evidence, which is what we are seeking.

Now the version of Bayes' Theorem in which Swinburne is interested can be expressed as follows (where P means probability):

$$P(h/e.k) = \frac{P(e/h.k)}{P(e/k)} \times P(h/k).$$

The first term, P(*h/e.k*), is what we are trying to derive; it is the overall probability of *h* given *e* and *k*. The large middle term, the one that appears after the = and before the ×, is the explanatory power of *h*, i.e., its ability to explain *e*. It will have a greater value to the extent that *h* makes *e* probable. The upper term, P(*e/h.k*), is a measure of *h*'s predictive power, i.e., of how likely the evidential phenomena *e* are if *h* is true. The lower term, P(*h/k*) is the prior probability of *h*, i.e., quite apart from *e*. One of Swinburne's claims is that the prior probability of *h* is a function not just of its fit with *k* but also of its simplicity (as well as what Swinburne calls scope).

The entire theorem, then, says that the probability of *h*, given *e* and *k*, is a function of the probability of *e* occurring given *h*, divided by the probability of *e* occurring whether or not *h* is true. That is, the probability of *h* is a function of its prior probability and of its explanatory power with respect to *e*.

Suppose that *h* is 'God exists.' This claim will of course have a certain prior probability before we even consider the evidence for and against it. Swinburne argues that that probability may be low, but is much higher than the probability of any of the alternatives to *h*. Furthermore, in evaluating competing theories of great scope, simplicity is the most important consideration. And theism, Swinburne argues, is a simple theory both because all explanation is ultimately reduced to personal explanation, i.e., explanation in terms of having been caused by an agent for a purpose, and because a being of unlimited powers like God is more simple than beings with limitations. This is because questions about why certain limitations on power, knowledge etc. exist do not come up.[35] Now suppose *e* is the evidence of apparent design that we see in the world (as noted, Swinburne actually understands *e* much more broadly than this). Since 'God exists' has both a higher prior probability than alternative hypotheses and a high explanatory power (as Swinburne argues, design is very probable if God exists and improbable if God does not exist), the overall probability of 'God exists' is quite high.

The probability that God exists thus equals the prior probability that God exists multiplied by the extent to which the existence of God makes the evidence of design (and other evidence cited by Swinburne) more to be expected than it would otherwise have been. Swinburne's claim is that the existence of God is well able to explain phenomona like the very existence of a world, like the design that we see in the universe, like the existence of conscious beings in the world – phenomena that would be very difficult to explain if God did not exist.

Swinburne's overall conclusion is that while the prior probability of theism may not be high, the phenomena that we group together as *e* call out for explanation; and theism is by far the best explanation of *e*. Accordingly, Swinburne says, 'on our total evidence theism is more probable than not. An argument from all the evidence considered in this book to the existence of God is good P-inductive argument [i.e., an argument whose premises make the conclusion probable].'[36]

It is clear that Swinburne's work constitutes a genuine and important advance in the tradition of offering proofs for the existence of God. Quite apart from his own views on the traditional arguments such as those discussed in this book, Swinburne's attempt to create an overall cumulative case argument for the existence of God, as well as his use of Bayes' Theorem, represent significant new departures in the philosophy of religion. Although I have discussed critically other of Swinburne's arguments elsewhere in this book, I do not propose here to offer a detailed critique of his use of Bayes' Theorem.

My one worry concerns divine simplicity, and the worry is exacerbated by Swinburne's (in my view, quite correct) reliance on the criterion of simplicity in determining the prior probability of a hypothesis. In one sense, Swinburne is correct that theism is a simple hypothesis – it does hold that one substance (God) is the cause of all other things; it does ultimately reduce all explanation to personal explanation; and it is true that theists do not have to answer questions about why God has certain limitations (as do, say, Deists and Process theologians). But anybody who is familiar with current issue in the philosophy of religion knows how many highly complex and difficult topics concerning the nature of the God of theism are being debated. To name just a few: What does omnipotence consist in? What does omniscience consist in? Is divine omniscience consistent with human freedom? Does God have middle knowledge? Is God able to do moral evil? Is God immutable? If so, is divine immutability consistent with divine omniscience? Is God timeless? If so, what does timelessness means and how can a timeless being be related to temporal realities?

I do not claim that there is a contradiction here, nor do I consider the problem unsolvable. But the challenge for Swinburne is to explain precisely what simplicity consists in and to show how a being like God – whose nature philosophers and theologians debate in terms like these – can be simple. In a later book, Swinburne argues that all God's properties (1) fit together (omnipotence, omniscience, benevolence, etc. are not just an *ad hoc* collection of predicates) and (2) can be expressed as God having the single simple property of 'pure unlimited, intentional power.'[37] Indeed, for Swinburne, this is what divine simplicity consists in – God's properties all being included in the one property that Swinburne mentions. He insists, quite rightly, that the simplicity of a hypothesis is a matter of the simplicity of the state of affairs that it postulates, and not necessarily of the complexity of the human sentences which describe that state. The complexity that philosophical theologians struggle with is not a complexity in the divine nature itself.

I certainly agree with the first point (I, too, hold that God has a unified nature), but it is not easy to understand the one predicate Swinburne mentions as a *simple* predicate. Swinburne claims that one hypothesis is simpler than another if it postulates fewer 'ultimate facts' than the other.[38] Now if the nature of God can be expressed via one claim (*viz.*, that God is 'pure, unlimited, intentional power'), then one can at least understand Swinburne's claim that theism is a simple theory. But a problem remains nonetheless: it isn't true that all the attributes theists consider essential to God are captured or entailed by this one predicate. Those theists who are Christians, for example, claim that God is essentially a Trinity, and of course that is not entailed at all.[39] Moreover, it is not easy to see how God can be simple. Since there exists in any omniscient mind a complete specification of the actual world (let alone other possible worlds), the nature of God is presumably going to be as logically complex as the universe God created.

NOTES

1. See William L. Rowe, *The Cosmological Argument* (Princeton, New Jersey: Princeton University Press, 1975), pp. 4–5.
2. Edith Hamilton and Huntington Cairns (eds), *The Collected Dialogues of Plato* (New York: Pantheon, 1961), pp. 1,455–79 (894A–899C).
3. Thomas Aquinas, *Summa Theologica* (New York: Benzinger Brothers, 1947), I, 2, 3.
4. All quotations from Paley are from the excerpts from his *Natural Theology* that are reprinted in William L. Rowe and William J. Wainwright, *Philosophy of Religion: Selected Readings* (New York: Harcourt Brace Jovanovich, 1973), pp. 149–56.
5. David Hume, *Dialogues Concerning Natural Religion*, ed. by Henry D. Aiken (New York: Hafner Publishing Company, 1959), p. 17.
6. Hume, *Dialogues*, p. 34.
7. Hume, *Dialogues*; these quotations are from pp. 52, 53, and 54–5, respectively.
8. Hume, *Dialogues*, pp. 38–41.
9. Peter Payne, *Design in the Universe: The Design Argument From the Perspective of Natural Law* (Claremont, California: Claremont Graduate School, 1996). Payne's fine dissertation has been of assistance to me at several points in writing the present chapter.
10. Richard Swinburne, *The Existence of God* (Oxford: Oxford University Press, 1979), p. 141.
11. Hume, *Dialogues*, p. 69.
12. I have tried to do so in *Encountering Evil: Live Options in Theodicy* (Atlanta, Georgia: John Knox Press, 1981).
13. Hume, *Dialogues*, pp. 18, 21–5, 42–3, 47–8, 50.
14. Swinburne, *The Existence of God*, p. 117.
15. Richard Dawkins, *The Blind Watchmaker: Why the Evidence of Evolution Reveals a Universe Without Design* (New York: W. W. Norton and Co., 1986), p. 10.
16. See F. R. Tennant, *Philosophical Theology*, 2 vols (New York: Cambridge University Press, 1928).
17. There are many contemporary philosophers and scientists who cite examples of fine-tuning. Some good sources are: John Leslie, *Universes* (London: Routledge, 1989); John Leslie, 'The Prerequisites of Life in Our Universe', in G. V. Coyne, M. Heller, and J. Zycinski (eds), *Newton and the New*

Direction in Science (Vatican: Citta del Vaticano, 1988); John D. Barrow and Frank J. Tipler, *The Anthropic Cosmological Principle* (Oxford: Oxford University Press, 1986); and William L. Craig, 'The Teleological Argument and the Anthropic Principle', William L. Craig and Mark S. McLeod (eds), *The Logic of Rational Theism: Exploratory Essays* (Lewiston, Maine: The Edwin Mellen Press, 1990), pp. 127–53.

18. J. P. Moreland, *Scaling the Secular City: A Defense of Christianity* (Grand Rapids, Michigan: Baker Book House, 1987), pp. 52–3.

19. On several of the points made in this paragraph, see Stephen Hawking, *A Brief History of Time: From the Big Bang to Black Holes* (New York: Bantam Books, 1988), pp. 121–2; and Paul Davies, *The Accidental Universe* (Cambridge: Cambridge University Press, 1982), p. 89.

20. See John Leslie, 'Modern Cosmology and the Creation of Life', in Ernan McMullin (ed.), *Evolution and Creation* (Notre Dame, Indiana: University of Notre Dame Press, 1985), p. 112. See also Craig, 'The Teleological Argument and the Anthropic Principle,' p. 129.

21. Leslie, *Universes*, p. 34.

22. Craig, 'The Teleological Argument and the Anthropic Principle', p. 129. See also Payne, *Design in the Universe*, pp. 82–7.

23. For many of these points, see Paul Davies, *Other Worlds* (London: Dent, 1980), pp. 56, 160–1, 168–9.

24. See Michael Hart, 'Atmospheric Evolution, the Drake Equation, and DNA: Sparse Life in an Infinite Universe', in John Leslie (ed.), *Physical Cosmology and Philosophy* (New York: Macmillan, 1990).

25. See Craig, 'The Teleological Argument and the Anthropic Principle', p. 133; and Bernard Ramm, *The Christian View of Science and Scripture* (Grand Rapids, Michigan: Wm. B. Eerdmans, 1954), p. 148. Ramm's book is dated at many points, but is still a valuable piece of work.

26. Craig, 'The Teleological Argument and the Anthropic Principle', p. 134.

27. Barrow and Tipler, *The Anthropic Cosmological Principle*, p. 15.

28. Swinburne, *The Existence of God*, p. 138. On the issues discussed in this section, see also Craig, 'The Teleological Argument and the Anthropic Principle', pp. 135–46; Payne, *Design in the Universe*, pp. 105–98.

29. Physicist Hugh Everett is the author of this theory. See his 'Relative State Formulations of Quantum Mechanics', *Review of Modern Physics*, Vol. 29 (1957), pp. 454–62.

30. Davies, *The Accidental Universe*, p. 125.

31. Craig, 'The Teleological Argument and the Anthropic Principle', p. 143. Craig is actually quoting the late astronomer Beatrice Tinsley.

32. Leslie thinks this problem can be solved, but he admits that his suggestions are highly speculative. See his 'Modern Cosmology', p. 112.

33. Tim Maudlin argues that the many-worlds interpretation is incoherent. See his *Quantum Non-Locality and Relativity*, Aristotelian Society, Series 13 (Oxford: Blackwell, 1994), pp. 4–5.

34. Bayes' Theorem is not without controversy among confirmation theorists. Swinburne argues for its acceptance in his *An Introduction to Confirmation Theory* (London: Methuen, 1973). In *The Existence of God* he hold that it is true in the sense that 'all statements of comparative probability which are entailed by the theorem are true' (p. 65). It should be noted that Swinburne is not committed to any of the probabilities involved in his application of Bayes' Theorem to theistic proofs having exact numerical values. He is only committed to their having certain rough values; or, more precisely, he is committed to the statements of comparative probability (like, 'Theory A is more probable that theory B') which are entailed by the Theorem.

35. See *The Existence of God*, pp. 107, 282–3.

36. *The Existence of God*, p. 291.

37. See Richard Swinburne, *The Christian God* (Oxford: Oxford University Press, 1994), pp. 126, 154–68.

38. *The Existence of God*, p. 167.

39. This despite Swinburne's attempt to argue in Chapter 8 of *The Christian God* that the Trinitarian nature of God *is* entailed by God having the property of being 'pure, unlimited, intentional power.'

7

Religious Experience

I. INTRODUCTION

Very many human beings claim to have had religious experiences. Many of those people interpret their experiences in terms of 'the presence of God'. Accordingly, there is a long tradition of using the fact of religious experience as an argument in favor of theism. The resulting argument is usually called 'the argument from religious experience' (ARE). Such an argument can take many forms, but it needs to be pointed out that the late twentieth century is a time of great interest in the argument, with many philosophers debating it.

But is the ARE a theistic proof? Well, a theistic proof, as we noted in Chapter 1, is an argument whose conclusion is 'God exists'. The result here is metaphysical; a claim is made about the existence of something. What we might call an 'argument for the rationality of theism', on the other hand, is epistemological; such an argument tries to show not that God exists but that belief in the existence of God is rational or warranted or intellectually acceptable.[1]

Some of those who use the ARE mean it to be not a TP but an argument for the rationality of theism. This is certainly true of William Alston, who specifically tells us that his argument in *Perceiving God* is not a TP.[2] But others clearly mean it to be interpreted as a TP. This is certainly true of Richard Swinburne, although the actual use he makes of the ARE in *The Existence of God* turns out to be not all that different from the treatment of it by Alston.[3] It should also be pointed out that Swinburne means the ARE to be assessed not primarily as a discrete TP, but rather as part of a cumulative case that can be made, along with other arguments, for the existence of God. In a book on theistic proofs, we will treat the ARE as a TP, and accordingly will focus more on Swinburne's argument than on Alston's. The question then will be whether the fact of religious experience can constitute a successful argument for the existence of God.

Let us define an 'experience' as simply an event or occurrence that one consciously lives through (whether as a direct participant or as an observer) and about which one has feelings, opinions, and memories. Let's define the term 'religious experience' quite broadly, that is, as any experience which one *takes to be* religious. Normally this means an experience in which one senses the presence of God or some supernatural being or force. God or the impersonal absolute itself might be manifest in the experience; or what is experienced might be some event or action or even other human being that is taken as in some sense manifesting the divine reality. When I say, 'in which one senses the presence of God', I use the word 'senses' in such a way as not necessarily to entail the reality of what one senses. That is, the sentence 'Jones senses the presence of *x*' does not entail that *x* is present or even that *x* exists. So a religious experience is any experience which a person takes to be (whether it is or not) an experience of God or something ultimate.

Now this is a book about theism, that is, proofs for the existence of *God*. So I am going to focus in this chapter on religious experience in a theistic context. That is, I will not emphasise the religious experiences of those who claim to have encountered something quite unlike the God of theism – some god among other gods like Thor or Zeus or some impersonal absolute like Brahman or the Dharmakaya or Absolute Emptiness. (The issue of the great variety of human religious experiences will come up later as a criticism of the ARE, and we will deal with it there.) This restriction is not in any sense meant to be dismissive of such experiences or of the religions in whose contexts they occur. It simply reflects the topic of the present book.

II. RELIGIOUS EXPERIENCE AS A THEISTIC PROOF

Religious experience is obviously highly important to the phenomenon that we call religion; indeed, some people consider it the heart of religion. Encountering God or ultimate reality constitutes the core and germ of religion. There would be no religion without religious experience. Saints, mystics, and sages claim to encounter God, but so do ordinary believers. Thus Moses encountered God as follows (Exodus 3: 1–6):

> Moses was keeping the flock of his father-in-law Jethro, the priest of Midian; he led his flock beyond the wilderness, and came to Horeb,

the mountain of God. There the angel of the Lord appeared to him in a flame of fire out of a bush; he looked, and the bush was blazing, yet it was not consumed. Then Moses said, 'I must turn aside and look at this great sight, and see why the bush is not burned up.' When the Lord saw that he had turned aside to see, God called to him out of the bush, 'Moses, Moses!' And he said, 'Here I am.' Then he said, 'Come no closer! Remove the sandals from your feet, for the place on which you are standing is holy ground.' He said further, 'I am the God of your father, the God of Abraham, the God of Isaac, and the God of Jacob.' And Moses hid his face, for he was afraid to look at God.

And Isaiah describes this religious experience which initiated his calling as a prophet (Isaiah 6: 1–6):

In the year that King Uzziah died, I saw the Lord sitting on a throne, high and lofty; and the hem of his robe filled the temple. Seraphs were in attendance above him; each had six wings; with two they covered their faces, and with two they covered their feet, and with two they flew. And one called to another and said: 'Holy, Holy, Holy is the Lord of hosts; the whole earth is full of his glory.' The pivots on the thresholds shook at the voices of those who called, and the house filled with smoke. And I said: 'Woe is me! I am lost, for I am a man of unclean lips, and I live among a people of unclean lips; yet my eyes have seen the King, the Lord of hosts.'

And Saul, later the Apostle Paul, had this experience on the road to Damascus (Acts 9: 3–9):

Now as he was going along and approaching Damascus, suddenly a light from heaven flashed around him. He fell to the ground and heard a voice saying to him, 'Saul, Saul, why do you persecute me?' He asked, 'Who are you, Lord?' The reply came, 'I am Jesus, whom you are persecuting. But get up and enter the city, and you will be told what you are to do.' The men who were traveling with him stood speechless because they heard the voice but saw no one. Saul got up from the ground, and though his eyes were open, he could see nothing; so they led him by the hand and brought him to Damascus. For three days he was without sight, and neither ate nor drank.

Countless other examples outside the Bible could be added – from the Koran or from other writings – of theists who claim to have encountered God. Here, for example, is St Teresa's account of one of her religious experiences:

> One day when I was at prayer . . . I saw Christ at my side – or, to put
> it better, I was conscious of Him, for I saw nothing with the eyes of
> the body or the eyes of the soul [the imagination]. He seemed quite
> close to me and I saw that it was He. As I thought, He was speaking to
> me. Being completely ignorant that such visions were possible, I was
> very much afraid at first, and could do nothing but weep, though as
> soon as He spoke His first word of assurance to me, I regained my
> usual calm, and became cheerful and free from fear. All the time Jesus
> Christ seemed to be at my side . . .[4]

And William James reports these words from an anonymous 17-year-old
boy:

> Sometimes as I go to church, I sit down, join in the service, and before
> I go out I feel as if God was with me, right side of me, singing and
> reading the Psalms with me . . . And then again I feel as if I could sit
> beside him, and put my arms around him, kiss him, etc. When I am
> taking Holy Communion at the altar, I try to get with him and
> generally feel his presence.[5]

Now the question is, what sort of weight shall testimonies like these be
given? If they are veridical – indeed, if any *one* of them is veridical (that is,
really is an encounter with God) – then God exists. But *are* they veridical?
And how can we go about deciding? Notice that religious experiences
typically have certain common characteristics. For one thing, they are
almost always private, in the sense that they are had by one person alone,
even if other people are present. There may have been other people present
when Isaiah had his religious experience, and there definitely were other
people present when Paul had his, but none of the others had Isaiah's, or
Paul's, experience. For another, religious experiences of God – the kind we
are interested in – almost always involve a strong sense of the transcendence or otherness or greatness of God, and a corresponding sense of
one's own guilt or inadequacy or smallness. This was definitely Isaiah's
experience.

   An important distinction is often made between two sorts of religious
experiences. In the first sort, one strongly senses the presence and power
and holiness of God, but recognises throughout the experience one's
ontological distinctness from God. Let's call this 'religious experience'.
One can feel, in a religious experience, a sweet and wonderful sense of
unity with God, but this is a sense of being accepted or loved by God, or of
being united with God in purpose or spirit. There is still the dualistic sense
that God is one thing, and I am quite another. The second sort of religious

experience, which we can call 'mystical experience', involves a strong sense of ontological unity with God, of the disappearance of one's self as a thing distinct from God. This is also sometimes called a monistic (God is the only reality) or unitive mystical experience.

Richard Swinburne helpfully distinguishes among five sorts of religious experiences. (1) In some of them, the presence of God or divine reality is mediated through some object that is or can be perceived in a normal public way. Someone might look at a beautiful sunset or a flower and strongly see it as a revelation of God or as mediating God's presence. (2) Someone might experience the presence of God or divine reality through something highly unusual that one perceives and which (presumably) others could perceive if they were present, for example, a vision of the risen Jesus or of the Virgin Mary. This was Moses' experience – the presence of God was mediated to him through the bush that was burning but was not consumed. (3) Someone might experience God or divine reality as mediated through a private object – that is, something that can be perceived only by the person who has the experience – that can nonetheless be described in ordinary sensory language. Religious experiences in the forms of visions, dreams or voices would fit here. (4) Someone might experience God or divine reality through a private object or through sensations that cannot be described in ordinary sensory language. Indeed, a sense of ineffability – of being unable to put the experience into words – is common in mystical experience. One might sense or even 'see', for example, the presence of Christ near one, but be quite unable to explain or even defend the feeling. (5) Finally, one might experience God or ultimate reality in a way that does not seem to be mediated by anything sensory at all. Here one simply intuitively senses, say, the presence of God without feeling that one has 'seen' or 'heard' or had bodily sensations of anything.[6]

Religious experiences like these raise three epistemological questions that philosophers debate. Whether one holds that any ARE is a successful theistic proof will depend on how one answers these questions. First, if I have a religious experience – one in which I become convinced that I have encountered God – am I *justified* in accordingly believing that I have encountered God and thus that God exists? This question has been answered in both ways by philosophers. Some think the answer is obviously yes,[7] while others hold that no subjective experience can ever constitute a good argument for the existence of something external to the consciousness of the experiencer.[8] Second, if I have a religious experience in which I become convinced that I have encountered God, is it possible that you, hearing my testimony to my experience, could be justified in accordingly believing that God exists? Or, could you be justified in so believing on the basis of the cumulative weight of the testimony of *many* religious experiencers? These questions too have been answered in both ways. Third (a closely related question), does the cumulative weight of the testimony of all those who claim to have experienced God, or a certain subset of them, constitute a successful TP?

Obviously, how these three questions are to be answered will depend in large part on the quality of the specific religious experience or religious experiences in question. It is widely recognised among philosophers that certain possible characteristics of an experience tend to call its reliability into question. Certain others tend to support it. For example, we will question the veridicality of a report of a religious experience by a person S that purportedly involves an encounter with a being B: (1) if S has proved unreliable in the past (for example, S is known to have delusions or to take LSD); (2) if the experience itself was made under circumstances that have proved unreliable in the past (for example, S is known not to have the experience or insight necessary to recognise B even when B is present); (3) if the existence or presence of B is highly improbable on the background evidence; or (4) if B, whether it was present or not, was probably not the cause of S's religious experience (this would be relevant in cases where S's experience can better be explained by another cause than B).[9] (We'll call these 'negative characteristics' of religious experiences.)

There are also certain possible characteristics of religious experiences which many philosophers agree count in favor of the veridicality of the experience. (We'll call these 'positive characteristics' of religious experiences.) For example, it will tend to support the believability of the experience if: (1) S's report of the experience is both internally consistent and consistent with other things we know to be true; (2) S's report agrees with the widely accepted exemplary and paradigmatic religious experiences of others, for example, those of various saints and mystics; (3) if the short-term and long-term consequences of the experience, especially in S's life but also in the lives of other affected people, are morally good (for example, S now leads a more praiseworthy moral life than previously); (4) the experience itself is deep, profound, sweet, and revelatory of spiritual insights. These are all public tests; none is to be considered conclusive on its own; but the idea is that an impressive combination of such characteristics as these counts strongly in favor of the veridicality of the experience.

People who push the ARE frequently point out the similarities, or alleged similarities, between religious experience and ordinary perceptual experience. Indeed, this is one of the central themes of Alston's important book *Perceiving God*. The overall moral that we are asked to draw is that religious experience is as trustworthy as ordinary perceptual experience – or, better, if it is rational to trust the one (as it surely is), it is or at least can be (in certain circumstances) rational to trust the other.

Let's compare my ordinary experience of perceiving a cat walking on the lawn outside my window with, say, Isaiah's experience of God in the temple. Some of the similarities are: (1) Both involve what we might call hypothetical reliability – that is, they are to be considered reliable only if certain conditions are satisfied. My perception of the cat is not to be trusted if it is too dark outside for me to tell for sure what it was that was moving on the lawn; and Isaiah's experience is not to be trusted if we know he frequently swallowed hallucinogens. This entails a further but closely related similarity – both perception and religious experiences can involve public procedures to check on reliability. (2) Both involve intentionality; that is, both are 'about' something or are aimed at or point toward something external (or at least putatively external) to the experiencer. In my case, it was the cat; and in Isaiah's case it was God. (3) Both simultaneously involve both privacy and publicness. My perception of the cat was (presumably) public in that anyone else who had stood beside me at the appropriate moment looking in the appropriate direction would also have seen the cat (cats are physical objects), and private in that nobody else could possibly have had 'my' experience of the cat; Isaiah's experience was public in that others who were in the temple could have observed at least some of what Isaiah reported (for example, the shaking of the pivots or even the vision's perceptable effect on Isaiah himself), and private in the obvious sense that it was a vision.[10]

A certain way of developing an ARE is based upon a claim that is frequently made specifically about mystical experience. It has been noted by many observers that the claims made by mystics in various periods of history and even in various religious traditions are amazingly similar, and that is taken by some commentators as evidence for the truth of those claims. The similarities are: the overcoming or eradication of the ontological distinctness between the mystic and the God or Absolute that is experienced; a sense that in such an experience one is experiencing reality (ontological monism is true; there is only one reality); and a powerful sense of bliss, peace, sweetness, and the absence of time. (The claim that the mystics all agree is sometimes disputed.)[11] In any case, a TP based on this claim might look as follows:

1. There is a large degree of unanimity among the mystics concerning the spiritual nature of reality.
2. When there is such unanimity among observers as to what they

believe themselves to be experiencing, it is reasonable to conclude that their experiences are veridical (unless we have good reason to believe they are deluded).

3. There are no positive reasons for thinking that mystical experiences are delusory.
4. Therefore, it is reasonable to believe that mystical experiences are veridical.[12]

But I am not going to emphasise this argument; the ARE that I want to discuss does not depend on mystical experience *per se* or on the claim that the mystics all agree.

The ARE that I am interested in discussing will look more like this:

5. Throughout human history, and in very many human societies and cultures, people claim to have experiences of God or of some Godlike being.
6. The claim that those experiences are veridical is more probable than the claim that they are delusive.
7. Therefore, probably, God or some Godlike being exists.

Or perhaps like this:

8. Religious beliefs generated by religious experiences of type A are generally reliable.
9. S's religious beliefs were generated by religious experiences of type A.
10. Therefore, probably, S's religious beliefs that were generated by S's religious experience are true.

The reference to 'type A' may include various conditions, but important among them will be conditions like not possessing any of the negative characteristics listed above and including all or many of the positive ones.

III. SWINBURNE'S ARGUMENT

It is time that we looked at the case Swinburne makes for the existence of God based on religious experience. Some of the points that he makes have been introduced already; let us look at several of his other central claims.

Important to Swinburne's version of the ARE is a principle called the principle of credulity. Swinburne argues that this is a principle that we all use and act on in ordinary life, and indeed that apart from the principle we would be stuck in a sceptical morass, never sure what to believe. He says: 'I suggest that it is a principle of rationality that (in the absence of special considerations) if it seems (epistemically) to a subject that x is present, then probably *x* is present; what one seems to perceive is probably so. How things seem to be is good grounds for a belief about how things are.'[13]

Now if this principle applies to all experiences, it certainly applies to religious ones. If someone claims to have had an experience of God, that constitutes *prima facie* evidence that that person *has* experienced God. As Swinburne says, 'In the absence of special considerations, all religious experiences ought to be taken by their subjects as genuine, and hence as substantial grounds for belief in the existence of their apparent object – God, or Mary, or Ultimate Reality, or Poseidon.'[14]

The 'special considerations' that tend to impugn the veridicality of a religious experience are the possible 'negative characteristics' of religious experiences that we discussed earlier. If there is good reason to think any of them is true of the religious experience in question (for example, the subject was hallucinating at the time), that will overcome the *prima facie* evidence in favor of the veridicality of the experience provided by the principle of credulity, and the veridicality of the experience ought to be doubted.

Swinburne then argues against the various attempts of religiously sceptical philosophers to restrict the range of the principle of credulity to nonreligious contexts. Some, for example, argue that the principle itself is not valid apart from inductive justification ('in most cases in the past where I seemed to see a chair present, there *was* a chair present'), and that that justification is not available in religious cases. But Swinburne argues that the principle of credulity does not require inductive support, and indeed any attempt to provide it will be circular. An induction from past experience to a present experience will only be valid if we consciously remember past cases, but what grounds do we have to suppose that we remember past cases accurately? An inductive argument that we do indeed remember correctly would obviously be circular. So the principle of credulity must be taken as basic, as not requiring further justification.[15]

It is important to note that the principle of credulity applies to other people as well as to the person who has the experience. If it seems to me that I have had an experience of a chair or of God, then in the absence of special circumstances, that constitutes a reason both for me *and for you* to believe that I have experienced a chair or God.

This leads to a second principle, namely, the principle of testimony. It says that what others tell us that they have perceived, we think (other things being equal) probably happened. Swinburne amplifies the point as follows: 'By "other things being equal" I mean the absence of positive grounds for supposing that the others have misreported or misremembered their experiences, or that things were not in fact as they seemed to those others to be. Clearly most of our beliefs about the world are based on what others claim to have perceived.'[16] This entails both that (probably) other people have the experiences that they report, and that (probably) things are as someone's experience suggests that they are.

Well then, do we have to believe whatever anyone tells us, so long as it is a report of an experience? Of course not. As we have seen, there are lots of things that can happen that can and should make us sceptical of a report. But Swinburne argues that the possible 'negative characteristics' of experiences that tend to limit the applicability of the principle of credulity do not apply in all cases of religious experience. That is, there are no general arguments that legislate on the irrelevance of our two principles to religious experience. Here is how his argument goes:

(1) It is true that some reports of religious experiences are made by unreliable people, but this is hardly a general critique of all reports of religious experiences. Most such reports are made by people who normally make reliable perceptual claims, not by people who (for example) habitually lie or have recently taken hallucenogenic drugs. (2) It is true that some reports of religious experiences are made in circumstances that have proved unreliable in the past, but again this hardly rules out all such reports. We might have here a powerful general critique of the veridicality of theistic experiences if it could be proven that God does *not* exist, Swinburne admits, but there is no such proof. But doesn't the fact that religious experiences notoriously conflict with other religious experiences constitute a general refutation of them?[17] (We will deal with this point in more detail in the next section.) Swinburne argues that conflicting religious vocabularies do not in themselves entail conflicting descriptions of God, because 'God may be known under different names to different cultures.'[18] Furthermore, Swinburne says, if one description of the object of religious experience conflicts with another, that constitutes a challenge to a particular detailed description of the object of religious experience, but is hardly a reason to reject all the claims of religious experience. (3) It is true that some reports of religious experiences suggest the existence of some thing or being whose existence is highly improbable on the background evidence, but this does not constitute a critique of all religious experience. If God exists, God is everywhere, and can presumably be experienced anywhere. So in order to have a general disproof of the veridicality of all theistic experience, we would again

have to have an argument or reason for thinking that very probably God does not exist, but there is no such reason or argument.

(4) It is true that some reports of religious experiences are made in circumstances where it is rational to think that the experience was caused by something other than the cause that is suggested by the reporter. But again this is not a general refutation of all theistic religious experience. If God exists, Swinburne argues, it is always going to be difficult to prove that God did not cause someone's religious experience. In one sense, any experience of anything will have God deeply involved in the causal chain that produced the experience. The crucial point again appears to be the existence of God. Swinburne concludes: 'A religious experience apparently of God ought to be taken as veridical unless it can be shown on other grounds significantly more probable than not that God does not exist.'[19]

On the basis of other arguments in *The Existence of God*, Swinburne thinks that the prior probability of the existence of God is significantly greater than the probability of the non-existence of God. Accordingly, we have good reason (other things being equal) to accept the veridicality of theistic religious experience. If there is a God, it is highly probable that people will have experiences of God. Thus, unless it can be shown that God probably does not exist (and nobody has ever shown that), the fact of religious experience tends to increase significantly the probability that God exists.

IV. OBJECTIONS TO THE ARGUMENT

Let us now consider objections to the ARE. Some will apply primarily to Swinburne's version of it, and some are more general.

(1) *Plausible naturalistic explanations of religious experience are available*

No one will deny that people have religious experiences; the question is how to explain that fact. Many critics of the ARE argue that plausible psychological explanations of religious experiences are available, explanations that do not require God. Sigmund Freud, for example, claimed that religious experience is the result of psychological need, for example, the desire to project a father image on to the universe. At some stage of life, all children come to recognise that their father, whom they once viewed as infallible and omnipotent, is fallible, human, and finite; but people subconsciously retain the inner need for a father figure who will care for and protect them in this life and the next; and so they project that need on to the universe; they come to believe in an all-powerful and perfectly good God, a cosmic father. But of course this is a myth, Freud said; no such God exists.[20]

Freud's theory seems completely irrelevant to those religious experiences that have nothing to do with God or with anything like a father figure. Still, since as noted I am emphasising theistic religious experience, I will not press the point. More importantly, Freud's explanation, *even if it is true*, does nothing to disprove the existence of God or show that God is a myth. Maybe God exists and uses our natural desire for a cosmic father figure as a way to bring people to need and long for God. But of course the current objection to the ARE is not limited to Freudian theories. The general critical point is that religious experiences – in perhaps some as yet unknown way – are caused not by God but by certain needs or emotions in the experiencers themselves, and therefore do not constitute evidence in favor of the existence of God.

To my knowledge, no one seriously argues that all reports of religious experiences are consciously deceptive, that is, that what we have in religious experience is a massive case of fraud. But it is still possible that unconscious deception of some sort is going on. Perhaps it is a kind of self-deception based on something like wishful thinking: most people very much *want* to believe in God or in some benevolent force ruling the universe, and so they do. But is it plausible to believe that in countless cases of religious experiences, people deceive themselves into believing that Christ is present when he isn't, or that a voice was heard when it really wasn't, or that a bright light was seen that really wasn't there?

What are the mechanisms that might cause such massive acts of self-deception? Are they psychological ('Mystics are all schizophrenic'), social ('Society causes people to expect to have religious experiences'), political ('People have religious experiences because the ruling class, as an instrument of oppression, wants them to have religious experiences'), medical, dietary, or what? And what reason do we have, independently of the desire to refute the ARE, to believe that the purported mechanism really works in the indicated way?

Evidence is needed that the theory really works, because simply to assume that it works is to assume that religious experiences are non-veridical, which simply begs the question against the ARE.[21] Notice that we only seek explanations of why someone believes something in cases where we are convinced that what the person believes is false. One doubts that Freud would ever have been tempted to give elaborate 'projection'-type explanations of why a certain person believed that grass is green, or even that God does not exist.

The 'genetic fallacy' is the mistake of thinking that you have refuted a claim once you have explained why a person makes the claim. 'You only believe p because you were brainwashed into believing p by your misguided parents; therefore, p is false.' Obviously, this sort of argument is fallacious because the question of why somebody believes something is quite unrelated to the truth value of what is believed. It seems that the 'plausible psychological explanation' objection to the ARE constitutes a classical example of the genetic fallacy.

But even if we waive this point, another serious objection looms. If religious experiences were caused in some as yet unknown way by human needs, it would seem to follow that they would be uniformly pleasant and comforting. But the fact is that they are sometimes intensely painful, troubling, and even life-changing. St Paul's experience cited earlier brought about blindness, massive confusion, and an eventual turn-about in the entire orientation of his life. Maybe there is some way that such an unpleasant experience can be reconciled with the 'human need' theory, but such an explanation will probably seem more like a far-fetched epicycle to a hard-pressed theory than a legitimate explanation. I conclude that the suggested 'plausible naturalistic explanations' of religious experience are not particularly plausible.

(2) *Contrary to the claims of many versions of the ARE, religious experience is not like ordinary perception*

This objection amounts to pointing out important dissimilarities between perception and religious experience, the implication being that we should ordinarily trust the one but not the other. Perception is very common while religious experiences are relatively rare; perception yields a great deal of information about the world while religious experience (even on the most sympathetic treatment of it) yields little information about God; all human beings have the capacity to perceive while few apparently have the capacity to have religious experiences; perceptual experience is sensory (the object perceived always has certain sensory qualities like, say, red) while the object purportedly experienced in religious experience does not (nobody wants to say that God is red or tall or soft; the idea rather is that God has non-sensory properties like goodness, power, and knowledge).[22]

Wallace Matson, for example, admits that if one has an experience of perceiving a tree, that normally (that is, in the absence of reasons to doubt) constitutes good grounds for believing in the existence of the tree. But he also notes that there are several crucial conditions, at least some of which must be met before a questionable or abnormal perceptual experience can rationally be believed. For example, the perception might have been seen and corroborated by others. But publicity and corroboration are notor-iously not met in reports of religious experience. Thus, unless there is independent reason for us to believe in the existence of God (in which case we might sensibly *expect* to have experiences of God), no report of a religious experience can ever count as good reason to believe in the existence of God.[23]

Furthermore, we have no criteria in cases of religious experience for distinguishing between normal and abnormal cases. As Ralph Clark says, in cases of religious experience, 'there is no objectively specifiable set of circumstances such that should a normal human being be in those circumstances, that person would have the religious experience in ques-tion, were the experience genuine. As a consequence of this, the sort of philosophical treatment that is appropriate for assessing the evidential value of experiences such as seeing colors and feeling pain under normal circumstances is not appropriate regarding religious experiences.'[24]

Much of this is true, but it is not clear that these disanalogies between religious experience and ordinary perception refute the ARE. It may still be the case that religious experience has a similar epistemic structure to perception; and the question whether the one is to be trusted like the other (in the absence of reasons to doubt) really amounts to the question of the reliability of the principle of credulity, to which we turn next.

(3) *Swinburne's principle of credulity is implausible*

Some philosophers argue that Swinburne's principle of credulity is too strong and thus too generous toward religious experience. Recall that Swinburne's version says that in the absence of special considerations, if it seems to a certain person that x is present, then probably x is present. So, in the absence of reasons to think otherwise, if it seemed to Saint Teresa that Jesus was present to her, then, probably, Jesus *was* present to her. Gary Gutting is one such critic of Swinburne. He prefers to say that religious experiences purportedly of God give *prima facie* evidence of the existence of God, but that further support (rather than merely the absence of reasons to be sceptical) is needed before the *prima facie* evidence can become convincing evidence.

He gives a counter-example: suppose Gutting walks into his office one day only to see, clearly and distinctly, what looks to be his recently deceased aunt sitting in his chair. Now Gutting claims (surely correctly) that this experience could happen in such a way that none of the four 'negative characteristics' recognised by Swinburne (and discussed in Section II above) applies. Gutting has not proved unreliable in the past, isn't drunk, the lighting is good, etc.; Gutting knows nothing of circumstances in which experiences of the dead by apparently normal people in the past have turned out false or unreliable; Gutting knows nothing about the habits or powers of the dead and so has no reason to think that his aunt could not be in his study or, even if present, could not be seen by him. But notice, Gutting says, that even though none of the defeating conditions recognised by Swinburne applies, it is obvious that Gutting is not rationally entitled, in the absense of other evidence, to believe that he has seen his aunt.[25]

Perhaps the differences between Swinburne and Gutting are not large enough to be considered crucial to evaluating the cogency of the ARE. Both philosophers hold that other things need to be true before a report of a religious experience can be considered veridical. Swinburne thinks that it must merely be true that there are no 'negative characteristics', and Gutting thinks that there must be both the absence of 'negative characteristics' and the presence of further 'positive' factors. In the dead-aunt-in-the-office case, these factors would include factors like other people having had similar experiences, the aunt staying for a long time and acting in ways that Gutting's aunt should behave, the aunt giving information that only she could possibly know, etc. Only then can the experience of the aunt be considered strong enough to support rational belief that the aunt still exists (beyond death).

I will not try to adjudicate the dispute between the two philosophers. I will only defend Swinburne at this point – he can sensibly claim that the dead-aunt-in-the-office case *does* satisfy one of his listed 'negative conditions', namely, the one (number (3)) that says that the event experienced is highly improbable on the background evidence. Surely Gutting's seeing his known-to-be-dead aunt alive and well in his office is highly improbable on the background evidence. Thus Swinburne (contrary to Gutting's claim) does not have to allow that Gutting's experience is veridical even in the absence of other, positive, considerations. Swinburne can certainly agree with Gutting's claim that if there is some reason to question the veridicality of a religious experience, then further evidence is needed before it can be believed.

The deep issue is whether theistic religious experience, *all by itself*, constitutes evidence for the existence of God. Swinburne and Gutting agree that the answer is no, and so do I. Swinburne thinks that theistic religious experiences that we have no reason to doubt significantly contribute to a cumulative case that can be made for the existence of God. Gutting thinks that only those theistic religious experiences that we have no reason to doubt *and* that are corroborated by positive considerations significantly contribute to a cumulative case that can be made for the existence of God. I am inclined to agree with Swinburne; but also to add *à la* Gutting that the cumulative case is obviously made stronger if there is other positive evidence that tends to confirm the religious experience.

(4) *Religious experiences differ enormously; whose experiences are veridical?*

We now return to the issue mentioned earlier, namely, the fact that there is a great diversity of religious experiences, some of them theistic and some of them not. Moslems tend to have religious experiences of Allah; Catholics of the Virgin Mary; Vedantic Hindus of Brahman. The problem for the ARE is that if religious experience is to constitute evidence for the existence of God (as opposed, say, to the 'Voidness' of some versions of Buddhism), then what do we do about non-theistic religious experiences? Or what do we do about *any* religious experience that contradicts theism, or one's own brand of theism, at some point? Do we simply ignore them? On what rational basis? If we restrict our coverage (as I have been doing) to theistic religious experience, what prevents Vedantic Hindus from using their religious experiences as evidence for the existence of Brahman?[26]

Of course, if *any* one religious experience or type of experience, theistic or non-theistic, is veridical, that at least accomplishes one important goal for theistic provers, namely, that of refuting naturalism. If, say, Shankara's religious experience of Brahmin was veridical, that at least shows that something else beside physical reality exists, that the world is morally governed (by karmic laws), and that there is life beyond death (through reincarnation). In other words, perhaps there is something like a common core of all religious experience, namely, that there is a power beyond ourselves and indeed beyond physical reality which is of ultimate concern to us and with which we can be in contact.[27]

But the question still remains whether theistic religious experience can be used as the basis of the ARE in the light of the fact that religious experience is so diverse, with much of it not theistic at all. I believe the answer is largely no. There is no rational way – short, that is, of question-begging – simply to rule out non-theistic religious experience and thus use religious experience as the basis of a proof of the God of theism. People who are already theists can certainly use theistic religious experience as a way of corroborating their beliefs; convinced theists as they are, they can simply say that non-theistic religious experience is mistaken, or is an experience of God that is misinterpreted. Or perhaps they can make use of other TPs, or other sorts of arguments from natural theology, to show that Ultimate Reality, or the object of religious experience, is personal rather than impersonal in nature. But the ARE, as a stand-alone proof of the existence of God, will always face the problem that not all of religious experience is experience of God and that much of it purports to be experience of realities that are inconsistent with the existence of God.

V. CONCLUSION

Still, the other objections to the ARE do not seem compelling. So it looks as if there are versions of the ARE that *can* constitute a successful proof that anti-religious naturalism is false. What it apparently cannot do – not, at least, by itself – is constitute a successful proof that the God of theism exists.[28]

NOTES

1. Successful theistic proofs have epistemological consequences, of course. If it can be proved that God exists, it follows that belief in the existence of God is rational.
2. William Alston, *Perceiving God: The Epistemology of Religious Experience* (Ithaca, New York: Cornell University Press, 1991), pp. 3, 222, 284.
3. Richard Swinburne, *The Existence of God* (Oxford: Oxford University Press, 1979), pp. 244–76.
4. St Teresa of Avila, *The Life of St Teresa of Avila by Herself*, cited in Alston, *Perceiving God*, p. 13.
5. William James, *The Varieties of Religious Experience* (New York: The Modern Library, 1936), p. 71.
6. Swinburne, *The Existence of God*, pp. 250–1.
7. This is the view of William James. See *The Varieties of Religious Experience*, p. 414.
8. Gary Gutting, despite being a defender of the ARE, argues that no experience, taken by itself, makes it reasonable to believe that any external object exists. This, he thinks, is the valid core of Descartes' dream argument. In other words, 'given an experience that purports to be of X, we need to know more before we are entitled to believe that X exists' (Gary Gutting, *Religious Belief and Religious Skepticism* (Notre Dame, Indiana: University of Notre Dame Press, 1982), pp. 145–6).
9. Swinburne, *The Existence of God*, pp. 260–4.
10. These point are taken from J. P. Moreland's discussion of religious experience in *Scaling the Secular City: A Defense of Christianity* (Grand Rapids, Michigan: Baker Book House, 1987), pp. 235–7.
11. The issues are laid out and discussed skilfully in William Rowe, *Philosophy of Religion: An Introduction*, 2nd edn (Belmont, California: Wadsworth Publishing Company, 1993), pp. 54–72.
12. I quote from Louis Pojman's summary of the argument in his *Philosophy of Religion: An Anthology*, 2nd edn (Belmont, California: Wadsworth Publishing Company, 1994), p. 99.
13. Swinburne, *The Existence of God*, p. 254.
14. Swinburne, *The Existence of God*, p. 254.
15. This is not Swinburne's only argument against the present objection, nor is it the only objection to the principle of credulity to which he replies. But it is enough to give a sense of where his argument is going.
16. Swinburne, *The Existence of God*, p. 271.
17. As Antony Flew argues. See his *God and Philosophy* (New York: Delta Books, 1966), pp. 126–7.
18. Swinburne, *The Existence of God*, p. 266.
19. Swinburne, *The Existence of God*, p. 270.
20. Among his other writings, see Sigmund Freud, *The Future of an Illusion* (New York: Norton Books, 1961).
21. This point is made nicely by Gary Gutting in *Religious Belief and Religious Skepticism*, pp. 161–3.
22. See Michael Peterson, William Hasker, Bruce Reichenbach, and David Basinger, *Reason and Religious Belief: An Introduction to the Philosophy of Religion* (Oxford: Oxford University Press, 1991), p. 18.
23. Wallace Matson, *The Existence of God* (Ithaca, New York: Cornell University Press, 1965), pp. 3–40.

24. Ralph W. Clark, 'The Evidential Value of Religious Experiences', *International Journal for Philosophy of Religion*, Vol. 16, No. 3 (1984), p. 189.
25. Gutting, *Religious Belief and Religious Skepticism*, pp. 147–9.
26. Although it is not in the context of treating religious experience as a TP, Alston devotes Chapter 7 of *Perceiving God* to this problem.
27. See Gutting, *Religious Belief and Religious Skepticism*, pp. 169–2.
28. Gutting reaches essentially the same conclusion. See *Religious Belief and Religious Skepticism*, pp. 169–70.

8

Other Theistic Proofs

In this chapter I wish to explain and discuss four additional theistic proofs. Three of them are versions of arguments that we have already considered, and one is new. Each raises fascinating issues. Fortunately, they can be discussed more briefly than many of the other TPs that we have considered.

I. ONTOLOGICAL ARGUMENT NUMBER 2

In *Proslogion* Chapter III, Anselm offered a version of the ontological argument that sounds similar but is different from the argument of *Proslogion* II that we discussed earlier. Actually, there is no evidence that Anselm himself saw the two arguments as logically distinct. Let us say that two arguments are logically distinct just in case it is logically possible for one to be valid and the other invalid. The fact that the arguments of *Proslogion* II and III are logically distinct was not noticed until the twentieth century, when theologian Karl Barth[1] and philosopher Norman Malcolm[2] (apparently quite independently of each other) pointed it out.

In *Proslogion* III, Anselm made a distinction between things that 'can be conceived not to exist' (which we have been calling contingent beings) and things that 'cannot be conceived not to exist' (which we have been calling necessary beings). He went on to argue that necessary beings are greater than contingent beings. Now in the first OA, as we have seen, Anselm referred to God as 'that than which nothing greater can be conceived' (or the GCB, as we are saying), and Anselm retained that terminology here. He then crucially said: 'Hence, if that, than which nothing greater can be conceived, can be conceived not to exist, it is not that, than which nothing greater can be conceived. But this is an irreconcilable contradiction. There is, then, so truly a being than which nothing greater can be conceived to exist, that it cannot even be conceived not to exist; and this being thou art, O Lord, our God.'[3] Perhaps the argument, in logical form, is meant to look something like this:

1. Either the GCB exists or the GCB does not exist.
2. If the GCB exists, the GCB's existence is necessary.
3. If the GCB does not exist, the GCB's existence is impossible.
4. The GCB is not an impossible thing.
5. Therefore, the GCB's existence is necessary.
6. Therefore, the GCB exists.

Obviously, this requires some explanation.

Premise (1) seems beyond reproach; indeed, it is a substitution-instance of one of the laws of logic, the Law of Excluded Middle, which says that every proposition is true or, if it is not true, then false. The statement 'The GCB exists', is accordingly either true or, if it is not true, then false.

Premise (2) is true because there are only two sorts of existing things: contingently existing things and necessary things (if there are any necessary beings). Now no GCB can be a contingently existing thing like you or me or the trees outside. Since no contingently existing being can be the GCB (all contingent beings depend for their existence on some other being or beings), it follows that if the GCB exists the GCB is a necessary being.

Premise (3) is true because there are only two sorts of non-existing things: contingently non-existing things and impossible things. The first category covers non-existing things like unicorns and my ninth daughter, things which for logical reasons might or could well exist but do not happen to exist. The second category includes things like married bachelors and square circles which for logical reasons cannot exist. Now Anselm cleverly recognised that no GCB can be a contingently non-existing thing like a unicorn because then it could be brought into existence by something else and *if it were to be brought into existence*, it would be dependent for its existence on that thing and so would not be the GCB. Thus if the GCB fails to exist, it must be an impossible thing rather than a contingently non-existent thing.

Premise (4) is true because there seems to be no contradiction or other sort of incoherence in the notion or concept of the GCB or in the words 'that than which nothing greater can be conceived'. It might be difficult strictly to *prove* that these concepts are coherent, but they surely seem to be so. Assuming that the GCB is a possible being, which follows from its not being an impossible being, it follows from premises (1), (2) and (3) that the GCB is a necessary being (5) and thus that the GCB exists (6).

Let us try to conceptualise this same argument in a slightly different way. Suppose we draw up a box containing six categories of sorts of things, ways in which things might exist or fail to exist.

(A) contingent existing things	(D) contingent non-existing things
(B) necessary existing things	(E) necessary non-existing things
(C) impossible existing things	(F) impossible non-existing things

These categories are meant to be exhaustive; there are no possible or impossible things, or existing or non-existing things, that do not fit into one or another of the six categories.

Now let's ask this question of each category: *Can there conceivably be such a thing as the sort of thing here described?* With category (A) the answer is yes. Not only can there be conceivably existing things – there actually exist such things. I am a contingently existing thing, and so are all other human beings, together with all the rocks and trees and molecules and galaxies. With category (B) the answer also seems to be yes: it certainly seems that there *can conceivably exist* necessary things (there is no contradiction in the notion of a necessary being); whether any *do in fact exist* is another matter and is one of the issues at stake in the OA. With category (C), we must say no: for logical reasons, there can be no such thing as an impossible thing (a thing whose definition or concept is incoherent, like a square circle or a married bachelor) that actually exists. With category (D) the answer is again yes: there *can* conceivably be such things. Unicorns, my ninth daughter, and Abraham Lincoln are all contingent things that do not exist. That is, they could or might exist, or even once did exist, but do not now happen to exist. With category (E) the answer is again no: for logical reasons, there can be no such thing as a necessary non-existing thing, that is, a necessary being that does not exist. And with category (F) the answer is yes: there not only can be but in fact are impossible non-existing things, like the married bachelor who just entered my office or the prime number between seven and nine. (There are other complications and difficulties with this method of argumentation, but I'll ignore them because I am not proposing to defend the argument.)

Now let us ask this question of each remaining category: *Can the GCB be such a being as this?* We have already excluded categories (C) and (E) on the grounds that there logically can be no such beings, and of course if there can be no such being, then, obviously, the GCB cannot be such a being. So we need to ask our present question about the remaining four categories, i.e., (A), (B), (D) and (F).

Can the GCB fit in category (A)? Clearly not: as Anselm cogently argued, if it is greater to exist necessarily than to exist contingently, then no contingently existing thing can be the GCB. For a similar reason, the GCB cannot fit in category (D): as Anselm argued with equal cogency, any contingently non-existing thing can possibly come into existence (this does not mean it *will* do so), and if it did, it would depend for its existence on whatever things or forces brought it into existence, and so it would not be the GCB. Nor does it seem that the GCB fits category (F): the way that we go about discovering whether some defined or named thing is an impossible thing is to examine its concept or definition; if the concept is incoherent, contradictory, or logically illicit in some sense (like the definition 'Unmarried adult male who is married'), then we conclude that the thing defined is an impossible thing. But there appears to be no contradiction or logical incoherence in the words 'Greatest Conceivable Being' or 'That than which nothing greater can be conceived'. Accordingly, we are within our intellectual rights in concluding that the GCB does not fit in category (F).

The only remaining category, then, is (B): since all the others have been ruled out, the GCB must be a necessarily existing thing. And if the GCB is a necessarily existing thing, then the GCB exists. QED.

Formidable as it may seem at first glance, this argument is unsuccessful. In order to explain why, let me introduce a being that I will call the 'ontologically impossible being' (or OIB). (I need to emphasise here that I am not talking about a *logically* impossible being.) The OIB has three defining properties:

a. it does not exist;
b. it can possibly exist (that is, is not logically impossible); and
c. if it were to exist, it would be a necessary being.

Now let's think carefully about these properties. Property (a) says that the OIB does not exist, that is, does not exist now. But since the OIB does not exist at some one moment in time, namely, the present moment, it follows that it never has and never will exist. This is because of property (c), which says that if the OIB were to exist it would be a necessary being. (Obviously, there is no such thing as a necessary being that has a finite lifespan, that exists at certain times and not at others.) So, despite the fact that at any moment the OIB *might* or *could* possibly exist (property (b) entails that there is no contradiction or incoherence in the notion of its existing), at no time *does* the OIB exist.

Here is a crucial question that must be asked: in which of the six categories noted above does the OIB fit? And the answer seems to be: in none of them. Categories (A), (B), and (C) are ruled out because these concern *existing* things, and as noted the OIB does not exist. Category (D) is ruled out because the OIB is clearly not a *contingently* non-existing thing like a unicorn or like my ninth daughter, things that do not now exist but might well come to exist. Category (F) is ruled out because property (b) says that the OIB is not a logically impossible thing like a square circle. Thus only category (E) remains, but the problem here is that there can be no such thing as a necessary being that does not exist; all necessary beings (if there are any) exist. The OIB is not a necessary being but rather, as property (c) explicitly says, the OIB *would be* a necessary being if it (contrary to fact) existed.

Now the (A)–(F) categories were supposed to be exhaustive; every sort of being was supposed to fit one of the categories or another. But if the OIB fits nowhere in the schema – and that seems to follow from our discussion – the so-called Second Version of the OA fails. The argument is not able to rule out the possibility that the GCB is an OIB – a thing that might exist, would be a necessary being if it existed, but in fact does not exist.

And it should be pointed out that the OIB is not just an esoteric philosopher's counter-example, the result of some analytic flight of fancy. That God is an OIB is just what many atheists want to say about God. Now probably some atheists think that God is logically impossible; they hold that the concept of God is contradictory or otherwise incoherent. But clearly many of them want to say something like this about God: 'Yes, I agree with you theists that God, if God were to exist, must be a necessary being (a contingent being would not be God); and I further agree that there is no logical incoherence in the concept of God; it is possible for God to exist; but as a matter of fact God does not exist.' That is, many atheists have some sort of being like the OIB nascently in mind when they talk about God. Accordingly, it is a deep failing of the so-called Second Form of the ontological argument that it is not able to rule out the possibility that the GCB is an OIB.[4]

Of course the mere fact that I have defined the OIB as a possible thing (see property (b)) does not guarantee that it *is* a possible thing. Just adding the property 'is a possible thing' to the properties (for example) of a square circle ('plane four-sided geometrical figure all of whose points are equidistant from the centre') does not suddenly make square circles possible things. One must, in the case of the OIB or any other being, examine its properties to see if the being *is* possible.

Now someone might argue in favour of Anselm here as follows: in spite of property (b), the OIB is an impossible thing; accordingly it fits in category (F); and accordingly it does not constitute a counter-example to Anselm's second OA. But why should we hold that the OIB is an impossible thing? The critic must show, and not just say, that the OIB is impossible. I can detect no contradiction in the concept of the OIB, and the fact that many atheists nascently have the OIB in mind when they speak of God strengthens my conviction that the OIB is a possible thing. If I am right, the second OA fails as a theistic proof.

II. A GENERIC COSMOLOGICAL ARGUMENT

We discussed the cosmological argument earlier. Let me now present a version of it that I call the 'generic CA' (or GCA) because I can find no philosopher to whom to attribute this precise rendition, although it clearly has affinities with eighteenth-century versions of the CA. Moreover, the GCA does contain most of the important themes that we associate with the CA, especially with the Thomistic 'Third Way':

13. If the universe can be explained, then God exists.
14. Everything can be explained.
15. The universe is a thing.
16. Therefore, the universe can be explained.
17. Therefore, God exists.

Let me now set out to clarify the GCA. Premise (13) simply claims that if there is any explanation of the existence of the universe, then God (or some sort of divine reality or realities) must exist as the explanation. This premise seems sensible because if God exists, then the explanation for the existence of the universe is simply this: 'God created it.' And that seems about the only sort of explanation that *could* be given. If no God or Godlike creator of the universe exists, it seems that the universe will have no explanation. Its existence will simply be a brute fact.

Premise (14) is the PSR, which we discussed earlier. The PSR says that everything that exists has a reason for its existence. As we saw, it does not seem possible to prove the PSR, but as Richard Taylor argues, the PSR is presupposed in all our thinking.[5] We never encounter some existing thing without assuming that there is a reason why it exists, and there are no existing things that we know for sure have no explanation for their existence.

Premise (15) represents what we might call the 'lumping together' strategy that we see in many versions of the CA. The normal move is to lump together all the existing things, or all the contingent things that have ever existed or will exist, and call it 'reality' or 'the universe' or 'the world'. Then causal questions are asked about this huge aggregate – questions like 'Who made it?' or 'Where did it come from?' or 'Why is it here?' or 'What is its cause?' Premise (15) simply says that the aggregate that we call the universe is itself a thing about which such causal questions can coherently be asked.

Premise (16) is entailed by (14) and (15). That is, if it is true, as premise (15) says, that the universe is a thing; and if it is true, as premise (14) says, that everything can be explained; then it strictly follows, as (16) says, that the universe can be explained. It is impossible for (14) and (15) to be true and (16) false. The conclusion of the GCA follows from (13) and (16). If it is true, as (13) says, that if the universe can be explained, then God exists; and if it is true, as (16) says, that the universe can be explained; then it strictly follows, as (17) says, that God exists. Because of the argument form known as *modus ponens*, it is impossible for (13) and (16) to be true and (17) false.

Now the GCA looks at first glance like a fine theistic proof, but I will argue that it is based on a mistake. In order to expose the error, I shall refer to the transcript of a famous 1948 debate on BBC radio. The topic of the debate was the existence of God, and featured Bertrand Russell, the famous atheist philosopher, and Father Frederick Copleston SJ, the eminent historian of philosophy. In a discussion of the CA, Copleston said: 'Well, my point is that what we call the world is intrinsically unintelligible, apart from the existence of God.'[6] Copleston thus endorsed premise (13) of the GCA. But Russell consistently took the position that the world has no explanation, and that it is illegitimate to ask for its explanation. Russell thus insisted on denying premise (14) of the GCA, the PSR. 'I should say that the universe is there, and that's all,' Russell said; 'the notion of the world having an explanation is a mistake.' The debate over the CA then ground to an inconclusive halt, with Russell unwilling to grant the PSR and Copleston unable to convince him of its truth. As Copleston wrote at the end of his own discussion of Aquinas' Five Ways, 'If one does not wish to embark on the path which leads to the affirmation of transcendent being . . . , one has to deny the reality of the problem, assert that things "just are" and that the existential problem in question is a pseudo-problem. And if one refuses even to sit down at the chess-board and make a move, one cannot, of course, be checkmated.'[7]

What the Russell–Copleston exchange shows, I believe, is that at least some versions of the CA, including the GCA, can be said to fail because they commit the fallacy of begging the question. Recall our discussion of question-begging from Chapter 1. There we concluded that there is more than one way for an argument to beg the question, and that one way amounts to this – an argument begs the question if it contains a premise that will only be acceptable to those who already accept the conclusion.

The premise of the GCA that is begged is

14. Everything can be explained,

which is the PSR. Let me put the point in this way: it is clear that the GCA is formally valid, but are the premises true? Well, premises (13) and (15) appear to be beyond reproach, and can be accepted by any sensible person. But what about (14)? Well, *I* think that premise (14) is true. Accordingly, *I* think that the GCA is a fine argument; *I* think it is both formally valid and (since *I* think its premises are all true) sound.

Now the pronoun 'I' has been italicised in the last two sentences for a reason – it is to emphasise the fact that I (Stephen Davis) accept the truth of premise (14) and thus the soundness of the GCA. But why is this true about me? Obviously, it is because of another crucial fact about me – I already believe in God; I accept (17). Believing in God as I do, I naturally accept the notion that everything can be explained. Ultimately I think everything can be explained in terms like 'it was created by God.' But, obviously, no atheist like Bertrand Russell will have the slightest inclination to grant premise (14). Such a person will hold that some existing things – such as the universe – have always existed and cannot be explained; they are simply brute facts.

If the cosmological arguer who uses the GCA can find a way of arguing for the PSR that does not appeal to or presuppose the existence of God, then the GCA might constitute a good theistic proof. In the absence of such an argument, the GCA fails because it requires a premise that should not be granted by those at whom the GCA is aimed, viz., atheists and agnostics. Accordingly, since even defenders of the PSR admit that it cannot be proved, the GCA fails as a theistic proof. One of its crucial premises will only be acceptable to those who already accept its conclusion. I am not saying that only theists accept the PSR. Some atheists affirm it. I *am* claiming that, following Russell's example, atheists *should* not affirm it. In order to be consistent, they must hold that there is no explanation of why there is any reality at all. Accordingly the GCA begs the question.[8]

III. THE MORAL ARGUMENT

Some theists argue for the existence of God on the basis of moral considerations. The most famous philosopher to do so was Immanuel

Kant. Despite the fact that Kant was not offering a TP in the sense that we have been using that term in this book (he was instead arguing that God is a postulate of moral reason), Kant's argument set the agenda for virtually all later moral arguments.[9] Never as popular as the other theistic proofs, the heyday of the moral argument was undoubtedly the nineteenth and early twentieth centuries. It was given an enormous boost by C. S. Lewis' appeal to it in *Mere Christianity*,[10] and has recently been impressively defended by Robert M. Adams,[11] Linda Zagzebski[12] and others. I will present a version of the moral argument that is more influenced by Lewis' presentation than by those of others.

The point at which all moral arguments for the existence of God begin is our human experience of the phenomenon of moral obligation. The vast majority of human beings believe and presuppose that they are under obligation to an objective moral law. The word 'objective' here means that our being under that obligation does not depend on what any human being believes or does. Some things are morally right, and other things are morally wrong. We are obliged to do things that are morally right and to avoid doing things that are morally wrong. For example, we strongly and confidently hold that it is morally wrong to torture children just because you want to do so.

Contemporary defenders of the moral argument must at this point defend the thesis of the objectivity or absolute nature of the moral law. This is obviously because of the great appeal of moral relativism to many people today. There are various forms of moral relativism, but what unites them all is the idea that what is morally right and wrong is not objective but relative. It depends on who you are, or what group you belong to, or what you sincerely believe. Now we are used to the idea that some sorts of judgements are 'subjective' – whether chocolate ice cream tastes better than vanilla, for example. It just depends on who you are, and what your tastes are. There is no 'objective truth' here. But we also think that other judgements are 'objective' – whether San Francisco is north of Los Angeles, for example. Here the truth does not depend on who you are or what you happen to think.

Now ethical relativists place moral judgements on the subjective side. Something might be morally right for you and morally wrong for me, even where the only morally relevant difference between you and me is our divergent moral beliefs. If relativism amounts to the theory that something is morally right for you to do just because you, or the members of your society, believe that it is morally right for you to do it, criticisms of relativism are not hard to find. What about the Nazis: were they morally right in murdering six million Jews just because they truly thought – as many of them surely did think – that they were doing the right thing? And what about raising children – is there any moral reason for us to try to teach them to do one thing rather than another if their nascent moral opinions (for example, 'Never share your toys unless you have to') are just as 'true for them' as ours are for us? In short, there seems to be no standpoint from which the moral beliefs or behavior of others can be criticised unless there is an objective moral law.

A final point: those who argue for moral relativism often do so on the basis of an appeal to tolerance – they think the best way to ensure the moral value of tolerance is to teach that everybody's moral views and practices are 'true for them'. That way – so the reasoning apparently goes – no one has the moral right to impose one's views on others. But clearly this move carries with it the grave danger of inconsistently introducing at least one absolute moral value – the need to be tolerant – through the back door.

Once it is established that the moral law is objective, the next point is to argue that there must be a lawgiver. This lawgiver must be morally superior to us, in order to explain the sense of authority that we feel the moral law has over us, and indeed the lawgiver must be or possess a mind. Lewis argues strongly against the idea that the moral law is grounded simply in matter. This is because science, which is the study of material reality, only tells us what *is* in fact the case. Indeed, this is the *only* thing that science can do. The moral law, on the other hand, tells us what *ought to be* the case. Only something mental or at least intentional can issue commands about what we must do. Scientists can tell us how things are, but that has nothing to do with what *ought* to be. As Lewis pointedly says, 'you can hardly imagine a bit of matter giving instructions.'[13] Furthermore, although both nature and morality are law-intensive, there is this important difference: we have no option but to obey the laws of nature (I have no ability to leap over a tall building), but we are free either to obey, or not to obey, the commands of the moral law.

The third and concluding point of the moral argument is that the source and fountain of the moral law must be God or a Godlike being. If the source of morality must be mind, then it is either God or human beings. Clearly it is not human beings, Lewis says, because we know that we are under obligation to 'a real law which we did not invent and which we know we ought to obey'.[14] The only other option is God.

It is clear that there are many debatable points here. Because I agree with it, I will not dispute the argument that morality must be objective, although establishing the point is more difficult than perhaps Lewis saw – or at least than my quick summary of his argument implies.[15] The deepest issue that arises in assessing the moral argument concerns the question of whether it is possible to give a compelling account of morality in purely naturalistic terms. Since the Enlightenment, a great deal of philosophical effort has been spent in the attempt to provide purely naturalistic ways of grounding ethics. And although this fact proves nothing in itself, atheistic moral philosophers who are not relativists tend to get indignant at the merest suggestion that objective morality requires God.

For this reason I am inclined to judge the moral argument as inconclusive. If Lewis and others are right that God is needed as the foundation of objective morality, then the moral argument is on to something important. But to establish this point would require taking up each of the proposed substitutes for God as the foundation of morality – Aristotelian final causes, evolutionary arguments about the need to preserve the self or propagate the human species, contemporary moral intuitionism, etc. – and showing that they all fail. This project has not so far been convincingly carried out; it might however constitute an important research programme for some future defender of theism.

Here is one possible line of argument.[16] Can an ethicist who is an atheist and who rejects moral relativism find a way morally to justify heroic acts of self-sacrifice? The people who perform such acts – like the soldier who sacrifices his life for the sake of his buddies – are said to go 'above and beyond the call of duty'. We consider their deeds morally praiseworthy for just that reason – such people do *more* than is strictly required by morality. They are moral heroes. Now the question is not whether it is possible to explain the hero's *motivation* without bringing in God. All will admit that that is surely possible, at least in many cases. Probably many moral heroes are not religiously motivated and do not think about God when they decide to do their acts of moral heroism.

The real question is whether, in naturalistic terms, such deeds can be *justified*, whether it is possible to explain why they are morally warranted. For it would seem that apart from God such acts are irrational. Notice that moral heroes sometimes save people who are not close relatives; accordingly, such heroic deeds cannot be justified on the grounds that the heroes are at least ensuring that many of their genes will be passed on to the next generation. Nor (apart from God and the afterlife) will the heroic behaviour be rewarded or repaid *to the hero*. But if God exists, heroic self-sacrifice might be morally justified on the grounds that God will reward it, or on the grounds that God commands it of certain folk in certain situations. But apart from God, how can anything be more valuable to a person than his or her own life? Of course a naturalist could simply say that heroic deeds of self-sacrifice are *not* morally justified. But that answer at the very least will need justification because it is so counter-intuitive. We consider such deeds about as praiseworthy as any human acts can possibly be.

IV. THE KALAAM COSMOLOGICAL ARGUMENT

We have already discussed Thomistic versions of the CA. But now we will consider a quite different version of the CA, one that was advanced in the medieval period by Moslem philosophers al-Kindi (who died about 870) and al-Ghazali (1058–1111), and by John Locke in the modern period. Recently it has been skilfully defended by William L. Craig, and it is on his version that I will concentrate.[17] Like the Thomistic CA, it is an *a posteriori* theistic proof that assumes certain obvious facts about the world, and then proceeds via argument about the cause or explanation of those facts to the existence of God. The Kalaam cosmological argument (KCA) tries to argue for the existence of a first cause of the universe in time, that is, it argues against the idea of an infinitely long causal series stretching back into the past. Its most recognisable theme is the denial of all actual infinities.

We might summarise the KCA as follows:

18. A beginningless series of events in time is an actual infinite.
19. No actual infinite can exist.
20. Therefore, there can be no beginningless series of events in time.
21. Therefore, the universe began to exist at some past point in time.
22. Whatever begins to exist at some point in time has a cause of its existence.
23. Therefore, the universe has a cause of its existence.[18]

Premise (18) presupposes a distinction between an actual infinite and a potential infinite. A *potential infinite*, Craig says, is 'a collection that is increasing without limit but is at all times finite'.[19] A potential infinite typically occurs whenever we add to or subtract from something without stopping; it would be more accurate to call such a series *indefinite* rather than infinite, because the series is always finite but ever increasing toward the limit of infinity. An *actual infinite*, however, is an infinitely large collection of things, a complete but infinite totality. Premise (18) says that if past events in the history of the universe had no beginning, then the set of all past events would constitute an actual infinite.

Premise (19) is clearly the crucial premise of the argument. To support it, Craig displays Zeno-like paradoxes to demonstrate the absurdity of actual infinites existing. (Craig is not opposed to the mathematical use of the *concept* of actual infinites, of course – he is denying that any actual infinite could exist in the real world.) Suppose your university has a huge library, so huge that it has an infinite number of books in its collection. Suppose further that all the books happen to be colored either red or black, and that they are all placed alternately by colour on the shelves – red, black, red, black.

Now notice certain absurd facts about this infinitely large collection – for one thing, the number of red books would be equal to the number of black books and red books together. Notice also that the total number of books in the collection would not decrease in the slightest if we took away all the black books. Notice also that the number of books in the collection would not increase at all if we added ten books to it, or even if we added an infinite number of books to it. Indeed, we *cannot* add to the number of books in the collection. Suppose we put a different number (in the series 1, 2, 3 . . .) on the spine of each book in the library; then since there are an infinite number of books in the library, every possible number will be printed on some book or other, and there will be no new numbers to assign to new books.

Thus there can be no such thing as an actual infinite. Now an infinite number of past events or even moments would constitute an actual infinite, Craig says, because for every event in the past, there would be an event before it. Thus premise (20) says that there can be no beginningless series of events in past time. It follows from premise (20) that the universe had to begin at some past point in time, which is what premise (21) explicitly says. Premise (22) claims that nothing can come into existence at a certain point in time uncaused. Whatever began to exist at some past point in time had a cause of its existence. Now nothing can be the cause of itself. If premises (21) and (22) are true, then (says premise (23)) the universe must have had a cause of its existence.

Craig also argues that the cause of the universe must be personal rather than impersonal in nature. (Obviously, the cause must be one or the other.) Now it is not easy to describe the state of affairs before (this means *logically* rather than *temporally* before) the first event in the history of the universe. This is because there was no time and no matter or energy in existence. Having already established the fact that the first event could not have been uncaused, Craig goes on to argue that the necessary and sufficient conditions for the occurrence of the first event must have existed from all eternity, since what existed prior to (logically prior to) spatio-temporal reality must have been timeless and thus immutable (since change cannot exist apart from time).

We know that whenever the necessary and sufficient conditions for an event to occur obtain, the event occurs. There is no waiting. How then could the first event in the history of the universe both be caused and spontaneously arise from a timeless, changeless, spaceless state of affairs? It would seem that if the cause is timeless, the effect must be timeless too. That is, if the cause of the first event was timeless, it would seem that the universe would then have been timelessly coexistent with the cause. But it isn't. Since the cause was timeless and the effect temporal, it must be the case that the cause was a personal being who *decided* to create a spatio-temporal universe. That is, the whole scenario makes sense only if the event resulted from the free decision of some sort of personal being.

Let us consider two possible criticisms of the KCA. One issue concerns premise (22):

22. Whatever begins to exist at some point in time has a cause of its existence.

Now I certainly accept premise (22), but it seems that an atheist could appeal to some interpretations of contemporary physics in order to cast doubt on the claim that everything that begins to exist at some point in time has a cause of its existence. Quantum physics definitely holds that certain uncaused *events* occur. Or at least that is an interpretation with which the vast majority of physicists are comfortable.

Now Craig argues not for the strong claim that 'Every event has a cause,' but rather for the more guarded claim that 'Everything that begins to exist has a cause of its existence.' This allows for quantum indeterminacy. But whether a proper explanation of events that occur in quantum physics amounts to matter popping into existence uncaused is a controversial matter. Most physicists still hold that the conservation laws forbid such a thing. But other physicists say that a given electron can pass out of existence and then later return to existence, uncaused, in a different orbit around the nucleus. In any case, there is no way to track the electron's existence during the intermediate period between its appearances in the two orbits, if indeed it does exist then. But my main point is that a great deal of work remains to be done both in physics itself and in the philosophy of physics before we can be sure that (22) is true.

On the other hand, Craig can surely argue that (22) is plausible in and of itself and perhaps even more plausible than its denial. Now (22) states a principle that, apart from twentieth-century physics, would seem almost axiomatic to the vast majority of people. Quantum indeterminacy may cast some doubt on (22), but it surely does not rule it out. There are fully deterministic interpretations of quantum mechanics that are mathematically consistent and explain all the data, and there are eminent physicists who would have no trouble affirming (22). So whatever doubts might be raised about (22) – a principle, I repeat, that I certainly accept – they are not strong enough to refute the KCA.

The other, more important, problem has to do with what I am calling premise (18) of the KCA:

18. A beginningless series of events in time is an actual infinite.

My own view is that Craig is absolutely right in his analysis of the absurd paradoxes that result if we allow for actual infinites existing simultaneously. The library paradoxes show that. So premise (19), which says, 'No actual infinite can exist,' understood in that sense, is true. And I have no wish to deny that a beginningless series of events in past time is an actual infinite. Of course it is. What I do question is whether such a series is the sort of actual infinite that Craig's paradoxes rule out. It seems that a close look at Craig's arguments about the library etc. reveals that what they show is that no infinitely large set of things can exist *at any one time*. No library can simultaneously contain an infinite number of books. But what if instead of an infinitely huge library we think of a very small one with great longevity? Imagine this picture: the library keeps only one book at a time in its collection; every year it destroys that book and replaces it with another one that has never yet been in its collection; and, finally, the library has existed for an infinite number of years.

Here then truly would be a library with an infinitely large collection of books, but it would seem that Craig's paradoxes no longer apply. Taking away one book at any given time *would* reduce the collection in size (to zero); adding ten books *would* increase the size of the collection (to eleven), etc. If I am right, the critic of the KCA can argue that there is no incoherence in the idea of an infinite number of past events. As long as past time is infinite, the infinite number of past events can occur in serial order, one at a time (or any finite number at a time); at no one time do an infinite number of events occur. For all that the KCA can so far show, then, the universe might be infinitely old.

On the other hand, it must be pointed out that Craig has another, quite separate, argument against the infinity of the past. He calls it the 'second Kalaam argument'. This argument in effect responds to the objection to (18) that we have been discussing. Craig argues that it is impossible to form an actual infinite by successive addition. Suppose there is a person named Tristram Shandy who writes his autobiography so slowly that it takes him one entire year to record the events of a single day. Bertrand Russell argued that if Tristram Shandy were mortal he would never finish the book but that if he were immortal he would, since each day would correspond to a given year, and the number of both days and years is infinite.[20] Since all one needs, in order to write about an infinite number of days at the rate of one day per year, is an actually infinite number of years, Tristram Shandy should by now be finished writing his book. There appears to have been plenty of time for Tristram Shandy to complete his task.

Craig argues,[21] however, that the book will never be finished even if Tristram Shandy were to live forever; indeed, since the future is a potential infinite, as each year passes, Tristram Shandy will only get further and further behind in his work. Indeed, 'he would never finish, for every day of writing generates another year of work.' The longer he writes, the further behind he will fall. Furthermore, if Russell's argument were correct, Craig says, we could ask why Tristram Shandy did not finish his autobiography yesterday, or the day before, or at *any* day in the past, 'since by then an infinite series of events had already elapsed'. Indeed, on Russell's argument, at any past day that we can imagine, Tristram Shandy should have finished the book and will no longer be writing. But this is absurd, since the initial idea was that he has been writing from eternity.

The real moral of the Tristram Shandy paradox, Craig argues, is that 'an infinite series of past events is absurd.' No collection formed by successive addition can ever constitute an actual infinite. Thus, since the past is formed by successive addition of one event after another in time, the series of past events must be finite. Thus 'the temporal series of events is finite and had a beginning. Therefore, the universe began to exist.'

Here then is the ultimate dilemma that the Kalaam cosmological arguer asks atheists to face:

24. If the series of past events is beginningless, then it constitutes either a simultaneously existing actual infinite or a series formed by successive addition.
25. It cannot be a simultaneously existing actual infinite (first KCA).
26. It cannot be a series formed by successive addition (second KCA).
27. Therefore, the series of past events is not beginningless.

Doubtless much more than this can be said about the KCA. Still, this argument seems to me to constitute the first step of what might well constitute a plausible and powerful theistic proof.

NOTES

1. See his *Anselm: Fides Quaerens Intellectum* (London: SCM Press, 1960).
2. See his 'Anselm's Ontological Arguments', in John Hick (ed.), *The Existence of God* (New York: Macmillan, 1964), pp. 47–70.
3. Saint Anselm, *Basic Writings* (LaSalle, Illinois: Open Court, 1962), pp. 8–9.
4. It might be objected that my notion of 'OIB' is incoherent. By property (b), the OIB exists in some possible worlds but not in others, and by property (c) in those worlds in which it exists it is a necessary being. But–so it could be said–it is a standard axiom of modal logic that necessity does not vary from world to world. Accordingly, since there are some worlds in which the OIB exists

and is necessary, it follows that the OIB exists and is necessary in the actual world, which contradicts property (a). But in reply I need only point out that the doctrine that necessity does not change from world to world applies to *de dicto* necessity, the sort of necessity possessed by certain propositions (like 'All bachelors are unmarried'). It does not apply to *de re* necessity, the sort of necessity possessed by those beings which have *aseity*. These are beings that (1) exist at all moments of time, and (2) depend for their existence on no other beings. Even if some being B is (*de re*) a necessary being in some world, the *de dicto* claim that ' "B exists" is necessarily true' does not follow. Thus it seems quite possible for there to be a being that is a necessary being in some worlds and not exist at all in others. If so, the notion of the OIB is coherent, and the objection I have raised against OA number 2 still stands.

5. Richard Taylor, *Metaphysics*, 4th edn (Englewood Cliffs, New Jersey: Prentice-Hall, 1992), pp. 91–9.
6. See John Hick (ed.), *The Existence of God* (New York: Macmillan, 1964), pp. 174–7.
7. Reprinted in Hick, *The Existence of God*, p. 93.
8. This point has been made by Hick. See *The Existence of God*, pp. 6–7.
9. See Immanuel Kant, *Critique of Practical Reason* (Indianapolis: Bobbs-Merrill, 1956), pp. 128–36.
10. C. S. Lewis, *Mere Christianity* (New York: Macmillan, 1960), Book I.
11. Robert M. Adams. 'Moral Arguments for Theistic Belief,' in *The Virtue of Faith and Other Essays in Philosophical Theology* (New York: Oxford University Press, 1987), pp. 144–63.
12. Linda Zagzebski, 'Does Ethics Need God?', *Faith and Philosophy*, Vol. 4, No. 3 (July, 1987).
13. Lewis, *Mere Christianity*, p. 20.
14. Lewis, *Mere Christianity*, p. 17.
15. See, for example, the essays on moral relativism in Michael Krausz and Jack W. Meiland (eds), *Relativism: Cognitive and Moral* (Notre Dame, Indiana: University of Notre Dame Press, 1982).
16. A version of it is put forward by John Hick in his discussion of the moral argument. See *Arguments for the Existence of God* (New York: The Seabury Press, 1971), pp. 59–67.
17. See especially William L. Craig, *The Kalaam Cosmological Argument* (New York: Barnes and Noble, 1979).
18. It should be noted that Craig's defense of the KCA is subtle and detailed, and there are many facets of it that we will not be able to discuss here. For example, alongside his argument against an actual infinite, Craig has an argument to the effect that even if an actual infinite is possible, it cannot be traversed. He also buttresses the KCA with scientific evidence, especially concerning the Big Bang.
19. William L. Craig, 'Philosophical and Scientific Pointers to *Creatio ex Nihilo*,' in R. Douglas Geivett and Brendan Sweetman (eds), *Contemporary Perspectives on Religious Epistemology* (Oxford: Oxford University Press, 1992), p. 186.
20. Bertrand Russell discusses the 'Tristram Shandy paradox' in *The Principles of Mathematics*, 2nd ed. (London: Allen & Unwin, 1937), pp. 358–9.
21. See William L. Craig and Quentin Smith, *Theism, Atheism, and Big Bang Cosmology* (Oxford: Clarendon Press, 1993), pp. 33–5, 99–106. All quotations from Craig in this section are from these pages of this book.

9

Alternatives to Theistic Proofs

I. INTRODUCTION

Some philosophers of religion see little value in engaging in the enterprise of trying to prove the existence of God. In some cases, they reject theistic proofs because they are convinced that none of the theistic proofs yet proposed is successful. In other cases, they do so for religious or theological reasons. God is so mysterious and incomprehensible to humans – it is said – that there is no chance at all that God's existence could be proved. Or, theistic proofs are inconsistent with the nature of true religious faith.

But some philosophers of religion who eschew theistic proofs nevertheless want to defend religious belief. These philosophers typically turn to other sorts of arguments. We will consider two such efforts in this chapter. Both are examples of what might be called 'voluntaristic defences of theism', that is, defences that are designed to appeal to the will or faculty of choice. First we will consider Pascal's famous 'Wager'; then we will discuss William James' almost equally famous argument in his essay 'The Will to Believe.'[1]

II. PASCAL'S WAGER

Blaise Pascal (1623–62) was a French Catholic mathematician, philosopher and theologian. In his book *Pensées*, he offered an argument in favour of religious belief (indeed, in favour of Christian faith) that has come to be called 'Pascal's Wager'. It is, as noted, a voluntaristic defence of religion rather than a rational one. This does not mean, of course, that it is *irrational*; the Wager is meant to be a rational argument, and Pascal clearly wanted readers to use their reasoning ability in following it. But the point is that Pascal's main appeal in the argument is to readers' sense of their own self-interest. He wanted them to see that they should voluntarily decide in favour of Christian faith.

It is important to note that Pascal assumed that reason cannot by itself decide whether God exists or, if God does exist, what God is like. Neither atheism nor theism can be proved. He said: 'We know neither the existence nor the nature of God . . . If there is a God, He is infinitely incomprehensible, since, having neither parts nor limits, He has no affinity to us. We are then incapable of knowing either what He is or if He is.'[2]

Of course Pascal was a committed Christian who believed in the existence of God and believed he knew certain things about God. Indeed, as we will see, specific beliefs about what God is likely to do in certain circumstances play an important role in the Wager. These beliefs, Pascal held, were given to human beings by revelation and received 'by faith'. Pascal identified himself as one of those who has accepted them. His agnostic comments about the existence and nature of God, then, have to do with thinking about God apart from revelation and faith; they have to do with speaking about God, as he said, 'according to natural lights'. Either God exists or God does not exist, Pascal said, 'but to which side shall we incline? Reason can decide nothing here.'

If that much is true, Pascal asked, then why not simply decide not to decide whether God exists; why not simply suspend judgement? Indeed, Pascal's imagined interlocutor said of those who *have* chosen: 'I blame them for having made, not this choice, but a choice; for again both he who chooses heads and he who chooses tails are equally at fault, they are both in the wrong. The true course is not to wager at all.'

But Pascal wanted to insist that suspending judgement is not possible here. He said things like: 'You must wager. It is not optional.' 'You are under the necessity of playing.' You are 'forced to play'. 'I am forced to wager, and am not free.' I think it is best to understand Pascal's point in terms of a distinction made by William James that we will explore in more detail later in this chapter, namely, the distinction between an avoidable and a forced option. An avoidable option is one where two choices are given but there are actually others available. If a person says, 'Either call my theory true or call it false,' we can decide (for example) not to call it anything at all. But a forced option is an option where two choices are given and there are no others available. If a person says, 'Either accept this truth or go without it,' any decision that we might make – even if we decide not to decide whether to accept this truth or go without it – will be in effect a choice for one of the two alternatives.

Although Pascal did not use the term 'forced option', I think something like James' distinction was what he had in mind. The reason he held that you cannot opt out of the wager either for or against God is that whatever you decide to do – even if you decide not to wager at all – you will in effect be wagering one way or the other. A decision not to wager will be, in its consequences, a wager against God. So 'Either wager for God or against God' is a Jamesian forced option.

To be more precise, there is actually a disjunction and a forced option that Pascal thought that humans face. The disjunction is:

1. Either God exists or God does not exist;

and the forced option is:

2. Either I will have religious faith or I will not.

In neither case can reason, by itself, decide which is true (as in the case of (1)) or optimal (as in the case of (2)). Let's assume – as Pascal does – that the expression 'wagering for God', means both *believing that God exists* and *living in a religious manner*. You can 'wager against God' by failing to do either or by failing to do both. The claim that (1) and (2) are forced options, then, means that there is no neutrality; there is no way of avoiding choice; there is no third possible choice. As Pascal put it, 'you must wager.'

If we must choose, and if reason cannot decide, how then do we choose whether to wager for or against God? Pascal recommended that you decide on the basis of prudential considerations, that is, of possible gains and losses for yourself. That is, you should decide on the basis of considerations of personal interest.

Here is the heart of the wager argument:

> Let us weigh the gain and the loss in wagering that God is. Let us estimate these two chances. If you gain, you gain all; if you lose, you lose nothing. Wager, then, without hesitation, that He is.

There are actually two possible wagers, although Pascal only spoke of the first. First, *suppose I wager for God*. As already noted, this means both that I believe in the existence of God and that I live a religious life. Now there are two possible outcomes if I make this wager – I might be right and I might be wrong. If I am right (that is, God does exist), the outcome, Pascal says, is that I gain everything. By this he means eternal salvation. And if I am wrong (that is, God does not exist), I lose nothing. (Some might see here what economists call an opportunity cost and change the word 'nothing' to 'little'. Presumably I will lose something, namely, the chance to have all the sinful fun I could have had had I wagered against God. But of course Pascal might with some justification reply that compared to eternity a few years of sinful pleasures will not amount to much.)

Second, *suppose I wager against God*. This means that I do not believe in the existence of God and/or do not live a religious life. Again, there are two possible outcomes – I might be right and I might be wrong. If I am right (that is, God does not exist), Pascal would say, I gain nothing. Or again perhaps we should say little – I *would* gain a few brief years of sinful pleasures. And if I am wrong (that is, God does exist), I lose everything. That is, I will spend eternity apart from God in hell.

Notice how obvious it is that the first is the better bet. It gives me the chance of gaining everything against the chance of losing little, while the second wager gives me the chance of gaining little against the chance of losing everything. No wonder Pascal said, 'Wager, then, without hesitation that He is.' Any intelligent gambler, indeed any sane person, must recognise that wagering for God is the thing to do. What I must clearly do is believe in the existence of God and set out to live a religious life.

But what about those persons who have been convinced by the wager, who truly want to 'wager for God' (which as noted includes both behaving religiously and believing in the existence of God), but somehow cannot manage belief in God? These are people, Pascal says, 'who would like to attain faith, and do not know the way'; they 'would like to cure [themselves] of unbelief, and ask the remedy for it'. In a famous passage, Pascal gave such folk this advice:

> Learn of those who have been bound like you, and who now stake all their possessions. These are people who know the way which you would follow, and are cured of an ill of which you would be cured. Follow the way by which they began: by acting as if they believe, taking the holy water, having masses said, etc. Even this will naturally make you believe, and deaden your acuteness.

Pascal's surprising advice to people who do not believe but who want to do so seems then to be this: you should learn from those who have already been cured of the malady of unbelief and who have committed their lives and possessions to God; you should imitate their behaviour. Doing so will deaden the acuteness of your doubts, and you will come to believe.

III. CRITICISMS OF THE WAGER

Pascal's Wager has been criticised in many ways, some theological and some philosophical. Let us discuss four objections.

(1) *Can we make ourselves believe?*

Although this point is probably not at the heart of the issues raised by the Wager, Pascal's concluding advice about taking the holy water and having masses said has often been criticised. Our beliefs are not under our control, it is said. People who are convinced by the Wager that it is in their best interest to wager for God can surely decide, if they want, to start to *behave* religiously, but they cannot, just because they want to do so, start to *believe* religiously. Our beliefs do frequently change, but that is normally because the evidence – or our awareness of it – changes. There is no way that people who do not believe in God can consciously and voluntarily, so to speak, make themselves believe in God. Merely pretending that you believe something will not make you believe it.[3]

Let us be clear on exactly what Pascal was claiming. Consider a proposition p which I do not believe but would like to believe. Can I come to believe p not because of convincing evidence or cogent arguments in favour of p but because I *want* to believe p, where I want to believe p because I recognize that it is in my interest to believe p? Pascal seems to suggest that I can successfully make myself believe p as long as four criteria are satisfied:

a. The truth or falsity of p is not discoverable by reason.
b. I strongly desire to believe p.
c. I understand that belief in p is warranted for me because of prudential considerations.
d. I act as if I believe p.

I interpret Pascal as claiming that under these conditions I can cause myself to believe p. Let's call the claim that this is true 'Pascal's doctrine'.

We will now discuss each criterion briefly. Criterion (a) rules out counter-examples like this: Suppose an eccentric millionaire who owns an infallible lie-detecting machine offers me a million dollars if I can make myself genuinely believe that somewhere hidden in the university library is a twenty-foot-tall live rhinoceros covered with pink polka dots. Probably I could *not* make myself believe this proposition, but that does not refute Pascal's doctrine, since the presence or absence of such a rhinoceros in the library *is* 'discoverable by reason'. Criterion (b) rules out counter-examples like this: Suppose an eccentric millionaire with an infallible lie-detecting machine offers me a million dollars if I can make myself genuinely believe that my life will be a miserable and unhappy failure, million dollars or not. Possibly I could *not* make myself believe *that*; but since I have no desire at all to believe this particular proposition, the suggested counter-example does not refute Pascal's doctrine.

Criterion (c) is important because it entails that I understand that my believing *p* is warranted – warranted for prudential rather than evidential reasons. So Pascal's doctrine has nothing to do with my making myself believe propositions that have no bearing on my own interests. Suppose our eccentric millionaire offers me a million dollars if I can genuinely make myself believe that Thadeus Smithson ought to be elected dog-catcher of Yankton, South Dakota. Since this proposition has no bearing on my personal interests, it would not constitute a counter-example to Pascal's doctrine even if I could not make myself believe it. Another point emerges here: since it is rationally warranted for me to believe in God, then clearly what prevents me from believing, and what must be overcome, are non-rational factors. Pascal called them 'passions', by which he seems to have meant emotions or dispositions that attract people to worldly things. Unbelief, then, is a matter of habit.

Criterion (d) needs some spelling out. What does it mean to 'act as if you believe *p*'? Pascal thought it means doing the things that believers in *p* do, for example, taking holy water and having masses said. In other words, I need to change my bad habits, form new dispositions. I should not only attend religious services but also strive to change my moral behaviour. I should, as Pascal says, do my best to become 'faithful, honest, humble, grateful, generous, a sincere friend, truthful'. Going beyond Pascal's specific advice, it seems I could also associate regularly with believers, commit myself publicly to the religious life, look for evidence that supports the existence of God, have long conversations with intelligent apologists for belief in God, never question or criticise the central claims or practices of religion, look for new interpretations of the evidence that causes me to doubt, read the books of great theologians, etc.

Pascal was saying, then, that if these criteria are satisfied, I will come to believe *p*. It is important to note that he was not claiming that I can make myself believe *p* directly, that is, simply decide to believe *p*. (Perhaps Hume was right about that.) He was instead saying that under the stated circumstances I can take certain steps that will indirectly bring it about that I believe *p*. He did not say how long it would take; perhaps for some people it will take some considerable time. But, eventually, it will happen: I will find myself believing *p*.

My own view is that Pascal's doctrine is correct, but I know of no way to prove it. The question is not strictly or completely a philosophical one; perhaps it is an issue in psychology. Those who accept Pascal's doctrine will hold that it is a psychological fact about human beings that given the stated conditions we can make ourselves believe a proposition we did not originally believe. The doctrine seems sensible; to some extent our beliefs are caused by our experiences; and to some extent we can exercise control over the experiences we have. It seems to follow, then, that to some extent our beliefs are under our control.[4]

(2) *Following Pascal's Wager is intellectually dishonest*

This criticism follows directly from the first. The claim here is that to follow Pascal's advice violates the ethics of belief. To pretend that I believe something that I do not in fact believe is a kind of self-deception, a way of lying to myself. J. L. Mackie, for example, admits that Pascal's doctrine is true ('indirect voluntary belief is possible') but argues that to attempt to cause myself to believe in God is 'a hopeful delusion, a self-deception'. He says:

> Deliberately to make oneself believe, by such techniques as [Pascal] suggests – especially by playing tricks on oneself that are found by experience to work upon people's passions and to give rise to belief in non-rational ways – *is* to do violence to one's reason and under- standing . . . In deliberately cultivating non-rational belief, one would be suppressing one's critical faculties . . . To decide to cultivate belief in God, when, epistemically, the odds are n to one against his existing, and n is some large number, is deliberately to reject all rational principles of belief in uncertainty.[5]

But Mackie's criticism is based on a misunderstanding of Pascal. Mackie apparently takes the expression 'non-rational belief', to mean belief in propositions that are highly improbable or contrary to the preponderance of available evidence. But then Mackie is wrong in interpreting Pascal as recommending non-rational belief. For two reasons, the Wager has no relevance to such beliefs. First, Pascal was only concerned with proposi- tions in which belief is warranted (although that warrant is prudential). Second, Pascal limited himself to propositions whose truth or falsity is not discoverable by reason. So the Wager has nothing to say on the question whether I should ever believe, or cause myself to come to believe, a proposition against whose truth the odds are n to one (where n is some large number).

But quite apart from Mackie's misinterpretation, the criticism of Pascal that he is driving at can still be pushed. The criticism will now say that it is irrational and intellectually immoral under *any* circumstances to believe a proposition for prudential reasons alone. A counter-example might even be suggested: Suppose our eccentric millionaire makes another offer – a million dollars if I can make myself genuinely believe that it will rain in Claremont on 25 April, AD 2031. Even if I could make myself believe this proposition – so the objection would run – to do so would be an immoral affront to reason, a violation of the ethics of belief. What I ought to do is simply suspend judgement on the truth of the proposition until conclusive evidence is available. Beliefs ought to aim at truth, not benefit, and the benefits of my believing the proposition in question have no bearing whatsoever on its truth and thus on its believability.

But in response to this criticism we must return to Pascal's claim that wagering is not optional. Perhaps we *should* suspend judgement on the question of whether it will rain in Claremont on 25 April 2031. But if Pascal is right, we *cannot* suspend judgement on the question of whether to wager for God. Here there is no third alternative beside wagering or not wagering; if I decide not to decide whether to wager for or against God, I will wager against God. If suspension of judgement is impossible in the case of wagering for or against God, the criticism we are discussing cannot even get going.

Suspension of judgement is psychologically possible, of course. Pascal knew that. Indeed, it was at people who had suspended judgement that he was directing his Wager. Pascal's point was that for the one who has suspended judgement, the pragmatic consequences will be the same as they are for the one who chooses to wager against God. Accordingly, we can conclude as follows: if reason is unable to determine the truth or falsity of *p*, and if it is in my interest to believe *p*, and if I *must* decide either to believe *p* or not to believe *p*, then I am within my intellectual rights in believing *p*.

(3) *The Wager presupposes a low view of God and religious faith*

A pointed statement of this criticism is found in William James:

> We feel that a faith in masses and holy water adopted wilfully after such a mechanical calculation would lack the inner soul of faith's reality; and if we were ourselves in the place of the Deity, we should probably take particular pleasure in cutting off believers of this pattern from their infinite reward.[6]

In other words, the sort of faith in God Pascal seems to be recommending bears little resemblance to real religious faith. Pascal's recommended attitude – a kind of scheming, calculating regard for the potential rewards and punishments of the two possible wagers – seems irreligious. And what kind of God would be pleased by the sort of attitude we see here – an attitude we associate more with professional gamblers or venture capitalists than genuine religious believers? For such people undeniably sense the presence of God in their lives; they love God disinterestedly; they commit themselves wholeheartedly to the service of God and the welfare of others.

But this is a strange criticism. Pascal nowhere says that the path of the Wager is the only or even the optimal route to faith. Indeed, in the Wager argument Pascal was clearly formulating a desperate, last-ditch appeal to a certain sort of person, namely, a person who is perched precariously on the fence separating belief and unbelief. Perhaps this person's heart inclines her toward religion, but her passions or her intellectual scruples will not allow her to move in that direction. Similarly, Pascal nowhere says that the impulse toward God and religion that the Wager might stir in me constitutes the fulness of religious faith. His hope doubtless was that this impulse would grow into mature faith, into the kind of sure sense of the presence of God and disinterested love of God that we see in genuine believers.[7]

Will God be pleased by the calculating psychological egoism of the wagerer? In certain cases, perhaps not. We can easily imagine with James that God will be displeased by a person who comes to believe via Pascal's Wager and whose faith never progresses beyond the stage of shrewd self-regard or bare intellectual assent. But perhaps in other cases God will not mind, especially if the actions and beliefs produced by the Wager are essential first steps toward genuine faith. For Pascal was presumably envisioning something like this: people who are convinced by the Wager will later have confirming experiences that will reduce their doubt, strengthen their faith, and lead them to certainty. Thus Pascal said: 'At each step you take on this road, you will see so great certainty of gain, so much nothingness in what you risk, that you will at last recognize that you have wagered for something certain.'

(4) The 'many Gods' objection

The final objection that we will consider is the most profound. If it does not refute Pascal's argument, it certainly limits severely its applicability. The objection is that Pascal does not consider all the possible Gods or gods that might exist. It is true that

1. Either God exists or God does not exist

is a forced option. But given his Christian orientation, it is clear that Pascal interprets (1) as

1a. Either the Christian God exists or the Christian God does not exist.

Pascal needs to assume (1a) because his arguments about how God is likely to respond to humans who wager either for or against God depend on his Christian beliefs. And (1a), too, is a forced option. There is no third possibility.

But the problem is that in the Wager, Pascal actually seems to be working with another, quite different option. This is the one his Wager argument depends on:

1c. Either the Christian God exists or no God exists.

And this is not a forced option. Indeed, there are scores of other Gods or gods that are actually worshipped in the religions of the world, and there is no guarantee that they will dispense rewards and punishments in the way that Pascal says that the Christian God will do. There are also an infinite number of possible or conceivable Gods of whom no one has ever heard, including a God who rewards everyone with eternal bliss *except* those folks who have ever taken 'the holy water' or had 'masses said' or tried to live a Christian life, whom this God sends straight to hell.

The Wager is flawed, then, because Pascal illicitly assumes (1c). He does not rule out any of the many possibilities that involve some God other than the Christian God existing. Of course a defender of Pascal might respond that we do not have to consider all the logically possible Gods in Wager-type arguments, only the most probable ones. Perhaps we only need to consider seriously those Gods or gods that are actually worshipped and that have a developed and coherent system of beliefs and practices associated with them.[8] And it is at least possible that apologists for the Christian God might offer arguments designed to show that their God is the most probable, and that accordingly the two best options are (1) atheism and (2) Christianity.[9] Pascal himself may have thought that (1a) and (1c) were equivalent because of apologetic arguments whose conclusions were that no other religion than Christianity is even plausibly true. Whether there are such arguments we will not try to judge here.

The limitations of the Wager appear to be these: Pascal's argument has no relevance to committed atheists or religious sceptics who hold that reason *can* prove something here, namely, that religion is irrational. It has no relevance to hedonists who live only for the present moment or the near future; those who care nothing about long-term consequences will care little for Pascal's arguments about eternal heaven or hell. It has no relevance to those who perhaps believe in the existence of God but suspect that we can know little or nothing about God – and certainly nothing about how and under what conditions God is likely to reward or punish human beings. Finally, it has no relevance to people who face non-forced options in religion – like the person who is truly struggling with the issue of whether to be an atheist, a Christian or a Zen Buddhist.

If Pascal's Wager is a sound argument at all, it is so only for a person who: (1) thinks that both Christianity and atheism are intellectually unproven but are also unrefuted; (2) entertains a roughly Christian view of God; (3) is concerned about long-term consequences; and (4) is truly struggling with the option of whether to wager for God (that is, the Christian God) or against God.

IV. JAMES' ARGUMENT

William James (1842–1910) spent most of his life at Harvard. During his adult life, he moved from medicine to psychiatry to psychology and finally to philosophy. He is best known as the founder of the school of American philosophy known as Pragmatism. James himself was not religious in any orthodox sense – he was not associated with any church or denomination. But he did hold a vaguely theistic view of the world, and he definitely believed in the intellectual right of religious people to believe as they do despite their inability to produce cogent arguments or convincing evidence. The argument I am interested in is found most centrally in his early essay 'The Will to Believe' (1897), as well as in two other early essays, especially 'The Sentiment of Rationality' (1879) and 'Is Life Worth Living?' (1895).[10]

Let us define the term 'evidence-situation' as any circumstance in which a person wonders whether a given proposition is true, or argues for or against it. Obviously, evidence-situations are common; they typically occur when the truth of some proposition is challenged. A wide variety of evidence-situations occur, and there are many different ways of confirming or disconfirming propositions. Our behaviour in evidence-situations is normally guided by a principle that I will call 'Russell's Principle' (in honour of Bertrand Russell, whose words they are):

> Give to any hypothesis that is worth your while to consider just that degree of credence which the evidence warrants.[11]

Russell's Principle seems to be a commonly accepted criterion of rationality. That is, those who base their belief on evidence – both which propositions they believe and which they do not, and the *degree* of their belief or lack of it – are considered rational people. Russell's Principle is, then, a guide for cognitive attitudes and behaviour in evidence-situations.

There is a corollary of Russell's Principle, one that is almost as commonly accepted. A striking version of it is provided by W. K. Clifford, a nineteenth-century mathematician and philosopher: 'It is wrong always, everywhere, and for anyone to believe anything upon insufficient evidence.'[12] It is against this claim – especially as it relates to religious belief – that James explicitly argued in 'The Will To Believe'.

Let us further stipulate that there are five main categories of evidence situations. Any proposition *p* whose truth is challenged or wondered about will fit into one of these five categories:

1. There is adequate evidence for *p* (that is, evidence that is as good or convincing as it can or need be).
2. There is some evidence that *p*, but not adequate evidence that *p*. (Or the evidence that *p* outweighs the evidence that not-*p*, but not decisively.)
3. Either there is no evidence available relevant to the truth or falsity of *p* or else the evidence that *p* is neither stronger nor weaker than the evidence that not-*p*.
4. There is some evidence that not-*p*, but not adequate evidence that not-*p*. (Or the evidence that not-*p* outweighs the evidence that *p*, but not decisively.)
5. There is adequate evidence for not-*p* (that is, evidence that is as good or convincing as it can or need be).

It would appear that Russell's Principle dictates roughly the following cognitive attitudes toward *p*: in case (1) a firm commitment to the truth of *p*; in case (5) a firm commitment to the truth of not-*p*; in case (2) a tentative commitment to the truth of *p*; in case (4) a tentative commitment to the truth of not-*p*; and in case (3) a refusal to commit oneself at all (suspension of judgement).

In 'The Will to Believe', James was interested in evidence-situations that fit category (3), especially religious propositions (although his argument can be applied to claims that have nothing to do with religion). The central thesis of the essay is that we are sometimes warranted in believing a religious proposition on grounds other than the available evidence, where the truth of the proposition has not been established by evidence. James was attacking the implicit claim of Russell's Principle that in all cases of ambiguous evidence, the only rational behaviour is suspension of judgement.[13]

Of course James was not allowing for rational belief in any or all non-evident propositions. Indeed, he stressed that his argument was only relevant to a certain sort of epistemic situation, and he described that situation – which he called a 'genuine option' – with some care. Notice that James used the term 'option' in two different senses: an option can be either an entire situation in which a choice must be made between two or more alternatives ('Your option is either steak or pizza') or it can be one of the two choices ('You may take the steak option or the pizza option'). James listed three criteria of genuineness – the option must be live, momentous, and forced – but it is important to note that an option must meet *four* criteria in order to be genuine. (James was always careful to add the fourth before bringing in his 'right to believe' doctrine.) Since it will simplify matters, I will call an option genuine only if it satisfies all four criteria.

6. The option must be live.
7. The option must be momentous.
8. The option must be forced.
9. The option must not be decidable 'on intellectual grounds'.

James' descriptions of the criteria are brief and vivid, but in some cases they raise questions that he does not answer. Let me discuss each criterion and, in some cases, try to clarify matters.

Liveness

If I must choose between the two alternatives (or options) of an option, they can be either live or dead to me. A live option is one that appeals to me as a distinct possibility; it tempts me, so to speak; while a dead option does not. Here James gave the example of the Mahdi, who was a nineteenth-century Moslem religious and military leader. Speaking to the philosophy students at Yale and Brown, to whom his essay was originally addressed, James said that belief in the Mahdi 'makes no electric connection with your nature, – it refuses to scintillate with any credibility at all.'[14] Obviously, there is a degree of subjectivity here – what appeals to or tempts the belief of one person will not do so for another. So an option might be live for one person (if both its alternatives are live) and dead for another (if one or both alternatives are dead).

Momentousness

A momentous option is one in which something important and unique is offered, something that will be irrevocably lost if rejected. James said:

> If I were Dr. Nansen and proposed to you to join my North Pole expedition, your option would be momentous; for this would probably be your only similar opportunity, and your choice now would either exclude you from the North Pole sort of immortality altogether or put at least the chance of it into your hands.[15]

A trivial option is one in which the offered option is unimportant or repeatable. There appear to be three conditions here. An option will be momentous if and only if one of its alternatives is unique (this is my only chance for it), important (I consider it crucial), and irreversible (if I reject the option now, I will never have another chance). Obviously there will be some degree of subjectivism here too – an option may be momentous to one person and trivial to another.

Forcedness

As we noted with Pascal, a forced option is a dilemma based on a perfect disjunction in which I *must* choose one option or the other. The two alternatives are both mutually exclusive and exhaustive of all the possibilities. An avoidable option is one in which I need not choose one or the other of the offered alternatives. 'Either call my theory true or call it false,' James said, is an avoidable option, because I can choose (for example) not to call the theory anything at all. But 'Either accept this truth or go without it,' James said, is forced.[16] Whatever I decide to do, even if I decide not to decide whether to accept this truth or go without it, I will in effect be choosing one of the two offered alternatives. Of course even in the case of a forced option, nothing prevents me from suspending judgement or deciding not to decide – but James' point was that the consequences will be the same as they would have been had I consciously opted for one of the alternatives.

Ambiguity

The option must be one, James said, which 'the intellect of the individual cannot by itself decide'.[17] By this I take James to mean that the evidence must be ambiguous as to which of the two alternatives of the option is more probable. Obviously, where the truth *can* be settled on intellectual grounds – for example, in determining whether San Francisco is north of Los Angeles – the 'right to believe' doctrine is irrelevant. Whenever conclusive evidence is available, it takes precedence and decides the case. James' fourth criterion, then, amounts to saying that in order for an option to be genuine, it must be what I called earlier a case (3) evidence-situation.[18] The available evidence, if there is any at all, is not sufficient in and of itself to warrant a choice.

Here, then, is the pay-off: in the unique case of a genuine option, and only in that case, we are justified in believing as our will or 'passional nature' directs. Thus James said:

> Our passional nature not only lawfully may, but must, decide an option between propositions, whenever it is a genuine option that cannot by its nature be decided on intellectual grounds.[19]

James never defined exactly what he meant by the 'passional nature', but it is clearly not the same as what Pascal meant by 'the passions'. What James means to exclude by this term is our 'intellectual nature' or 'pure intellect'. Let us simply stipulate that the passional nature consists of human needs that are emotional, moral, aesthetic, religious, or practical. With full epistemic justification, then, we can choose (on the basis of our hopes and needs) to believe any proposition that is one of the alternatives of a genuine option. (Of course this does not mean that the proposition is true – the point of the ambiguity criterion is that its truth is unknown – but simply that we are warranted in believing it.)

However, when we look carefully, it appears that two of James' criteria are somewhat superfluous. Liveness and momentousness might have some value in limiting the range of James' 'right to believe' argument to situations of actual concern to people. And without momentousness, people might not particularly care which option is chosen. Still, liveness and momentousness are not strictly needed. If Russell's principle tells us that in all cases of ambiguous evidence, including religion, the rational thing to do is suspend judgement, then James' reply can be simpler than he imagined. He only needs two criteria:

10. There is a forced option between two alternatives, that is, the two alternatives are mutually exclusive and are exhaustive of all possible choices.
11. The evidence is ambiguous on the truth or falsity of the two alternatives.

James wanted to show that Russell's Principle does not always hold. But surely if an option is forced – we *must* decide – it does not matter whether it is also live or momentous. Thus criterion (10) rules out the possibility of not choosing and criterion (11) rules out the possibility of choosing on the basis of evidence. All that is left, then, is to choose on some basis other than evidence, for example, a passional basis, which was what James was trying to show. The point is that a belief (religious or not) in the sort of case that James has in mind is fully epistemologically justified; the person who holds the belief cannot be criticised as gullible or credulous or soft-headed; the person is morally right, according to the ethics of belief, in holding the belief.

Clearly, then, James saw himself as having supplied a warrant for belief in God quite apart from any sort of theistic proof. This is always provided, of course, that the two crucial criteria are satisfied. That is, 'I will believe in God or I will not believe in God' must be a forced option (which, stated in that way, it surely is) and the evidence relative to the existence of God must be ambiguous, that is, evenly balanced pro and con. (James' own terse discussion of what he calls 'The Religious Option' in Section X of 'The Will to Believe' is vague and of questionable relevance, let alone coherence, so I will not discuss it here.)[20]

Now it is obvious that not all religious options are forced – there may be someone who is facing the option 'Shall I become a Christian, an atheist, or a Zoroastrian?,' and that is not a forced option. It is equally obvious that on many religious questions, the evidence is not ambiguous – maybe someone somewhere is trying to decide whether to believe that the universe was created in 4004 BC – and the evidence is quite clearly and decisively against this claim. But I will take it as given that some people, on some occasions, face religious options in which the two criteria are satisfied.

A final point should be made here, a clear difference between James and Pascal that ought not to be overlooked. Pascal's Wager is essentially an evangelistic device: his argument was an attempt to convert people to religious faith. (James noticed this: he said that in the Wager Pascal 'tries to force us into Christianity.')[21] But James's 'right to believe' doctrine should not be viewed in this way. He was not trying to convince us that we should believe: he was only trying to convince us (if the belief is an alternative of a genuine option) that we are epistemologically justified in believing *if belief is what we want*. His doctrine also justifies refusing to believe (say, in God), if *that* is what we want. What James was opposing in the 'right to believe' doctrine is any insistence that suspension of judgement is *always* the *only* justified attitude in cases involving lack of adequate evidence.

V. OBJECTIONS TO JAMES' ARGUMENT

James' 'right to believe' argument has been criticised in a great number of ways. Let us consider three of the more easily answered objections before turning to a serious one.

(1) Some react with near-hysteria to James' argument. Is not James obviously wrong if he deems 'rational' the belief of paranoids that their friends are out to kill them or the belief of religious fanatics that the world will end tomorrow at noon or the belief of a man in a train that the unknown man in the same car is named Ebenezer Wilkes Smith (just because the first man has always desperately wanted to meet someone with that name)?[22] But the answer to this is that the ambiguity criterion is being ignored here. James' 'right to believe' doctrine does not warrant the holding of absurd or superstitious or highly improbable beliefs, for the ambiguity criterion is not satisfied in such cases.

(2) Others argue that James has opened the door of belief in non-evident propositions too widely; an enormous range of cases will fit his criteria,

and surely belief in non-evident propositions is habit-forming, and will spread to other areas.[23] But it seems that the door is only slightly ajar: the severe limitations James places on the range of his argument – even if we eliminate two of his four criteria – will prevent the virus from spreading. Furthermore, James stresses that those who believe a non-evident proposition in the case of a genuine option retain their rationality only if they keep an open mind to future evidence. The evidence one day may no longer be ambiguous.[24]

(3) Others have argued that the view of faith that James presupposes and defends has little to do with the living faith of the true religious believer.[25] Few believers carefully reason their way through to the conclusion that certain religious propositions are instances of genuine options and can accordingly be believed. Indeed, the very idea seems absurd. Believers are absolutely certain; they want to say that they *know* God. But while all of this is true, it is obviously not much of a criticism of James' argument. He was not, in 'The Will to Believe', trying to analyse religious faith – he was not claiming that religious faith is like a scientific hypothesis, gambled upon prudently but tentatively. He was doing philosophy of religion. He was showing how some religious beliefs can be warranted.

(4) By far the most serious objection to James' argument is that it amounts to a recommendation of wishful thinking. Let us treat this point a bit more extensively than the first three. Suppose we define 'wishful thinking' as believing a proposition not because of evidence that it is true but because of a desire that it be true. It is clear that wishful thinking, defined in this way, is an intellectual weakness or fault. When we note children or even adults engaging in it, we usually endeavour to correct them. As Dickenson Miller says, 'Our wishes and goals are one thing; the stubborn necessities of the world in which we have to attain them by action are another.'[26] Hick says that James' 'right to believe' doctrine 'authorizes us to believe . . . any proposition, not demonstrably false, which it might be advantageous to us, in this world or another, to have accepted.' It amounts to saying 'that since the truth is unknown to us we may believe what we like and that while we are about it we had better believe what we like most.'[27]

It is easy to see that Miller and Hick have misrepresented James. If he were recommending what they say he is recommending, James' argument would indeed be objectionable. But only someone who has not paid close attention to the strict limits James draws around his argument (that is, the criteria of genuineness) could argue that he was advocating 'believing a proposition because you want to believe it'. But pointing this out in defence of James, important as it is, does not make the 'wishful thinking' charge go away. For a more careful 'wishful thinking' critic would claim not that James was advocating 'believing whatever proposition you want to believe' but rather 'believing whatever proposition you want to believe *that is an alternative of a genuine option*'. James *was* advocating that. And the more careful critic could simply charge that to do so is to advocate wishful thinking.

The proper route for a defender of James is, I believe, not sternly to deny that this amounts to wishful thinking. It is rather cheerfully to admit that it amounts to (a species of) wishful thinking and then ask: But what precisely is wrong with wishful thinking in evidence-situations involving genuine options? There is, of course, Miller's previously-noted argument that wishful thinking spreads like a virus and if allowed in one area will extend to others. But, again, the careful limits of James' doctrine would surely prevent this. Here we see the real subtlety of James' argument: James was not stupidly flying in the face of Russell's Principle (as perhaps Miller and Hick assume); he was rather *questioning* the Principle, denying that it always holds.

Is there any way to test the 'right to believe' doctrine? One way might be to conduct the thought experiment of considering real or imagined cases of genuine options. The point would be to ask whether James' advice – believe what you would like to be true – seems sensible in those cases, or whether Russell's Principle still seems to hold.

Imagine the following situation: while entering a steep downgrade, a truck driver suddenly discovers that her brakes have failed. The truck is starting to pick up speed and the driver sees that soon she will be in danger. The driver is faced with a choice: she can either immediately jump from the truck, risking bruises and broken bones while escaping the greater danger of a possible crash farther down the hill. Or she can remain in the truck, risking a crash but hoping eventually to guide it down the hill to a level spot. But the driver does not know how long the downgrade is; she cannot see where it ends and this stretch of road is new to her.

It surely seems that this is a genuine option for the driver. It is live, because both possibilities appeal to her as distinct possibilities. It is forced, because there is no third option beside jumping now or staying with the truck (jumping later is a logical possibility, but is clearly too unsafe to be seriously considered). It is momentous, because her life is at stake. And the evidence is ambiguous because, let's say, neither possibility seems to her any safer or more dangerous than the other. Of course James had more reflective, intellectual situations in mind than this when he wrote 'The Will to Believe'; in our thought experiment the driver must make up her mind almost instantaneously on the basis of the limited evidence that is available to her. Still, if this case does amount to a genuine option, then James would claim that she now has the intellectual right to choose whichever option she wants to choose, to let her passional nature decide.

But the more careful 'wishful thinking' critic will now argue that the passional nature of the driver has nothing to do with the question of which is the safer choice. (We can imagine that one of the two options might prove to be objectively safer than the other to the driver and to other drivers and passengers on the road that day; experiments with many volunteer drivers in similar trucks trying out both options could be carried out.) The critic will claim that the driver has no other rational choice than to make up her mind on the basis of the (admittedly meagre) evidence that is available to her at the moment – her own driving abilities, the speed of the truck at the moment of decision, the appearance of the road ahead, the terrain at the side of the road (where she could possibly jump), etc.

In other words, the critic will argue that Russell's Principle still holds in cases such as this for the simple reason that the driver's passional nature might opt for the wrong alternative, the more dangerous one. But this leaves James the option of replying, 'What evidence is there, in this or any other case of a genuine option, that deciding on the basis of one's passional nature is more likely to lead to the wrong decision than deciding on the basis of the evidence, which we are granting is ambiguous?' He could go on and say: 'If this is a case that *can* (and thus *should*) be decided on the basis of evidence, then it is not a genuine option, and thus not a legitimate counter-example to the "right to believe" argument.'

Here, then, is one way that James' argument might be defended against the 'wishful thinking' criticism. The passional nature can justifiably determine choice in the case of any forced option where the available preponderance of evidence in favour of one alternative over the other is so slight that choosing on the basis of evidence gives no better chance of making what will turn out to be the correct choice than choosing on the basis of one's passional nature.

NOTES

1. C. Stephen Evans carefully discusses various versions of fideism in *Faith Beyond Reason* (Edinburgh: Edinburgh University Press, 1998).
2. Unless otherwise indicated, all quotations from Pascal in this chapter are from Section 233 of Blaise Pascal, *Pascal's Pensées*, trans. by W. F. Trotter (New York: E. P. Dutton, 1958). The 'Infinite/ Nothing' section (Section 233 in Brunschvicg's numeration) is on pp. 65–9.
3. Thus David Hume said: 'We may, therefore, conclude, that belief consists merely in a certain feeling or sentiment; in something that depends not on the will, but must arise from certain determinate causes and principles, of which we are not masters.' David Hume, *A Treatise on Human Nature*, ed. by L. A. Selby-Bigge (Oxford: Clarendon Press, 1988), Appendix, p. 624.
4. For further exploration of this issue, see Stephen T. Davis, 'Pascal on Self-Caused Belief', *Religious Studies*, Vol. 27, No. 1 (March, 1991), pp. 27–37.

5. J. L. Mackie, *The Miracle of Theism* (Oxford: Clarendon Press, 1982), p. 202.
6. William James, 'The Will to Believe', in *The Will to Believe and Other Essays in Popular Philosophy* (New York: Dover Publications, 1956), p. 6.
7. This point is made nicely by James Cargile in 'Pascal's Wager', in S. Cahn and D. Shatz (eds), *Contemporary Philosophy of Religion* (Oxford: Oxford University Press, 1982), p. 231.
8. See George Schlesinger, 'A Central Theistic Argument', in Jeff Jordan (ed.), *Gambling on God: Essays on Pascal's Wager* (Lanham, Maryland: Rowan and Littlefield, 1994), pp. 83–99.
9. See Thomas V. Morris, 'Wagering and the Evidence', in Jeff Jordan (ed.), *Gambling on God*, pp. 47–60.
10. All are found in William James, *The Will to Believe and Other Essays in Popular Philosophy*. In order to avoid confusion, I must note that I will be concerned with views James held *prior* to his explicit avowal of pragmatism and the pragmatic theory of truth. Let me also note that James' essay 'The Will to Believe' has been interpreted in a great variety of ways, some of them in my opinion hopelessly wrong. I offer my own interpretation in this chapter; it is developed more fully in Stephen T. Davis, *Faith, Skepticism, and Evidence: An Essay in Religious Epistemology* (Bucknell, Pennsylvania: Bucknell University Press, 1978), pp. 89–187.
11. It is found in Russell's discussion of James' 'Will to Believe' argument. See Bertrand Russell, *A History of Western Philosophy* (New York: Simon and Schuster, 1945), p. 816.
12. W. K. Clifford, *Lectures and Essays*, ed. by Leslie Stephen and Frederick Pollack (New York: Macmillan and Company, 1901), Vol. II, p. 186.
13. It is now recognised that there are two quite distinct theses in 'The Will to Believe' – what is called the 'Will to Believe' thesis (the claim that in some cases belief can be self-verifying, that is, sometimes believing *p* can make or help make *p* true) and the 'Right to Believe' thesis, the argument about belief policy and rationality that I am discussing in this chapter. I will not deal with the 'Will to Believe' thesis here. See Gail Kennedy, 'Pragmatism, Pragmaticism, and The Will To Believe – A Reconsideration', *The Journal of Philosophy*, Vol. 55 (1958), pp. 578–88.
14. 'The Will to Believe', p. 2.
15. 'The Will to Believe', p. 4.
16. 'The Will to Believe', p. 3.
17. 'The Will to Believe', p. 29.
18. James made this point in various places in 'The Will to Believe', using such expressions as: the available evidence is 'insufficient', 'doubt is still theoretically possible', belief would be 'going beyond the literal evidence', 'our mere logical intellect may or may not have been coerced', there is no objective 'proof' or 'evidence' because not all the evidence is yet 'in', 'there is no outward proof', the claim cannot be 'refuted or proved by logic' or be 'decided on intellectual grounds', etc.
19. 'The Will to Believe,' p. 11.
20. See Davis, *Faith, Skepticism and Evidence*, pp. 169–87 for discussion of it.
21. 'The Will to Believe', p. 5.
22. This last is Russell's criticism of James. See *A History of Western Philosophy*, p. 816. Sadly, Russell criticises nothing but a cruel caricature of James' argument. One almost feels he did not bother to read 'The Will to Believe'; he certainly did not read it carefully.
23. See John Hick, *Faith and Knowledge*, 2nd edn (Ithaca, New York: Cornell University Press, 1966), p. 42; and Dickenson Miller, 'James' Doctrine of "The Right to Believe"', *The Philosophical Review*, Vol. 51 (1942), pp. 557–8.
24. 'The Will to Believe,' p. 14.
25. See, among others, Hick, *Faith and Knowledge*, p. 55; Miller, 'James' Doctrine of "The Right to Believe"', pp. 547–8.
26. Miller, 'James' Doctrine of "The Right to Believe"', pp. 552–4.
27. Hick, *Faith and Knowledge*, pp. 42, 44.

10

Conclusion

I. INTRODUCTION

In this concluding chapter, I shall discuss three main issues. First, I will consider the question of what is at stake in debates over theistic proofs. That is, I want to ask how important an issue this is. I will argue that the existence of God is as important an issue as human beings ever face.

Second, we need to consider a question that has come up at various points in the book but has been postponed till now, namely, the question of whether any of the theistic proofs counts as a proof not just of the first mover or the designer of the universe but of the God of theism. Is the God of the theistic proofs the same God as the God who is worshipped, for example, by Jews, Christians and/or Moslems?

Third, we shall continue the conversation started in Chapter 1 about the value of theistic proofs. We will consider the motivation of those who offer theistic proofs; that is, we will ask what theistic provers try, or should try, to accomplish. We will also ask about reasons for the great variety of attitudes toward theistic proofs that we see in the history of theology and philosophy.

II. HOW IMPORTANT IS THE EXISTENCE OF GOD?

What then is at stake in the debate over theistic proofs? Or, more precisely, what is at stake when we debate the question whether the God of theism exists? The first point to be made is that there is obviously a certain degree of subjectivity here. Some people care deeply about the question whether God exists (even some atheists or agnostics), and some do not. But for other people, it would not matter much at all if a given theistic proof turned out to be successful, or even if they themselves believed or came to believe in the existence of God. Whether they believe in the existence of God or not, they live their lives as if God were absent; it makes no real practical or existential difference to them.

Wittgensteinian philosophers of religion sometimes stress the point that coming to believe that God exists is not like coming to believe that molecules or hyenas exist. This point is largely correct, although (as I argued in Chapter 3), I do not agree with everything that the Wittgensteinians think follows from it. The point is fairly made that coming to believe in God, for a person who was an atheist or agnostic, typically involves a change of life. My only caveat is that it *need* not do so. There are people who do not believe in God and who could come to believe in God with that change having little effect on their lives. They would not necessarily start praying or attending religious services.

For other people, however, the question of whether God exists is the most important question of all. I am one of them. I will give some arguments in favour of this point momentarily.

Let us look briefly at some of the views about God and the meaning of life advanced by Albert Camus (1913–60) in his 1941 book *The Myth of Sisyphus*.[1] Camus was an atheist who dealt honestly and even courageously with the question of the meaning of life in the absence of God. He seems clearly to have been a thinker whose philosophy would have had to change had he become convinced that God existed. (Camus's thought in the late 1950s seems to have been moving in a trajectory towards a less critical view of religion, but his death in a car crash in the south of France in 1960 cut short any further development in that or any other direction.)

Camus's basic assumption was that life is absurd. What this means, he said, is that human beings have certain questions that life does not answer and certain hopes that life does not satisfy. We long for some sort of Meaning in Life, but there is none. (Let's say that the expression 'Meaning of Life' in capital letters refers to a meaning that is there in reality to be discovered, and exists quite apart from what any human being thinks or does; and that the expression 'meaning of life' in lower-case letters refers to meanings that we create by our actions or projects.) We want there to exist a kindly, loving God, but no such being exists. Indeed, *no* God exists. We hope for life after death, but death is the end of our existence. We long for some sort of grand, over-arching explanation of life and history and human existence, but no such explanation is available.

In the light of life's absurdity, Camus said, we can do one of three things. First, we can embrace some kind of hope – typically a religious hope – that life is not absurd after all. Second, convinced that life is pointless and empty, we can commit suicide. Third, we can do what Camus calls live absurdly; we can 'revolt'. The central claim of Camus's book is that we should embrace this third alternative.

One of Camus' arguments for this conclusion – he had others – is based on his unstated but nevertheless clearly presupposed premise that life itself is of intrinsic value. Accordingly, he placed great emphasis on the amount of time that one lives. 'What counts', he said, 'is not the best living but the most living.'[2] Of course quality of life was also important for Camus – his strong ethical concerns are well known, especially in some of his later writings. But he really did emphasise, in a surprising way, quantity over quality. 'The point is to live,'[3] he said. Some people live longer than others – they are the lucky ones. Those whose lives are cut short are simply unlucky – 'A premature death is irreparable.'[4] Thus Camus said:

> Let us say that the sole obstacle, the sole deficiency to be made good, is constituted by premature death . . . Weighing words carefully, it is altogether a question of luck. One just has to be able to consent to this. There will never be any substitute for twenty years of life and experience.[5]

People who revolt, realising this, abandon hope for the future and make the most of what they have – a fleeting succession of present moments.

Why did Camus urge us to abandon hope in the future in favour of the transient but real joys of the present moment? He advanced several reasons in *The Myth of Sisyphus*, but two are crucial for our concerns. The first and most obvious is that Camus, an atheist, held that any hope that the world would not turn out absurd is illusory. There just is no Christian God to guarantee that we will live eternally. Nor are the secular hopes of the Marxists well founded – there is no good reason to believe that history is moving irrevocably toward a classless society. There is no Meaning of Life.

The second problem with hope is that it enslaves those who have it and accordingly lessens emphasis on the present moment. Religious people tacitly admit that they cannot carry the burden of their lives on their own shoulders; they are only able to live because the burden is placed on God's shoulders. They are happy only because they hope; without hope they are not strong enough to endure. But people who revolt are free to create their own lives in the present. They are bound neither to God nor to a given theory of history (as Marxists are), nor are they cowed by life's absurdity. 'A man devoid of hope and conscious of being so has ceased to belong to the future.'[6] 'A world remains of which man is the sole master. What bound him was the illusion of another world.'[7] The 'absurd man', as

Camus called him, decides to accept this absurd universe and 'draw from it his strength, his refusal to hope, and the unyielding evidence of a life without consolation'.[8] In the motto of *The Myth of Sisyphus*, Camus quotes Pindar:

> O my soul, do not aspire to immortal life, but exhaust the limits of the possible.

This is precisely what Camus's absurd man does. He is 'indifferent to the future', but has an unshakeable desire 'to use up everything that is given' – that is, the succession of present moments that is allotted to him. Devoid of a future, 'he lives out his adventure within the span of his lifetime'.[9]

Camus used the mythical figure of Sisyphus to complete his argument. Sisyphus was condemned by the gods to an everlasting and futile punishment – he had to push a large stone up a mountain, watch it roll back down, and then push it up again. Camus's point was that Sisyphus is the exemplar of the human condition in an absurd world. Human beings struggle mightily to achieve things in life, but there is no guarantee that they will be achieved, and no guarantee that, once achieved, they will prove significant. But Sisyphus – so Camus argued – can be 'happy' in his world without hope, and so can we. The gods thought that they had inflicted on him the most terrible possible punishment, but they had out-smarted themselves. Knowing he would never be released from his futile labour, Sisyphus was able to overcome the gods with his scorn and defiance of them and his unwillingness to despair. There is no Meaning of Life, Camus was saying, but we can give our lives meaning and, if we are lucky, even happiness.

Camus displayed with stark clarity the importance of the question of God. Religious believers, of course, part company with Camus from the opening page. They will not agree that life is absurd and that hope is accordingly illusory. Camus did not argue in *The Myth of Sisyphus* that life is absurd; he rather said that he took the absurd as his starting-point.[10] That is, the argument of the book is based on the assumption of the absurd. This is a perfectly acceptable procedure for Camus to follow; it is just that those who believe in God are unwilling to make the same assumption and so will be unconvinced by what follows from it. Believers will want to know, for example, where Camus learned that there is no God, afterlife, or Meaning of Life.

Does hope enslave? Are believers in God (or any sort of Meaning of Life) so bound to the future that they are less concerned with the present moment than they should be? (It should be noted that Camus did not hold that religious beliefs *per se* prevent one from revolting or living absurdly –

the problem is the specific religious belief in the afterlife.)[11] Perhaps Camus was right that there are certain religious believers who focus so insistently on the glories of the future that they ignore the present (of course some nonbelievers do this too). But not all religious believers do so, nor should they. Theists are folk who are enjoined to look at life here and now as a precious and worthwhile gift of God.

It is true that certain theists, for example Christians, hold that life has Meaning and that history is moving in a certain direction, that is, toward the kingdom of God. It is also true that they believe that this kingdom will be a time of joy far greater than can be found on earth. But how does this 'bind' them to the future or make them less 'available' to their fellow humans (as Camus charged), here and now? Camus's indictment of religious belief seems very much unproved.

The importance of the question of God can be put in terms of five theses. (It is important to note again that we are talking here about the God of classical theism, that is, the God of Judaism, Christianity, Islam, and perhaps other theistic traditions. The God of eighteenth-century deism, for example, is not in question.)

1. If God exists, God created us rather than vice versa.
2. If God exists, the world is ultimately intelligible.
3. If God exists, life has Meaning, and history is moving in a certain direction.
4. If God exists, human beings have a future destiny.
5. If God exists, there is an objective moral right and wrong, and it is our duty to do what is right.

Let us consider each of these points briefly. Each is complex and controversial, and requires more extended discussion than I am able to give here.

On point (1), atheists are committed to the idea that God is a creation of the human mind. Many accept the notion proposed by the classic nineteenth-century 'projection theorists' (Feuerbach, Marx, Freud *et al.*) that we created God in our own image and out of human needs. In any case, the main point atheists insist upon – as we saw with Camus – is that human being are free, autonomous, and under no obligation to any higher being. Most theists are committed to the opposite notion that we owe our existence to God, and that we were created in the image of God. It is for that reason, they say, that we have instrinsic value as persons. God relates to us lovingly and graciously. We become who we truly are, and who we are truly meant to be, when we are related to God correctly – that is, when we love, obey, and glorify God in our lives.

On point (2), we are reminded of the philosophy of Descartes, where the existence of God was the ultimate guarantor of the intelligibility of the universe. Without God, Descartes reasoned, there is no guarantee that our experiences are intelligible, that our interpretations of our experiences are reliable, or that our memories are accurate. Now I am not here adopting Cartesianism. (That would be an intellectually suicidal thing to do, since nobody nowadays, in either philosophy or theology, thinks that Descartes basically got things right.) But on this point I agree with him. I do not argue that atheists cannot consistently hold that the world is intelligible; I do argue that theists *must* hold that the world is intelligible.

On point (3), if God exists, life has Meaning and time is linear; history is moving in a certain direction. This is because God is the answer to the question of the origin and destiny of reality itself, and of human life. History is moving toward the ultimate triumph of God over all God's enemies, that is, toward the kingdom of God. The apparently aimless flux of reality is not random, but is moving toward a *telos* supplied by God. Despite all the apparent reasons for hopelessness and despair, if God exists, I can confidently affirm that my existence counts; my life matters; what I do has significance.

On point (4), if atheists are right, death is the end of human existence. Now it is possible to be an atheist and to affirm an afterlife (just as it is possible to affirm God and deny the afterlife), and there have been one or two examples of such folk in the history of recent philosophy. But the ideas of God and afterlife are so closely connected, and for such understandable reasons, that few will find such a position attractive. The question of God is a crucial question because almost everybody wants to know whether God or nothingness awaits them after death. If God exists, then it is possible for me confidently to affirm that my existence does not end with my death. Of course, my survival of death does not by itself mean that my life is meaningful and worthwhile; it is possible to imagine afterlives that are trivial, meaningless, or horrible. But the afterlives envisioned in the theistic traditions are not of this sort. They constitute aims or goals of human life that are infinitely worthwhile. They are grounded in our true natures as creations of God.

On point (5), if God exists, the concepts of moral right and wrong are 'objective'. What is morally right does not depend on who I am or what society I was raised in or what my opinions happen to be. Right and wrong depend upon the nature and commands of a loving God. In his brilliant dialogue *Euthyphro*, Plato raised a classic question which for our purposes can be put as follows: are moral things moral because God commands them, or does God command them because they are moral? Either alternative seems unacceptable to theists – either morality is entirely arbitrary (God could command that we torture babies, and if God did so, torturing babies would be right), or else morality is based on something outside of and morally superior to God. The theistic reply is that morality does depend on God but that it is not arbitrary or capricious because God is loving and good. Moral things are moral because they are commanded by a *loving* God.[12]

If God exists, the most important thing for any human being is, as noted, to be related correctly to God. Different theistic traditions give different recipes for that relationship, but the crucial ideas are always those of loving, honouring, and obeying God in one's life. The question of the existence of God takes on crucial importance, then, because obviously it is difficult to see how a person who does not believe in the existence of God can be correctly related to God.

Camus might object to these arguments as follows: God *lessens* rather than *heightens* meaning in life because the people who follow God simply accept what God has dictated that they must do; such persons have given up their autonomy; meaning in life only truly exists when freely chosen and created by individual persons.

Some of this is true. Human beings who choose to follow God's way are *not* autonomous. Indeed, they would be horrified at the idea. They accept the claims that they were created by God, are under God's authority, and have no ability on their own to create worthwhile destinies for themselves. Of course the choice to follow God is a free one; God does not coerce. And all that God does is in our best interests as human beings. It may be true that meaning in life must be freely chosen, but why say that meaning in life only exists when *created* by humans? That is a claim that no theist will accept.[13]

III. DO THEISTIC PROOFS PROVE THE EXISTENCE OF *GOD*?

We now move to the question of theistic proofs as proofs of *God*. Suppose that some, or even all, of the theistic proofs that we have discussed in this book are entirely successful arguments. Do they prove the existence of the God of theism? Or do they just prove the existence of some sort of less impressive first mover or source of religious experience or designer of the universe? It has seemed to many philosophers that the theistic proofs, quite apart from any internal problems that might render them unsound as arguments, fall short as proofs of God. If we were to make a list of the crucial attributes of the God of theism, the list would surely include attributes like:

- uniqueness (there is but one God);
- existing at all times (including now);
- all-powerful (omnipotent);
- all-knowing (omniscient);
- perfectly morally good; and
- personal (being a person and caring for us as persons).

But surely the theistic proofs fail to conclude in the existence of a being or beings with these properties (or so many philosophers have claimed).

Of course we would not expect theistic proofs to prove every attribute of the God of theism or even everything that we would like to know about God. Indeed, within the Christian branch of theism, there are truths about God – for example, the fact that God is a Trinity – that are said to be beyond the reach of natural theology or even of human reason. Such truths must simply be accepted as a part of revelation.

Let's talk first about Aquinas' theistic proofs. This is a good place to begin because questions about 'Is this God?' are often raised as criticisms of the Five Ways. The point frequently made is that Aquinas errs in each of his five closing lines, which say, respectively, 'this [the being just proved to exist] everyone understands to be God', 'to which everyone gives the name of God', 'this all men speak of as God', 'this we call God', and 'this being we call God'.[14] When Aquinas speaks of 'God', he of course means the Christian God, a being that has all the properties mentioned in the above paragraph as well as being the creator of the heavens and the earth and existing in the form of a Blessed Trinity.

Even if (let's say) the Third Way is a sound argument – so the objection goes – all that it proves is that a necessary being of some sort exists. But why must there be only one NB? Why must the NB of the Third Way be identical to the first mover of the First Way or the first cause of the second way or the intelligent being of the Fifth Way? Why must the NB be omnipotent or omniscient or morally good? Of course the NB whom Aquinas thinks he has proved *might* be God (nothing in the Third Way prevents its being omnipotent, etc.), but does not *have to be* God. Why could there not exist seventeen NBs, none of them omnipotent, omniscient, good creators of the heavens and the earth?

This criticism is essentially correct. Aquinas has not shown that the prime beings whose existence he has argued for can be none other than the God of theism, let alone the Christian God. Of course it must be pointed out that in the passage known as the 'Five Ways', Aquinas was not trying to prove that *God* exists. He was trying to prove the existence of a first mover, first cause, necessary being, and intelligent being,[15] which, as he said, 'everyone speaks of as God'. Aquinas' argument (as opposed to his claim) that the beings proved can be none other than God comes later in Part I of the *Summa Theologica*.

Now some would even question the modest claim 'this everyone speaks of as God'. Yet I think we can understand and defend what Aquinas was doing here even apart from later arguments in Part I of the *Summa*. He was, of course, connecting his philosophy and his theology. His method was first to prove the existence of a NB (as well as the first mover and first cause of the first two Ways and the intelligent being who directs the behaviour of unintelligent things of the Fifth Way). He then did an inventory, so to speak, of all the beings he believed to exist on other grounds (including theological grounds). Finally, he asked, which of them could be the same being as the being or beings proved to exist in the Five Ways? The answer he found, naturally enough, was that only *God* could be a first mover, first cause, necessary being, and intelligent designer. His mother could not do or be all those things, and neither could his confessor, the Pope, his brightest student, his cat, the Abbot's desk, *or any other such being* of which he could think. This was why he said, 'and this all men speak of as God'. Who else could a first mover be than God?

My own view is that this 'connecting' strategy – connecting one's philosophical proofs with one's empirical or theological convictions – is entirely acceptable. And this is surely the (usually implicit) strategy of many of those who, like Aquinas, offer TPs. If you successfully prove that a given being exists, and if on other grounds there is good reason for you to think that this being is God, then you have good reason to hold that you have successfully proved the existence of God. Or at the very least you have in some sense philosophically confirmed your belief in God.

But more than this can be said about the relationship between God and the TPs. Again, let's suppose for the sake of argument that the OA, the CA, the DA, the ARE, and the MA all have sound versions. This is of course a huge supposition; I suggest we make it because TPs that are *un*successful arguments have, in my opinion, nothing whatever to say about the existence or nature of anything, let alone God. If then each of the main TPs that we have discussed in this book has successful versions, what if anything would follow about the nature of God?

Consider the OA. If there are successful versions of it, then we know that there exists a 'greatest conceivable being'. This is a theologically rich description, doubtless the richest of the descriptions or titles or expressions used for the prime beings of the various TPs. Anselm himself clearly held that all the central Christian attributes of God were both logically interrelated and entailed by the expression 'that than which nothing greater can be conceived'. Indeed, Anselm appeared to have available a handy method – an algorithm, if you will – for assigning attributes to the GCB. In *Proslogion* V, he said of the GCB: 'Therefore, thou art just, truthful, blessed, and *whatever it is better to be than not to be.*'[16]

In the later chapters of the *Proslogion*, he specifically argued that divine necessary existence, creation of the world *ex nihilo*, eternity, omnipotence, omniscience, and perfect goodness followed from God's being the GCB.[17] In addition, the GCB's uniqueness follows directly from the suffix 'est' in the words 'Great*est* Conceivable Being.' Accordingly, either this term refers to nothing at all, or else (if some version of the OA using it is a successful argument), the GCB uniquely exists.

A way of summarising the point is to say that if some version of the OA is successful, an absolutely perfect being exists. This predicate either contains or entails most of the other properties that theists want to attribute to God. Whatever properties are great-making (in senses discussed in Chapter 1) or perfection-making, the GCB has them, and indeed has them to or in the degree that it is proper for a GCB to have them.

What about the CA? William Rowe discusses sympathetically Samuel Clarke's attempt to show that the NB proved to exist by the CA (on our assumption that it is a successful TP) must be everlasting. If a certain being comes into existence at a certain point in time, then either that being was brought into existence by some other being or else its existence is simply what Rowe calls 'a brute fact'. But in either case, the being cannot be a NB, that is, a being 'whose existence is entirely and solely accounted for by reference to its own nature. So, clearly, a self-existent being, if it exists, must have existed from everlasting, without beginning.'[18] Rowe also endorses, in a qualified way, Clarke's argument to the effect that the NB proved to exist by the CA must be omnipresent or everywhere present – otherwise the question why it exists in a certain place and not in another will have to be answered in terms of the causal activity of some other being or force.

As noted earlier, even if Aquinas' first three Ways are successful TPs, they do not strictly constitute proofs of God. There might well be a first cause that is not omnipotent, a first mover that is not personal or compassionate, a NB that is not omniscient. Still, the being Aquinas is trying to prove is the ground and explanation of all reality. And if such a being *is* successfully proved to exist, we have arrived at a being that is necessary, everlasting, uncaused, very powerful, and very intelligent (adding the Fifth Way into the equation). This is a metaphysically highly interesting result, and is surely a being that *could well be* (although it need not be) the God of theism.

What about the DA? There is a great deal that could be said here. The

DA doubtless points to a being of great power, knowledge, skill, and wisdom – indeed, to a being that possesses these attributes to a far greater degree than humans do. It does not necessarily point to omnipotence and omniscience, but is certainly compatible with them. Some argue that the evidence of design points definitely to *limited* power, knowledge, and especially goodness, and much will hang on whether that claim is true. The critic of the DA or of theism can make the best case with limited goodness. Although unlimited power and knowledge are perhaps not strictly needed to account for the evidence, it is hard to see how anyone could successfully argue that something less than omnipotent and omniscient is *required* by the evidence (this despite the arguments of Hume and Mill).[19] Whether perfect goodness is compatible with the amount of evil and suffering that exist in the world amounts to the classic 'problem of evil', and is beyond the scope of the present book.

Transcendence, in at least one sense, does seem to be indicated by the evidence of design. It is hard to see how a being that is part of the process of nature and is subject to its laws can account for them or be said to have organised (let alone created) them. If a given being is the universe's designer, I would take that to entail that that being cannot be identified with any thing, event, or process that exists or occurs in the physical world. And if that much is true, it also seems to follow that the designer of the universe must be non-physical or incorporeal (which is of course one of the crucial attributes of God).[20]

The designer must be personal in one sense of that word, since the order that we see in the universe seems to be the product of intentional design. Accordingly, the designer is intelligent, formulates plans, engages in courses of actions, has desires and wishes and the ability (possibly within limits) to satisfy them. The designer is an agent.

The designer of the universe is, then, a being that must be greatly admired and respected. Whether the evidence of design alone indicates that it is a being that is worthy of worship will depend in part on such attributes as being a person, being perfectly good, being compassionate, and being strong enough to bring about its ultimate triumph.

So far as the argument from religious experience is concerned, let us simply posit that if any version of that TP is a successful argument, a being that is the source or ground of religious experience, or at least some of it, exists. That would certainly give one grounds to question the truth of naturalism and at least to be open to a religious way of interpreting the world. And so far as the moral argument is concerned, let us say that if any version of that TP is a successful argument, a being that is the source of moral obligation exists. This being must be intelligent (it has wishes, issues commands) and is morally good. Its purposes and character 'are in accord with our most confident judgments of right and wrong'.[21] In addition, the being must have enormous knowledge, at least of ethical matters, which includes the moral comings and goings of human beings.

How many prime beings are there? Suppose that each of the seven TPs that we have seriously considered in this book has one successful version. Suppose further that each successful version proves the existence of no more than one being. Then we have arrived at the existence of (1) the GCB; (2) the first mover; (3) the first cause; (4) a NB; (5) the world's designer; (6) the source of religious experience; and (7) the source of moral obligation. How many separate beings are named here? Theoretically, it could be any number greater than zero and less than eight.

Considerations of simplicity might push us in the direction of one as opposed to seven, especially since the properties of each of the seven prime beings seem consistent with the properties of the other six. Nothing seems to prevent the NB of the Third Way from also being the ground of religious experience, etc. With the possible exception of the Hume–Mill line about the designer of the world being evil, and thus constituting a problematical source of moral obligation (an argument that I find less than convincing), there appear to be no obvious inconsistencies.

The OA is the key. If there are successful versions of the OA, and if Anselm's method for determining the properties of the GCB is also successful (the GCB has whatever properties it is better for the GCB to have than not to have), it follows that there is but one prime being. This is because the other six properties (being the first mover, the first cause, a NB, the world's designer, the source of religious experience, and the source of moral obligation) all appear to be great-making or (as we might say) better-making properties. In the case of each of the six, it is better for the GCB to have them than not to have them.

Even apart from the OA (which many philosophers reject out of hand and whose soundness few are willing to countenance), there are important commonalities among the seven properties that seem to argue for a number of prime beings far less than seven. For example, being the source of religious experience and being the source of moral obligation appear to go together, since religious experience is virtually always moral experience and moral experience is often religious experience. The two sources could be separate, of course, but there appears to be no good reason pushing us in that direction. Similarly, the first mover, the first cause, and the world's designer can usefully be considered one and the same being. If this is true, then the DA shows that the first mover and the first cause are purposive beings.

If there are successful versions of our seven TPs, and if the seven beings proved to exist are all one and the same being, then clearly we have arrived at the existence of a being that is remarkably similar to the God of theism.

IV. THE VALUE OF THEISTIC PROOFS

In the final section of this chapter, we return to some of the issues that we discussed in Chapter 1. In particular, we shall try to reach a conclusion on the question of whether philosophising about TPs is an enterprise worth engaging in. Do TPs accomplish anything worthwhile?

Let's begin by asking why there is so much hostility to TPs among certain contemporary scholars (biblical scholars, historians of religion, historians of doctrine, theologians, philosophers of religion) who might be thought to have at least some professional interest in the issues raised by TPs. Maybe one reason, for some scholars, is a conviction that TPs have produced nothing serious in the past and a belief that that trend will continue. Another might be a methodological or theological conviction that TPs constitute a wrongheaded way of approaching issues like God and religious belief. Another might be the fact that the thinkers in question do not accept the basic assumptions of TPs discussed in Chapter 1 (many Wittgensteinian philosophers of religion and post-modern philosophers of religion perhaps fit here). Another might simply be a firm conviction that God does not exist, and that, accordingly, no TP can possibly be successful. (Obviously, this explanation would not apply to theists who reject TPs.)

A few analytic philosophers of religion (both atheists, agnostics, and theists) and Thomistic philosophers are the ones who are now interested in TPs. The view that all the TPs are fallacious, but some are at least philosophically interesting and worthy of discussion, is commonly held, but very few philosophers of religion are willing to commit themselves to the view that a given TP, or a given set of TPs, is successful.

Suppose someone were to produce a proof, which no one is able to refute, for the existence of some being B. That is, suppose the premises of the argument are clearly true, the argument is clearly formally valid, and it clearly commits none of the informal fallacies like equivocation, question-begging, or arguing in a circle. This would raise for us the question: What exactly is B? Now let's suppose that B is something you have very good reason to believe does not exist (my ninth daughter, Napoleon Bonaparte, a square circle). Your reaction would probably be (and rationally *should* be) 'Something is wrong here; the proof of B *must* be fallacious in some way that I did not earlier see; one of the premises of the argument must be false, after all.'

Here we have a parallel to the attitude many atheists have toward TPs – since they are firmly convinced that God does not exist, no TP can successfully prove God. Here also is a parallel to the attitude many religious believers have toward TPs. If B is something you already know exists (your mother, Bill Clinton), it will seem pointless, foolish, even ridiculous to worry about proving B's existence. 'Who needs the proof?' you might ask. 'Doesn't it seem inappropriate or even vaguely unfaithful to your mother to try to prove her existence?'

I have used the word 'success' (as in 'The generic CA is not a successful TP') on many occasions throughout the book. It is time that we tried to lend a bit more precision to the term. For a TP, what does success consist in? As we saw in Chapter 1, this is not an easy question to answer. There are certain necessary conditions of success for a TP that are not hard to arrive at – it must be formally valid, informally valid, and sound. But this is clearly not enough. How one proceeds, in order to spell out the criteria of 'success', depends (as we also saw in Chapter 1) on one's views as to the goal or purpose of a TP.

I argued that the purpose of TPs is to demonstrate the existence of God. Of course, if a given argument succeeds in doing that, it also succeeds in demonstrating the rationality of belief in the existence of God. This entails, among other things, that the premises of a successful TP must themselves be more reasonable or plausible than their denials, which in most cases entails their being reasonable or plausible *per se*. The ideal would be that they be known to be reasonable or plausible by those (whether believers or nonbelievers in God) at whom the TP is directed, those who are to benefit from it. But we would doubtless consider a given TP successful if, among the other conditions we have noted, its premises were more plausible than their denials and if that fact *should* be known by any rational person.

But if the goal of TPs is to demonstrate the existence of God and thus the rationality of theism, there are several ways in which the second half of this goal can be envisioned. I shall mention five possibilities, moving from the weakest to the strongest. The purpose of a TP is to:

1. show that theists are rational in their belief in the existence of God;
2. show that it is more rational to believe that God exists than it is to deny that God exists;
3. show that it is more rational to believe that God exists than to be agnostic on the existence of God;
4. show that it is as rational to believe in God as it is to believe in many of the things that atheist philosophers often believe in (for

example, the existence of 'other minds' or the objectivity of moral right and wrong);[22] or

5. show that it is irrational not to believe that God exists (that is, it is irrational to be either an atheist or an agnostic).

As someone who is a theist, I naturally would applaud any argument that demonstrated that belief in God is or can be rational. Indeed, I do think there are TPs that succeed in doing that very thing. Goal (1) is very modest, however, especially in the light of the relativity of rationality (it is possible for belief in a given claim to be rational for one person and irrational for another), and my own hope would be for more than that from TPs. Indeed, one can imagine many atheists and agnostics not being bothered at all if some TP showed that theists are rational in believing in God, as long as that argument accomplished nothing more dramatic than that. An exception to this point would be atheist philosopher Kai Nielsen, who on a number of occasions has opined that 'for somebody living in the twentieth century with a good philosophical and a good scientific education, who thinks carefully about the matter . . . for such a person it is irrational to believe in God.'[23] If there exists a TP, or any other sort of argument, that demonstrates the rationality of theism for theists, Nielsen's claim will have been reduced to nothing more than bravado.

There are surely some arguments that almost everybody accepts as successful, especially in mathematics – the Pythagorean Theorem, for example. But it is hard to think of an argument for any substantive philosophical conclusion that almost everybody accepts as successful. Accordingly, I am not hopeful that goal or aim (5) can be achieved by any TP, and again this has to do with the relativity of rationality. No matter how logically impeccable a given TP is, no matter how obviously true its premises, an atheist who wants to resist its conclusion can simply find one of its premises to reject. 'I used to think that that premise was true,' the atheist will say, 'but I now see that it must be false.' (This is just what I would do if somebody were to publish in the *Journal of Philosophy* a logically impeccable proof of the non-existence of God based on premises all of which I accept, or accepted.)

So goal (1) is an acceptable aim for TPs, but it seems that a bit more is possible and needed. Goal (5) is too strong; for reasons that we have considered, it is unrealistic to think that any TP must be able to do that. (2) and (3) are stronger than (1), and I consider them too to be acceptable goals for theistic provers to aim at. It would be hard for one TP to show, by itself, that theism is a more rational position than atheism or agnosticism; a theistic prover might be more likely to attain that end by combining a TP or a set of TPs with an argument against the rationality of naturalism. I have not emphasised such arguments in this book – TPs constitute a big enough topic on their own for me to manage. Nevertheless, I would endorse this strategy as worth pursuing as a part of theistic apologetics. Goal (4) is also a worthwhile aim for theistic provers. Whether it is in fact a stronger goal or aim than (2) and (3) I am not sure. In any case, I believe this goal is quite possible to attain. Indeed, I think Plantinga has achieved it in several of his essays.

Throughout this book, I have avoided defining success for a TP in subjective terms, for example in terms like *ability to convince*. There can be no such thing as a subjectively fool-proof TP. But it would be unwise to allow that a proof whose ability to convince is zero could be a successful proof, because it is reasonable to believe that human beings, most of the time, believe and behave rationally. We should not expect that there will be a TP that convinces every atheist (short, perhaps, of the kingdom of God). On the other hand, it seems unacceptably weak to take the position that TPs are, so to speak, for internal use only, that TPs only state the theist's interpretation of reality. Rather, successful TPs *should* convince atheists that God exists.

Let's distingush between *objective success* and *subjective success* for a TP. A TP is objectively successful, let's say, when it is formally and informally valid, and its premises are known to be true by the people (whoever they are) at whom the TP is aimed. Such a proof, we might say, *should* convince any rational person that God exists. A TP is subjectively successful, let's say, when it *does* convince people (we'll leave open questions like how many people, or what percentage of its readers, or whether they were already theists) that God exists. Obviously, the two criteria are quite separable, are not always satisfied together.

Equally obviously, no theistic prover is interested in presenting a TP that is objectively unsuccessful, even if it is also subjectively successful. The theistic prover would probably be delighted that certain folk have come to believe in God. But the fact that the TP is objectively unsuccessful spoils everything. In the first place, the people who come to believe in God because of it believe in God for a weak reason. In the second place (and more importantly), the objective weakness of the TP will soon be discovered and pointed out, and it will then no longer be subjectively successful.

Probably the best strategy for theistic provers who hope that atheists and agnostics come to believe in God, is: (1) to present TPs that are as objectively successful as possible; (2) to hope and pray that those who are not theists will come to believe in God, perhaps some of them by being convinced by the TP; and (3) to leave the rest up to the grace of God.

It is sometimes said that the problem with TPs – or at least with objectively successful ones – is that they take away our cognitive freedom *vis-à-vis* God. It is surprising that such views are so often expressed, for they are quite mistaken. It is true that God placed us in a world where we are free to love or hate God, obey or rebel against God, honour or curse God. It is also true, as John Hick has argued on many occasions, that one aspect of that cognitive and moral freedom is epistemic. God must hide, but not too well; it must be possible to look for and find God; but the reality of God must not be so obvious to us as, say, the reality of our parents, or our automobiles.

Suppose that what God wants from us is (1) a freely decided-upon choice to love and obey God (not coerced or forced upon us), that is made (2) by use of the best of our rational faculties. (Perhaps God wants us to use the best of our emotional or even physical faculties too, but we'll leave that out of the argument.) If so, it follows that God cannot make it epistemically irrational to be an atheist (or to be anyone who does not love and obey God). If God's aims are to be realised, if humans are to be rational and rationally free in deciding to love and obey God, God cannot allow there to exist any state of affairs that would make atheism irrational.

Now I am not here to endorse the details of the argument I have just outlined (although I think something like it can be defended). I was just trying to flesh out the argument that God cannot allow there to exist an objectively successful TP because the existence of such a TP would take away our cognitive freedom *vis-à-vis* God. *That* argument is clearly mistaken, and (among other things) for reasons that we have had before us throughout the book. It is one thing to come to believe in the existence of God. It is quite another to commit one's life to God, to set out to love, obey, and honour God in one's life. No TP could ever have the effect of taking away one's freedom on the question of whether or not to do that.

Theists would hold that the truth is more like this: God gives us the freedom to be irrational. If there were no epistemic distance between us and God, if God's existence were as obvious to us as is the existence of our own bodies or as (say) trees, we would be so epistemically overwhelmed that nonbelief in God's existence would be epistemically impossible. But what God does – so theists say – is to create us (1) at an epistemic distance from God (2) but with the intellectual resources available to come to know that God exists. Perhaps TPs are part of those resources.

It is part of the argument of this book that rational discussion of theistic proofs is worthwhile. But in the end it does seem that theistic proofs are very much *optional* for theists. The fact of the matter is: I enjoy discussing theistic proofs, consider the enterprise valuable, and even consider that there do exist successful theistic proofs. Nevertheless, the reason I am a theist has almost nothing to do with theistic proofs. It has a great deal to do with experiences I have had that I interpret in terms of the presence of God – experiences I find myself interpreting in terms of divine forgiveness, divine protection, divine guidance. That is why I would be extremely suspicious of any apparently successful atheistic proof. That is why I claim to know that God exists.

NOTES

1. Albert Camus, *The Myth of Sisyphus* (New York: Vintage Books, 1955). We will not consider any other of Camus's writings.
2. Camus, *Myth of Sisyphus*, p. 45.
3. Camus, *Myth of Sisyphus*, p. 48.
4. Camus, *Myth of Sisyphus*, p. 62.
5. Camus, *Myth of Sisyphus*, pp. 46–7.
6. Camus, *Myth of Sisyphus*, p. 24.
7. Camus, *Myth of Sisyphus*, p. 87.
8. Camus, *Myth of Sisyphus*, p. 44.
9. Camus, *Myth of Sisyphus*, p. 49.
10. Camus, *Myth of Sisyphus*, p. 2.
11. Camus, *Myth of Sisyphus*, p. 83.
12. For a careful defence of 'divine command ethics', see the essays collected in Part III of Robert M. Adams' *The Virtue of Faith and Other Essays in Philosophical Theology* (Oxford: Oxford University Press, 1987).
13. These and related issues are skilfully discussed by J. P. Moreland in Chapter 4 of his *Scaling the Secular City: A Defense of Christianity* (Grand Rapids, Michigan: Baker Book House, 1987).
14. Thomas Aquinas, *Summa Theologica* (New York: Benzinger Brothers, 1947), I, 2, 3.
15. I am ignoring here – as I have throughout the book – Aquinas' Fourth Way. This is because I have never been able to think of any construals of that argument that seem plausible.
16. Anselm, *Basic Writings* (LaSalle, Illinois: Open Court, 1962), p. 11.
17. See Anselm, *Basic Writings*, *Proslogion*, Chapters V, VI, IX, XII, XIII, XIX, XX and XXIII.
18. William Rowe, *The Cosmological Argument* (Princeton, New Jersey: Princeton University Press, 1975), p. 226.
19. See David Hume, *Dialogues Concerning Natural Religion* (New York: Hafner Publishing Company, 1959), pp. 38–41; John Stuart Mill, *Theism* (New York: Liberal Arts Press, 1957), Part II.
20. There are other possibilities that I will not explore. One is the possibility that God created the universe in some sense out of its own being. Another is the Process or Whiteheadian theory that makes God not entirely transcendent over physical reality and yet qualitatively different from it.
21. Robert M. Adams, *The Virtue of Faith*, p. 149; see also pp. 150, 160.
22. This strategy has been followed for years by Alvin Plantinga in many of his writings on the philosophy of religion.
23. J. P. Moreland and Kai Nielsen (eds), *Does God Exist? The Great Debate* (Nashville, Tennessee: Thomas Nelson, 1990), p. 48.

Bibliography

Adams, Marilyn McCord, 'Praying the *Proslogion*: Anselm's Theological Method,' in Thomas D. Senor (ed.), *The Rationality of Belief and the Plurality of Faith* (Ithaca, New York: Cornell University Press, 1995), pp. 13–39.

Adams, Robert M., *The Virtue of Faith and Other Essays in Philosophical Theology* (Oxford: Oxford University Press, 1987).

Alston, William P., *Perceiving God: The Epistemology of Religious Experience* (Ithaca, New York: Cornell University Press, 1991).

Alston, William P., *A Realist Conception of Truth* (Ithaca, New York: Cornell University Press, 1996).

Anselm, *Basic Writings* (LaSalle, Illinois: Open Court, 1962).

Aquinas, Thomas, *Summa Theologica* (New York: Benzinger Brothers, 1947).

Aquinas, Thomas, *Summa Contra Gentiles*, trans. by Anton C. Pegis (Notre Dame, Indiana: University of Notre Dame Press, 1955).

Aristotle, *Metaphysics*, trans. by Richard Hope (Ann Arbor, Michigan: University of Michigan Press, 1960).

Barrow, John D. and Tipler, Frank J., *The Anthropic Cosmological Principle* (Oxford: Oxford University Press, 1986).

Barth, Karl, *Anselm: Fides Quaerens Intellectum* (London: SCM Press, 1960).

Braithwaite, R. M., 'An Empiricist's View of the Nature of Religious Belief', in B. Mitchell (ed.), *The Philosophy of Religion* (Oxford: Oxford University Press, 1971).

Burrill, Donald R., *The Cosmological Arguments* (Garden City, New York: Anchor Books, 1967).

Camus, Albert, *The Myth of Sisyphus* (New York: Vintage Books, 1955).

Cargile, James, 'Pascal's Wager', in S. Cahn and D. Shatz (eds), *Contemporary Philosophy of Religion* (Oxford: Oxford University Press, 1982).

Clark, Ralph W., 'The Evidential Value of Religious Experiences', *International Journal for Philosophy of Religion*, Vol. 16, No. 3 (1984), pp. 189–202.

Clarke, Samuel, *A Demonstration of the Being and Attributes of God* (Oxford: Oxford University Press, 1969).

Clarke, Samuel, *British Moralists 1650–1800*, ed. D. D. Raphael (Oxford: Oxford University Press, 1969).

Clifford, W. K., *Lectures and Essays*, ed. Leslie Stephen and Frederick Pollack (New York: Macmillan and Company, 1901).

Copleston, Frederick C., *Aquinas* (Baltimore, Maryland: Penguin Books, 1961).

Craig, William, *The Kalaam Cosmological Argument* (New York: Barnes and Noble, 1979).

Craig, William, *The Cosmological Argument from Plato to Leibniz* (New York: Barnes and Noble, 1980).

Craig, William, 'The Teleological Argument and the Anthropic Principle', in William L. Craig and Mark S. McLeod (eds), *The Logic of Rational Theism: Exploratory Essays* (Lewiston, Maine: The Edwin Mellen Press, 1990), pp. 127–53.

Craig, William, 'Philosophical and Scientific Pointers to *Creatio ex Nihilo*', in R. Douglas Geivett and Brendan Sweetman (eds), *Contemporary Perspectives on Religious Epistemology* (Oxford: Oxford University Press, 1992).

Craig, William and Smith, Quentin, *Theism, Atheism and Big Bang Cosmology* (Oxford: Clarendon Press, 1993).

Davies, Paul, *Other Worlds* (London: Dent, 1980).

Davies, Paul, *The Accidental Universe* (Cambridge: Cambridge University Press, 1982).

Davis, Stephen T., 'Anselm and Gaunilo on the "Lost Island"', *The Southern Journal of Philosophy*, Vol. XIII, No. 4 (Winter, 1975), pp. 435–48.

Davis, Stephen T., 'Anselm and Question-Begging: A Reply to William Rowe', *International Journal for Philosophy of Religion*, Vol. VII, No. 4 (Winter, 1976), pp. 448–57.

Davis, Stephen T., 'Does the Ontological Argument Beg the Question?', *International Journal for Philosophy of Religion*, Vol. VII, No. 4 (Winter, 1976), pp. 433–42.

Davis, Stephen T., *Faith, Skepticism, and Evidence: An Essay in Religious Epistemology* (Lewisburg, Pennysylvania: Bucknell University Press, 1978).

Davis, Stephen T. (ed.), *Encountering Evil: Live Options in Theodicy* (Atlanta, Georgia: John Knox Press, 1981).

Davis, Stephen T., *Logic and the Nature of God* (London: Macmillan, 1983).

Davis, Stephen T., 'What Good Are Theistic Proofs?', in Louis Pojman (ed.), *Philosophy of Religion: An Anthology* (Belmont, California: Wadsworth Publishing Company, 1987).

Davis, Stephen T., 'Why God Must Be Unlimited', in Linda J. Tessier (ed.), *Concepts of the Ultimate: Philosophical Perspectives on the Nature of the Divine* (London: Macmillan, 1989).

Davis, Stephen T., 'Pascal on Self-Caused Belief', *Religious Studies*, Vol. 27, No. 1 (March, 1991), pp. 27–37.

Davis, Stephen T., 'Hierarchical Causes in the Cosmological Argument', *International Journal for Philosophy of Religion*, Vol. 31, No. 1 (February, 1992), pp. 13–27.

Davis, Stephen T., 'Against "Anti-Realist Faith"', in Joseph Runzo (ed.), *Is God Real?* (London: Macmillan Press, 1993).

Davis, Stephen T., 'Anselm and Phillips on Religious Realism', in Timothy Tessin and Mario von der Ruhr (eds), *Philosophy and the Grammar of Religious Belief* (New York: St Martin's Press, 1995).

Dawkins, Richard, *The Blind Watchmaker: Why the Evidence of Evolution Reveals a Universe Without Design* (New York: W. W. Norton and Co., 1986).

Dennett, Daniel, *Darwin's Dangerous Idea: Evolution and the Meanings of Life* (New York: Simon and Schuster, 1996).

Descartes, René, *The Philosophical Works of Descartes*, ed. E. Haldane and G. R. T. Ross, Vol. I (Cambridge: Cambridge University Press, 1970).

Edwards, Paul, 'The Cosmological Argument', in Donald R. Burrill (ed.), *The Cosmological Arguments* (Garden City, New York: Anchor Books, 1967).

Egner, Robert and Denonn, Lester E., *The Basic Writings of Bertrand Russell* (New York: Simon and Schuster, 1961).

Evans, C. Stephen, *Faith Beyond Reason* (Edinburgh: Edinburgh University Press, 1998).

Everett, Hugh, 'Relative State Formulations of Quantum Mechanics', *Review of Modern Physics*, Vol. 29 (1957), pp. 454–62.

Flew, Antony, *God and Philosophy* (New York: Delta Books, 1966).

Freud, Sigmund, *The Future of an Illusion* (New York: Norton Books, 1961).

Garcia, Laura L., 'Natural Theology and the Reformed Objection', in C. Stephen Evans and Merold Westphal (eds), *Christian Perspectives on Religious Knowledge* (Grand Rapids, Michigan: Wm. B. Eerdmans, 1993), pp. 112–33.

Geach, P. T., 'Commentary on Aquinas', in Donald Burrill (ed.), *The Cosmological Arguments* (Garden City, New York: Anchor Books, 1967).

Gerson, L. P., *God and Greek Philosophy: Studies in the Early History of Natural Theology* (London: Routledge, 1990).

Gilson, Etienne, *The Christian Philosophy of St Thomas Aquinas* (New York: Random House, 1956).

Greco, John, 'Is Natural Theology Necessary for Theistic Knowledge?', in Linda Zagzebski (ed.), *Rational Faith: Catholic Responses to Reformed Epistemology* (Notre Dame, Indiana: University of Notre Dame Press, 1993).

Grube, Dirk-Martin, 'Religious Experience After the Demise of Foundationalism', *Religious Studies*, Vol. 31, No. 1 (March, 1995), pp. 37–52.

Guth, Alan and Steinhart, Paul, 'The Inflationary Universe', in Paul Davies (ed.), *The New Physics* (Cambridge: Cambridge University Press, 1989).

Gutting, Gary, *Religious Belief and Religious Skepticism* (Notre Dame, Indiana: University of Notre Dame Press, 1982).

Hamilton, Edith and Cairns, Huntington (eds), *The Collected Dialogues of Plato* (New York: Pantheon, 1961).

Hart, Michael, 'Atmospheric Evolution, the Drake Equation, and DNA: Sparse Life in an Infinite Universe', in John Leslie (ed.), *Physical Cosmology and Philosophy* (New York: Macmillan, 1990).

Hasker, William, 'Proper Function, Reliabilism, and Religious Knowledge', in C. Stephen Evans and Merold Westphal (eds), *Christian Perspectives on Religious Knowledge* (Grand Rapids, Michigan: Wm. B. Eerdmans, 1993), pp. 66–86.

Hawking, Stephen, *A Brief History of Time: From the Big Bang to Black Holes* (New York: Bantam Books, 1988).

Helm, Paul, *Faith and Understanding* (Edinburgh: Edinburgh University Press, 1997).

Hick, John (ed.), *The Existence of God* (New York: Macmillan, 1964).

Hick, John, *Faith and Knowledge*, 2nd edn (Ithaca, New York: Cornell University Press, 1966).

Hick, John, *Arguments for the Existence of God* (New York: The Seabury Press, 1971).

Hick, John, 'Comment on Stephen Davis', in Linda J. Tessier (ed.), *Concepts of the Ultimate: Philosophical Perspectives on the Nature of the Divine* (London: Macmillan, 1989), pp. 32–3.

Hume, David, *Dialogues Concerning Natural Religion*, ed. Henry D. Aiken (New York: Hafner Publishing Company, 1959).

Hume, David, *A Treatise on Human Nature*, ed. L. A. Selby-Bigge (Oxford: Clarendon Press, 1988).

James, William, *The Varieties of Religious Experience* (New York: The Modern Library, 1936).

James, William, *The Will to Believe and Other Essays in Popular Philosophy* (New York: Dover Publications, 1956).

Kant, Immanuel, *Critique of Practical Reason* (Indianapolis: Bobbs-Merrill, 1956).

Kant, Immanuel, *Critique of Pure Reason*, trans. by Norman Kemp Smith (New York: St Martin's Press, 1965).

Kennedy, Gail, 'Pragmatism, Pragmaticism, and The Will To Believe – A Reconsideration', *The Journal of Philosophy*, Vol. 55 (1958), pp. 578–88.

Kenny, Anthony, *The Five Ways* (London: Routledge and Kegan Paul, 1969).

Krausz, Michael and Meiland, Jack W., *Relativism: Cognitive and Moral* (Notre Dame, Indiana: University of Notre Dame Press, 1982).

Leibniz, Gottfried, *Leibniz: Selections*, ed. Philip Wiener (New York: Charles Scribner's Sons, 1951).

Leslie, John, 'Modern Cosmology and the Creation of Life', in Ernan McMullin (ed.), *Evolution and Creation* (Notre Dame, Indiana: University of Notre Dame Press, 1985).

Leslie, John, 'The Prerequisites of Life in Our Universe', in G.V. Coyne, M. Heller and J. Zycinski (eds), *Newton and the New Direction in Science* (Vatican: Città del Vaticano, 1988).

Leslie, John, *Universes* (London: Routledge, 1989).

Lewis, C. S., *Mere Christianity* (New York: Macmillan, 1960).

McDonald, Scott, 'Aquinas' Parasitic Cosmological Argument', *Medieval Philosophy and Theology*, Vol. I (1991).

Mackie, J. L., *The Miracle of Theism* (Oxford: Clarendon Press, 1982).

Malcolm, Norman, 'Anselm's Ontological Arguments', in John Hick (ed.), *The Existence of God* (New York: Macmillan, 1964).

Matson, Wallace, *The Existence of God* (Ithaca, New York: Cornell University Press, 1965).

Maudlin, Tim, *Quantum Non-Locality and Relativity*, Aristotelian Society, Series 13 (Oxford: Blackwell, 1994).

Mavrodes, George, *Belief in God* (New York: Random House, 1970).

Messer, Richard, *Does God's Existence Need Proof?* (Oxford: Clarendon Press, 1993).

Meynell, Hugo, 'Faith, Foundationalism, and Nicholas Wolterstorff', in Linda Zagzebski (ed.), *Rational Faith: Catholic Responses to Reformed Epistemology* (Notre Dame, Indiana: University of Notre Dame Press, 1993).

Mill, John Stuart, *Theism* (New York: Liberal Arts Press, 1957).

Miller, Dickenson, 'James' Doctrine of "The Right To Believe"', *The Philosophical Review* Vol. 51 (1942), pp. 541–58.

Mitchell, Basil, *The Justification of Religious Belief* (New York: Oxford University Press, 1981).

Moreland, J. P., *Scaling the Secular City: A Defense of Christianity* (Grand Rapids, Michigan: Baker Book House, 1987).

Moreland, J. P. and Nielsen, Kai (eds), *Does God Exist? The Great Debate* (Nashville, Tennessee: Thomas Nelson, 1990).

Morris, Thomas V., 'The God of Abraham, Isaac, and Anselm', *Faith and Philosophy*, Vol. 1, No. 2 (April, 1984).

Morris, Thomas V., 'Wagering and the Evidence', in Jeff Jordan (ed.), *Gambling on God* (Lanham, Maryland: Rowan and Littlefield, 1994), pp. 47–60.

Murphy, Nancey, *Beyond Liberalism and Fundamentalism: How Modern and Postmodern Philosophy Set the Theological Agenda* (Valley Forge, Pennsylvania: Trinity Press International, 1996).

O'Collins, Gerald, SJ, *Retrieving Fundamental Theology: The Three Styles of Contemporary Theology* (New York: Paulist Press, 1993).

Pascal, Blaise, *Pascal's Pensées*, trans. by W. F. Trotter (New York: E. P. Dutton, 1958).

Payne, Peter, *Design in the Universe: The Design Argument from the Perspective of Natural Law*, doctoral dissertation (Claremont, California: Claremont Graduate School, 1996).

Peterson, Michael, Hasker, William, Reichenbach, Bruce and Basinger, David, *Reason and Religious Belief: An Introduction to the Philosophy of Religion* (Oxford: Oxford University Press, 1991).

Phillips, D. Z., *Religion Without Explanation* (Oxford: Basil Blackwell, 1976).

Phillips, D. Z., *Faith After Foundationalism* (London: Routledge, 1988).

Phillips, D. Z., 'At the Mercy of Method', inaugural lecture (Claremont, California: Claremont Graduate School, 1993).

Phillips, D. Z., 'Authority and Revelation', *Archivo Di Filosofia*, Vol. LXII, Nos 1–3 (1994).

Plantinga, Alvin, *God and Other Minds: A Study of the Rational Justification of Belief in God* (Ithaca, New York: Cornell University Press, 1967), pp. 16–18, 35.

Plantinga, Alvin, *The Nature of Necessity* (Oxford: Clarendon Press, 1974).

Plantinga, Alvin, 'The Reformed Objection to Natural Theology', *Proceedings of the American Catholic Philosophical Association*, Vol. 54 (1980) pp. 49–62.

Plantinga, Alvin, 'Reason and Belief in God', in Alvin Plantinga and Nicholas Wolterstorff (eds), *Faith and Rationality: Reason and Belief in God* (Notre Dame, Indiana: University of Notre Dame Press, 1983), pp. 16–93.

Plantinga, Alvin, 'Is Theism Really a Miracle?', *Faith and Philosophy*, Vol. 3, No. 2 (April, 1986), pp. 109–34.

Plantinga, Alvin, 'Positive Epistemic Status and Proper Function', *Philosophical Perspectives*, Vol. 2 (1988).

Plantinga, Alvin, 'The Prospects for Natural Theology', in James Tomberlin (ed.), *Philosophical Perspectives*, 5th edn (Atascadero, California: Ridgeview Publishing Co., 1991), pp. 311–12.

Plantinga, Alvin, 'Dennett's Dangerous Idea', *Books and Culture: A Christian Review*, Vol. 2, No. 3 (May–June, 1996).

Plantinga, Alvin and Wolterstorff, Nicholas (eds), *Faith and Rationality: Reason and Belief in God* (Notre Dame, Indiana: University of Notre Dame Press, 1983).

Pojman, Louis, *Philosophy of Religion: An Anthology*, 2nd edn (Belmont, California: Wadsworth Publishing Company, 1994).

Quine, W. V. and Ullian, J. S., *The Web of Belief*, 2nd edn (New York: Random House, 1978).

Quinn, Philip L., 'In Search of the Foundations of Theism', *Faith and Philosophy*, Vol. 2, No. 4 (October, 1985), pp. 468–86.

Quinn, Philip L., 'The Foundations of Theism Again: A Rejoinder to Plantinga', in Linda Zagzebski (ed.), *Rational Faith: Catholic Responses to Reformed Epistemology* (Notre Dame, Indiana: University of Notre Dame Press, 1993), pp. 14–47.

Ramm, Bernard, *The Christian View of Science and Scripture* (Grand Rapids, Michigan: Wm. B. Eerdmans, 1954).

Ross, James F., *Philosophical Theology* (Indianapolis: Bobbs-Merrill, 1969).

Rowe, William, 'The Ontological Argument', in Joel Feinberg (ed.), *Reason and Responsibility: Readings in Some Basic Problems of Philosophy*, 3rd edn (Encino, California: Dickenson Publishing Co., 1973), pp. 8–17.

Rowe, William, *The Cosmological Argument* (Princeton, New Jersey: Princeton University Press, 1975).

Rowe, William, 'The Ontological Argument and Question-Begging', *International Journal for Philosophy of Religion*, Vol. VII, No. 4 (1976), pp. 425–32.

Rowe, William, 'Comments on Professor Davis' "Does the Ontological Argument Beg the Question?"', *International Journal for Philosophy of Religion*, Vol. VII, No. 4 (1976), pp. 443–7.

Rowe, William, *Philosophy of Religion: An Introduction*, 2nd edn (Belmont, California: Wadsworth Publishing Company, 1993).

Rowe, William and Wainwright, William J. (eds), *Philosophy of Religion: Selected Readings* (New York: Harcourt Brace Jovanovich, 1973).

Runzo, Joseph, *Reason, Relativism, and God* (New York: St Martin's Press, 1986).

Russell, Bertrand, *Introduction to Mathematical Philosophy* (London: Allen & Unwin, 1919).

Russell, Bertrand, *The Principles of Mathematics*, 2nd edn (London: Allen & Unwin, 1937).

Russell, Bertrand, *A History of Western Philosophy* (New York: Simon and Schuster, 1945).

Russell, Bertrand, 'Logical Atomism', in *Logic and Language* (London: Allen & Unwin, 1956).

Schlesinger, George, 'A Central Theistic Argument', in Jeff Jordan (ed.), *Gambling on God: Essays on Pascal's Wager* (Lanham, Maryland: Rowan and Littlefield, 1994), pp. 83–99.

Schopenhauer, Arthur, *On the Fourfold Root of the Principle of Sufficient Reason and on the Will in Nature*, trans. by K. Hillebrand (London: 1888).

Swinburne, Richard, *The Existence of God* (Oxford: Oxford Univeristy Press, 1979).

Swinburne, Richard, *The Christian God* (Oxford: Oxford University Press, 1994).

Taylor, Richard, *Metaphysics*, 4th edn (Englewood Cliffs, New Jersey: Prentice-Hall, 1992).

Tennant, F. R., *Philosophical Theology*, 2 vols (New York: Cambridge University Press, 1928).

Tessier, Linda J. (ed.), *Concepts of the Ultimate: Philosophical Perspectives on the Nature of the Divine* (London: Macmillan, 1989).

Tillich, Paul, *Systematic Theology*, I (Chicago: University of Chicago Press, 1951).

Wykstra, Stephen, 'Toward a Sensible Evidentialism: On the Notion of "Needing Evidence"', in William Rowe and William Wainwright (eds), *Philosophy of Religion: Selected Readings* (New York: Harcourt Brace Jovanovich, 1989), pp. 426–37.

Wykstra, Stephen, 'Externalism, Proper Inferentiality and Sensible Evidentialism',
   Topoi, Vol. 14 (1995), pp. 107–21.
Zagzebski, Linda, 'Does Ethics Need God?', *Faith and Philosophy*, Vol. 4, No. 3
   (July, 1987), pp. 249–303.
Zagzebski, Linda, (ed.), *Rational Faith: Catholic Responses to Reformed Epistemology*
   (Notre Dame, Indiana: University of Notre Dame Press, 1993).
Zeis, John, 'Natural Theology: Reformed?', in Linda Zagzebski (ed.), *Rational Faith:
   Catholic Responses to Reformed Epistemology* (Notre Dame, Indiana: University of
   Notre Dame Press, 1993).

Index